RESTAURANT
LAW BASICS

Stephen Barth

David K. Hayes

Jack D. Ninemeier

JOHN   WILEY   &   SONS,   INC.
New York   Chichester   Weinheim   Brisbane   Singapore   Toronto
OCM 45917059

Library of Congress Cataloging-in-Publication Data:

Barth, Stephen C.
   Restaurant law basics / Stephen C. Barth, David K. Hayes, Jack D. Ninemeier.
     p. cm.
   Includes index.
   ISBN 0-471-40272-9 (cloth : alk. paper)
     1. Restaurants—Law and legislation—United States.   2. Restaurateurs—Legal status, law, etc.—United States.   3. Restaurant management—United States.   I. Hayes, David K. II. Ninemeier, Jack D.   III. Title

KF2042.H6 B37 2001
343.73'07864795'068—dc21

                                      2001017846

Printed in the United States of America.

10 9 8 7 6 5

CONTENTS

PREFACE

Restaurant managers have one of the most difficult and exciting jobs available in today's economy. An effective restaurant manager must combine the skills of managing guest relations, culinary arts, finance, accounting, supervision, marketing, and increasingly, the law, to his or her everyday decision making. Indeed, a serious mistake made in the legal area can cost a manager business, a good employee, or even his or her job! Few managers, however, are attorneys, nor are they likely to become attorneys.

The good news is that managers do not need to be attorneys to make sound ethical decisions that follow the law. This book was designed to help restaurant managers avoid making the wrong legal decision by emphasizing an approach that seeks to prevent legal difficulties from occurring. By making the proper decision, based on knowledge of the law, and teaching employees to do the same, managers can most often avoid litigation. This book is designed to help managers do just that. It is the only hospitality-related legal guidebook on the market to be supported and supplemented by its own website;

www.HospitalityLawyer.com. This free-to-the-user site, with its management tools, checklists, forms and procedures, as well as legal libraries, and continuously updated content makes this book an invaluable tool for managers.

We have created a tool that we believe should be put to use by every restaurant manager responsible for the production and service of food and beverage products. In the daily operation of a restaurant, it is the manager, not a licensed attorney, who will most influence the company's legal position. Restaurant managers and their staff make decisions every day based on their interpretation of the law. The quality of these decisions determines whether lawyers and the expense of fees, trials, and potential judgments will become necessary. The legal issues faced by managers are varied. Consider the following:

- A guest angrily demands his money back from a meal that has been substantially eaten. Should the guest's money be refunded?
- A long-term employee states that she has converted to a religion that prohibits work on Sunday. Can the employee still be required to work on that day in violation of her religious beliefs?
- A franchisor demands to see the daily receipt totals from a franchisee's sales rather than monthly totals. Must the franchisee share this information?
- A manager wishes to buy her own restaurant. Which organizational structure will be best for tax considerations?
- A guest is choking in the dining room. Is the restaurant required to assist? What if, because of such assistance, the guest is injured further? Who would be responsible?
- What should managers do when they are notified that they or their businesses are being sued?

These are just a few of the hundreds of questions that managers must answer on a regular basis. The format of this book, unlike a law textbook, was developed to make it a useful, practical guide to legally appropriate decision making in food service management.

CONCEPTUAL DEVELOPMENT OF THE BOOK

Years of teaching hospitality law at the undergraduate, graduate, and continuing professional education level, as well as years in the operation of commercial and nonprofit food service management have helped to shape the concept of this book. The result of this experience was a recognized need for a resource that can be used to teach managers what they have to know about managing in today's litigious environment.

Prior to the development of this book, a survey of attorneys and human resource directors at the top 100 U.S. hospitality organizations was completed. The participants were asked to identify the primary areas they believed were critical in avoiding legal difficulties in the hospitality industry. The most significant areas of interest focused on the ability to manage correctly and thereby reduce the potential for legal liability.

Thus, preventing liability through a proactive management of the law is the dominant theme of this book. In all cases, where issues of content, writing style, and design were involved, the touchstone for inclusion was simply: "Does this add to managers' ability to do the right thing?" That is, will this feature improve their ability to manage the law in their own operations? If so, it was considered critical. If not, it was quickly deemed superfluous. For that reason, this book will look and read very differently from any other book on the market. The legal information in it has been carefully selected to be easy to read, easy to understand, and easy to apply.

THE CONTENT AND FORMAT OF THE BOOK

This book has been designed to foster within managers an attitude of "compliance and prevention" in their work ethic and personal management philosophy. Compliance and prevention means teaching ways to prevent or limit legal liability by complying with legal norms. Instead of approaching the topic of hospitality law from a traditional case study viewpoint, this book provides an understanding of the basic foundations and principles of the laws affecting the hospitality industry. It then goes on to provide guidelines and techniques that show how to manage preventively and apply a practical legal awareness to day-to-day actions.

In addition to the legal, safety, and security information the book contains, the following elements make the book reader friendly and practical.

Manager's Brief
The first element in each chapter is a short overview of what will be covered in the chapter and why it is important.

What Would You Do? and Consultant's Corner

A number of true-to-life situations, based on the information presented, are located throughout the book. Managers are asked to think about their own responses to each scenario (What Would You Do?). The second part of this element (Consultant's Corner, located at the end of each chapter), lets the reader know what an attorney might advise about that scenario. This element relates directly to the practical challenges managers face.

Internet Assistant

In the Internet Assistant boxes, readers will be directed to Internet addresses that can provide them with greater detail, information, or resources related to the topic under discussion.

Manager's "To Do" List

Each chapter includes a checklist of activities that can be undertaken by the reader to improve operations or knowledge. For example, a section of the book related to reducing credit card fraud results in a "To Do" item that advises the manager to implement written procedures for identity verification when accepting credit cards for payment.

www.HospitalityLawyer.com

HospitalityLawyer.com is the companion website to this book. Here, managers will find the most up-to-date hospitality-related legal, safety, and security information available anywhere. By simply registering, with no user fee, managers can access answers to frequently asked legal questions, find resources to help train staff or implement procedures, and keep up with the rapidly changing legal environment they encounter.

Despite the common notion that the law is either black or white, this book demonstrates that many legal issues are subject to debate, interpretation, and judgment. Our hope for managers is that they learn to operate their facilities in compliance with the law and that they manage in such a way as to bring honor to the hospitality profession by doing the right thing rather than the wrong thing. If this book helps managers acquire that ability, then it, like they, will indeed be a success.

ACKNOWLEDGMENTS

This book has truly been a community effort. It would be impossible to thank everyone over the years who has provided us with insight or ideas that made this book possible. Accordingly, for those of you whom we fail to mention personally, please know that it was not an intentional oversight.

Thanks go to those education professionals whose experience in the classroom, insights, and encouragement served to illumine this book. Reviewers can do a remarkable job of keeping the needs of the reader at the forefront of the writing effort, and the following individuals have been tremendous in this regard. Truly, this book contains the collective teaching acumen of some of hospitality education's very best and is thus a testament to their skill, commitment, and wisdom.

Tom Atkinson, Columbus State Community College
Thomas F. Cannon, University of Texas at San Antonio
Edward H. Coon, University of South Carolina

Edward Doherty, Endicott College

James M. Goldberg, Northern Virginia Community College

Joseph W. Holland, University of Wisconsin-Stout

Barry R. Langford, University of Missouri-Columbia

Charla R. Long, Grand Valley State University

Robert Alan Palmer, California State Polytechnic University-Pomona

George J. Pastor, Hillsborough Community College

Denver E. Severt, Eastern Michigan University

James R. Turley, New York Institute of Technology

Bruce S. Urdang, Northern Arizona University

A special thank-you also goes to those industry professionals who took time to respond to surveys and answer our questions.

We have benefited greatly from the guidance and expertise of JoAnna Turtletaub, Matt VanHattam, Jolene Howard, Millie Torres, and Valerie Peterson at John Wiley & Sons, Inc.

We have been very fortunate in our lives to have tremendously supporting and loving family and friends. Thank you all for your never ending support and enthusiasm for all of our projects. A special note of thanks goes to Jill Daniels, Fiona Leslie, Chel Lipschutz, and Debbie Ruff.

Stephen Barth

David K. Hayes

Jack D. Ninemeier

1

RESTAURANT MANAGERS
AND THE LAW

MANAGER'S BRIEF

Managers reading this chapter are given an overview of the legal environment within which a restaurant exists and a manager must work. The manager's legal role is examined, and a strategy (STEM—**S**electing, **T**eaching, **E**ducating, and **M**anaging) is presented to emphasize (1) the role employees play in reducing litigation risks and (2) the numerous opportunities the manager has to interact with employees in these efforts. Finally, the concept of ethics—what it is and how it relates to the law and possibility of litigation—is examined. As a result of reviewing this information, the manager will know about the significant impact that legal issues have on a restaurant's daily operation and will understand how planning to avoid litigation can be effective.

IS THIS YOU?

Trisha was the Manager of a 75-seat seasonal restaurant. The season was about to begin, but she still did not have a chef. She had been telephoning for background checks on the top three applicants she had interviewed and always received the same response from past employers: no information, or only the person's name and employment dates. Everyone was cautious, and she wondered whether it was worth her while to verify applicant information.

She had a copy of sanitation scores from the local health department inspection conducted last season. The violations were not serious, but the scores told her that the kitchen staff had let some things slip. A quick walk through the kitchen made her aware that the problems remained unresolved. She wondered why longtime standards seemed de-emphasized and how the new chef would react to a renewed emphasis on sanitation.

As Trisha returned to her office, she was thinking about the customer contact she enjoyed. However, this seemed to be less a part of her daily routine, with rules, regulations, and paperwork consuming most of her time. She needed to reprioritize her efforts, but many issues were important and she didn't know where to start.

As she scanned the newspaper, she noticed a headline: "City Restaurant Targeted in Lawsuit." The manager was a friend. Trisha knew that she had to minimize chances of a lawsuit being brought against her restaurant. She wondered whether her own efforts were enough and, if not, what she could do to improve them.

THE MANAGER AND THE LEGAL ENVIRONMENT

Restaurant managers must have many talents, including expertise in food and beverage, marketing, and accounting. They may also assume specialized roles such as employee counselor, interior designer, facility engineer, and computer systems analyst. The skills required for success today are broader than ever.

Restaurant management has always been challenging. Managers must purchase raw materials, produce a product or service, and sell it—all under one roof. This is different from the process used in manufacturing: one team produces and a separate team is responsible for retail sales. Most important, the manager has direct contact with guests—the ultimate end users of the products and services.

Managers frequently make decisions that have, in one way or another, legal implications. This does not mean that managers must be **attorneys;** they don't. However, their decisions may increase chances that an attorney's services will be needed.

> **ATTORNEY   A person trained and legally authorized to act on behalf of others in matters of the law.**

Think about a manager who is informed that a guest has fallen in the salad bar area. The guest reports that he had been serving himself and slipped on a piece of lettuce. Was this a simple accident? Could it have been prevented? Is the restaurant responsible? What medical attention, if any, should the manager be prepared to provide? What if the injury is severe? (Is the restaurant then responsible?) Can the manager be held personally responsible? What should the manager do when told about the incident? What, if anything, should the employees do? Who is responsible if the employees were not trained in the proper response(s)?

Managers can profoundly influence their property's legal position. Their actions influence the likelihood of the business and/or the manager becoming the subject of **litigation.**

> **LITIGATION   The act of initiating and carrying on a lawsuit; often refers to the lawsuit itself.**

There is a unique body of **law** relating to the hospitality (including food service) industry. These **hospitality laws** have developed over time as society and the courts have defined the relationship between the individual or business serving as the host, and the individual who is the guest. Managers need up-to-date information about these laws and relationships.

> **LAW   The rules of conduct and responsibility established and enforced by a society.**

> **HOSPITALITY LAWS   Those laws that relate to the industry involved with providing food, lodging, travel, and entertainment services to guests and clients.**

Restaurant managers are not lawyers. However, they can think like one. They can carefully consider how their personal actions and those of their employees will be viewed in a legal context.

THE MANAGER'S LEGAL ROLE

There are thousands of new federal and state laws in addition to all of the federal and state administrative rules issued annually. Some managers believe there is too much to cover in one book. They would also argue that because the law is constantly changing, knowledge learned today may be out of date tomorrow. These positions are understandable, but they argue for—not against—the need to study legal management.

Law is complicated, but certain basic principles and procedures can be understood to minimize a manager's chances of encountering legal difficulty. It is less important to know, for example, the specific rules of food safety in every city than to know the basic principles of serving safe food. Not even the best lawyer can know everything about all laws. Similarly, managers cannot have a thorough knowledge of every law or lawsuit that affects their industry. They must, however, know how to effectively manage their legal environment.

STEM: LEGAL MANAGEMENT IS PREVENTIVE MANAGEMENT

How can managers operate their properties to minimize chances of illegal actions? They must manage in a way that combines preventive legal management with sound ethical behavior. They must minimize the risk of litigation initially, rather than operate in a manner that unnecessarily exposes their operations to legal actions.

Every day, managers make decisions about hiring, firing, and/or providing benefits to employees. A manager may also approve a meeting space contract for a catered event that involves serving alcohol. These seemingly independent decisions have something in common: legal implications. With each decision, managers must be fair, operate within the law, and think and act preventively. If they do not and a lawsuit results, the courts may hold such managers **liable.**

LIABLE Legally responsible or obligated.

The need for preventive management becomes even more important when one recognizes that many lawsuits have something in common: a poorly trained employee. Injuries and resulting financial, physical, or mental damages often result from the improper training of a staff member. Staff members may omit a task (fail to clean up a salad bar spill) or engage in a prohibited activity (such as sexual harassment or arguing with a guest).

The increase in lawsuits is not caused solely by employees; the legal system itself, including some attorneys, have also created problems. Managers cannot

STEM CAN REDUCE LEGAL PROBLEMS

A process called STEM (**S**electing, **T**eaching, **E**ducating, and **M**anaging) helps reduce employee errors and omissions leading to litigation and liability.

- **Selecting.** Managers begin reducing litigation risks by *selecting* the right employee. Managers cannot hire "just anyone." Staff must be selected based on specific job qualifications, written job specifications (which relate to qualifications), and information derived from the best possible investigation of the candidate. These are important factors in hiring a busperson, waitperson, hostess, line supervisor, or assistant manager.

- **Teaching.** Managers must develop proper *teaching* (training) methods for employees, including evaluation to assess competencies to ensure training effectiveness.

- **Educating.** Effective managers are continuously *educating* themselves to ensure they know the principles and procedures in which employees must be trained.

- **Managing.** *Managing* the right way reduces chances for mistakes and litigation. Management involves several activities. One of them—motivating—is really what STEM is about. Managers must create a supportive work environment to gain the trust and respect of employees. When they do, employees will be motivated to do their best work, which will help avoid errors resulting in litigation.

delegate responsibilities. When an employee makes a mistake, it is often the result of management error. (In fact, some believe that most employee-related problems are caused by managers!) For example, the wrong person may have been hired, job duties may not be effectively communicated, the employee may have been improperly trained, and/or the employee may not be effectively supervised or motivated.

To create a motivating environment, managers first establish trust and respect. Managers must make a commitment to employees, must follow through, and must be willing to accept responsibility for mistakes. Managers must set an example: If a manager asks employees to be on time, managers must be on time; if managers expect employees to pay for food, beverages, and services, they must also pay for such items.

Managers must effectively communicate their vision and plans to those who are expected to attain that vision. The ability to communicate with skill and grace is critical to success.

Today's culturally diverse workforce requires a variety of motivating techniques: Different people are motivated by different things. Money is an example. To some, it is a strong motivating factor; others prefer more time off instead of additional pay. Managers must know their employees to determine what best motivates them as individuals and as a team.

The goal of STEM is to reduce employee mistakes. By continually encouraging and rewarding good performance, managers can create an environment to help reduce employee mistakes. Even though a goal is unattained, individual or group efforts still merit praise. Managers should try to catch their employees doing something right instead of trying to catch them doing something wrong!

WHAT WOULD YOU DO?

Suppose that another manager at your restaurant, who is your friend, tells you he has been arrested a second time in two years for driving under the influence of alcohol. His current case has not yet gone to trial. He is responsible for the night closing of your employer's restaurant.

What would you do?

ETHICS AND THE LAW

ETHICS Set of standards governing choices about proper conduct made by an individual in his or her relationships with others.

Sometimes it is not clear whether a proposed action is illegal or simply wrong. Managers and their employees must make this distinction. **Ethics** refers to the behavior of someone toward another individual or group. Ethical behavior relates to behavior that is "right" or the "right thing to do." Ethical behavior is influenced by a person's cultural background, religious views, professional training, and personal moral code. Consistently choosing ethical over nonethical behavior helps avoid legal difficulty. Managers may not know what the law requires in a given situation. However, in cases of litigation, a jury may make a determination about whether a manager's actions were intentionally ethical or unethical.

Guidelines for Ethical Decisions

Although it may be difficult to determine precisely what constitutes ethical behavior, the answers to the following questions provide useful guidelines to evaluate possible courses of action:

1. Is it legal?
2. Does it hurt anyone?
3. Is it fair?
4. Am I being honest?
5. Would I care if it happened to me?
6. Would I publicize my action?
7. What if everyone did it?

Let's see how a manager could use these ethical guidelines in a particular situation:

> You are a manager planning a New Year's Eve event. A large amount of wine and champagne will be needed. After conducting a competitive bidding process with suppliers, you place a large order with a single supplier. One week later you receive a case of very expensive champagne delivered to your home. Attached is a note stating that the order was appreciated. It also indicates a hope for more business in the future. What do you do with the champagne?

Ethical Analysis. Some managers will thank the supplier and keep the champagne. However, let's consider the ethical guidelines just presented.

1. Is it legal? The gift may not be illegal. However, there may be liquor laws prohibiting suppliers from giving alcoholic beverages as gifts. Consider, too, the property's own guidelines. Many companies have established gift acceptance policies, limiting the value of employee gifts. Violation of a company policy may cause disciplinary action or termination. Managers must be familiar with their company's ethics policy,

if any. Assume that accepting the champagne does not violate a law and/or company policy; however, there are other guidelines.

2. Does it hurt anyone? Can you be fair and objective when evaluating the next set of beverage bids, or will you be thinking about the champagne you received? Assume you do not think that accepting the gift will hurt anyone.

3. Is it fair? Recognize the stakeholders in this situation. How might others in your company feel about your gift? You agreed to work at the restaurant for established compensation. Should benefits from decisions made on duty accrue to the property or to you? Assume you decide it is fair to keep the champagne.

4. Am I being honest? Do you believe you can remain objective when purchasing and continue to seek the best price quality (value) when you know a supplier rewarded you and may do so again?

5. Would I care if it happened to me? If you owned the company and you knew a manager was given a gift, would you be concerned? Would you like all managers to receive such gifts?

6. Would I publicize my action? Would you keep the champagne if you knew your company's newsletter would contain the following headline:

> *"Manager Accepts Free Champagne After Placing Large Order with Supplier"*

7. What if everyone did it? If you keep the champagne, could others accept gifts? Could the Dining Room Manager receive furniture every time new furniture was ordered for the restaurant? Could the Chef receive several pounds of steaks for each order placed?

WHAT WOULD YOU DO?

Let's assume you decide that you should not keep the champagne. What would you do?

Ethical Codes and Policies

Some managers adopt (or modify) codes of ethics of their professional associations. Others state the company's ethical philosophy and/or policies in a section of the employee handbook.

Ethical codes and corporate policies generally emphasize the importance of following laws. Yet laws do not exist for every situation that managers encounter. Society's views of acceptable behavior, as well as specific laws, constantly change. Ethical behavior, however, is always important to the management of responsible and profitable restaurant operations.

WHAT WOULD YOU DO?

Assume your city is considering the passage of a law to prohibit the *sale* of all tobacco products by bars and restaurants but not by grocery stores. However, there is no current effort to prohibit smoking in cocktail lounges. Your restaurant has a cocktail lounge, and cigarettes are consumed and sold in the lounge. You are considering whether to address the local government body charged with creating this legislation.

What would you do?

A FINAL THOUGHT

Managers make many decisions with legal consequences. They cannot know all of the laws that can potentially affect an operation. Because litigation is widespread and laws change frequently, they must develop and practice a management philosophy of prevention such as STEM.

Just because a law does not prohibit a particular activity does not make the activity correct. Always follow a process to help determine the ethical and legal implications of your decisions.

MANAGER'S "TO DO" LIST

Review the following recommendations proposed in this chapter. Analyze your interest in and need for implementing these recommendations by completing the columns on the right side of the form. Remember, when task assignments are made, time requirements for completion should also be stated. Follow up, as improvement activities evolve, to ensure that your property is moving closer to the goal of minimizing litigation risks.

Recommended Procedures	In Place Now?			Needed to Implement			Assigned To	Completion Date
	Yes	No	N/A*	Policy	Training	Other		
The manager has constant access to a qualified attorney. The telephone number and other contact information is available and current.								
Current trade publications are available and read to keep up with changing laws and regulations.								
Managers are aware that their decisions and actions can influence the likelihood and outcome of legal actions.								
Managers accept their responsibility to be proactive in the management of their operations' legal environment.								
Managers recognize their responsibility to recruit, select, train, and supervise employees in the most effective way to minimize the possibilities of litigation.								
Managers use STEM (Selecting, Teaching, Educating, and Managing) as the basis for both a philosophy about avoiding litigation and as a process for managing employees.								
Managers "walk the talk"; they are role models and "do as they want employees to do."								
Managers and other employees are involved in an ongoing professional development and/or training program.								
Managers proactively create a work environment supportive of employees to help them become motivated to do their best work.								
Managers effectively communicate their vision and plans to attain that vision to employees.								

*N/A = Not Applicable

Recommended Procedures	In Place Now?			Needed to Implement			Assigned To	Completion Date
	Yes	No	N/A*	Policy	Training	Other		
Motivating techniques recognize the wants, needs, and interests of culturally diverse employees.								
Managers reward good performance and provide incentives for employees to do the expected work.								
Managers use an ethical analysis process similar to the seven-step process to decide in advance whether proposed actions are ethical.								
Written guidelines and policies relating to ethics are in place and consistently followed at the restaurant.								

For more information and suggestions log onto www.hospitalitylawyer.com.

*N/A = Not Applicable

CONSULTANT'S CORNER

What Would You Do? (page 6)

As a manager you have an obligation to do what is best for the business. Obviously, in this situation you are torn because you also feel an allegiance to your friend.

The legal issue here is that if, because of your friend's drinking problem, a customer or employee becomes injured at the restaurant, it could be argued that the restaurant knew or should have known of the problem because of your knowledge of the second arrest. Knowing of the problem and then failing to take any steps to correct it creates a danger for customers, other employees, or perhaps innocent third parties (e.g., the manager becomes intoxicated at the restaurant, has an accident driving home, and injures an innocent driver).

Accordingly, sharing this knowledge with your employer is the legally responsible thing to do.

It may also be helpful for you to revisit this dilemma after you have read the rest of the chapter, particularly the section on ethics, and answer the seven questions to aid in the ethical decision-making process.

What Would You Do? *(page 8)*

You have several alternatives. Listed here are a few; feel free to add your own.

1. If required by your company policy, notify the general manager or director of human resources about the gift and how you intend to dispose of it.

2. You can return the champagne to the vendor with a kind note of thanks for his or her generosity and explaining why it is inappropriate for you to accept the gift.

3. If legal in your state, you can give the champagne to the company either for use in its general inventory or for use at a social event for all employees.

4. You can let the vendor know that it is inappropriate for you to accept the champagne, but perhaps he or she might consider donating it to a charity of his or her choice to be auctioned off to raise money for the charity.

What Would You Do? *(page 9)*

Once again you are faced with an ethical dilemma. You have an obligation to maximize profit for your operation, so the loss of the revenue from the sale of cigarettes could be significant. However, you also have an obligation to your community and your employees' health. Apply the seven-question ethical decision-making process to this situation and see what you come up with after answering the seven questions. It is important to remember that as a business owner or operator in a community, you have the ability to influence legislation, certainly on a local level and perhaps on a state or even national level. Accordingly, you need to think through the consequences to all of the different constituencies and stakeholders that can be affected by your taking a position and/or influencing the outcome.

2

RESTAURANT CONTRACTS

MANAGER'S BRIEF

Managers reading this chapter will learn basic information about contracts. They will recognize the usefulness of written versus verbal contracts and will know about the components of an enforceable contract (legally valid, offer and acceptance, and consideration). Contract clauses essential for providing products and services to guests are analyzed, as well as others important in contracts to purchase products and services. Details about exculpatory clauses (which attempt to excuse a business from blame), a focus on preventive legal management, and discussions about contract breaches, remedies, statutes of limitations, and consequences of breaching an enforceable contract complete the chapter.

INTRODUCTION TO CONTRACTS

PLAINTIFF   A person or entity who initiates litigation against someone else; sometimes referred to as claimant, petitioner, or applicant.

DEFENDANT   A person or entity against whom litigation is initiated; sometimes referred to as respondent.

CONTRACT   An agreement or promise made between two or more parties that the courts will enforce.

Litigation against restaurants generally arises because the **plaintiff** believes that the **defendant** either:

- Did something he or she was *not* supposed to do

or

- Didn't do something he or she was *required* to do

It can be difficult for managers to know precisely what is expected of them when serving guests. It is also difficult to know what should reasonably be expected of the operation's suppliers. **Contracts** and laws surrounding them permit both parties to an agreement to understand more clearly what they have agreed or promised to do or not do.

WRITTEN AND ORAL CONTRACTS

Managers make promises and enter into many agreements every day. Although they may do so in good faith, problems can arise that may prevent an agreement from being fulfilled.

WHAT WOULD YOU DO?

Vincent's Landscaping Service offered to trim trees and bushes around the Olde Tyme Restaurant for $500. The manager agreed to the price and a start date of Monday. When the job was completed, the trees looked great, but a large amount of debris was neatly piled near bases of the trees. When the manager inquired about the removal of the brush, Vincent's stated that removing the brush was never discussed and was not included in the quoted price. The manager agreed that removal was never discussed but stated his assumption that when a company trims a tree, it will remove the brush.

What would you do if you were the manager?

Valid contracts may be established in writing or orally. Generally, written contracts are preferred because they make it easier to clearly establish each party's responsibilities. In addition, over time memories fade, businesspeople change jobs or retire, and recollections, even among well-intentioned people, differ. These problems are less likely to affect written contracts.

Even though written contracts have advantages, most hospitality transactions with guests are established orally. When a potential guest telephones to order pizza for home delivery, an oral contract is established. The guest agrees to pay for the pizza when delivered, and the restaurant agrees to prepare and deliver a quality product. It would not be practical to obtain a written agreement. Likewise, the guest who makes a reservation for eight people at 7:30 P.M. on Friday does not usually obtain a written agreement from the restaurant accepting responsibility to provide a table at that time. The guest simply makes an oral request, which is either accepted or denied. Sometimes transactions with guests are confirmed in writing. Appendix A shows a sample banquet contract.

Oral contracts are often used with suppliers and others who provide services. If a restaurant is required by law to have its fire extinguisher system inspected twice a year, the agreement to do so may not be committed to writing for each inspection. Perhaps the same company has done the inspection for years. To efficiently schedule staff, the inspection company—not the restaurateur—decides the exact day of inspection. The presence of the inspector, with access provided to the property and an invoice for services performed, along with a written inspection report, all serve as indications that an oral contract existed.

ELEMENTS OF AN ENFORCEABLE CONTRACT

All oral or written contracts must include specific elements to make them legally **enforceable.** If any are missing, the courts will consider a contract unenforceable.

To be enforceable, a contract must be legally valid and must consist of an offer, consideration, and acceptance.

> **ENFORCEABLE CONTRACT A contract recognized as valid by the courts and subject to the courts' ability to compel compliance with its terms.**

Legally Valid

Not all agreements or promises are legally valid. For example, if a ten-year-old child "agrees" to host friends at the local amusement park, the owner has no recourse if the child neglects to arrive with friends and pay admission fees. Society requires a minimum age before a party to a contract can legally commit to its promises. If that minimum age (usually 18) is not met, any contract would be considered unenforceable. In addition, an individual without the mental capacity to understand contract terms cannot enter into an enforceable contract.

Even if parties to a contract are considered legally capable, the courts will not enforce a contract that requires breaking a law. If a gourmet restaurant contracts with a foreign supplier to provide an imported food product that has entered the country without the proper inspection, the courts will not enforce the contract because the activity involved—selling uninspected food products—is illegal.

Offer

An **offer** states, as precisely as possible, exactly what the offering party is willing to do and what is expected in return. The offer may include specific instructions

> **OFFER   A proposal to per-form an act or pay an amount, which, if accepted, creates an agreement.**

about how, where, when, and to whom the offer is made. It may include time frames or deadlines for acceptance that are either clearly stated or implied. In addition, the price or terms of the offer are generally stated.

When guests read a menu, they are really reading a series of offers. Although the menu states, "16-Ounce Roast Prime Rib of Beef, $22.95," the contract offer could be stated as "The restaurant will provide Prime Rib, if the guest will pay $22.95."

When a manager orders produce, the offer is similar. The manager offers to buy the produce at a price quoted by the supplier. The offer sets the terms and responsibilities of both parties. The offer states, " I will promise to do this if you will promise to do that."

Think about the landscaping case discussed earlier. It is clear why the offer is important. In that example, the manager and the landscaping service had different ideas about what constituted the offer. Much litigation involves plaintiffs and defendants seeking the court's help to define what is "fair" about a legitimate offer when the offer has not been clearly identified. Courts enforce contracts with reasonably identifiable terms even if the terms are heavily weighted in favor of one party. It is important to clearly understand all terms of an offer before it is accepted. Then the manager can help minimize the potential for litigation.

Consideration

Consideration is the payment for, or cost of, the performance promised in an offer. In the case of the prime rib dinner discussed earlier, the consideration is $22.95 plus any taxes. The guest, by ordering the prime rib, agrees to pay $22.95 as consideration for the prime rib dinner.

> **CONSIDERATION** The payment (value) exchanged for the promise(s) contained in a contract.

Consideration may be something besides money: A restaurant may agree to provide a Christmas party to a professional decorating company in exchange for having the restaurant decorated for Christmas. The restaurant's consideration is hosting the decorator's Christmas party; the consideration for the decorator is the products and services used to decorate the restaurant.

Consideration can also be the promise to act or not to act. When a manager is hired at a certain salary, the restaurant's consideration is money and the manager's consideration is the work (acts) to be done while managing the property. Sometimes consideration requires that one of the contracting parties does *not* act. Suppose a couple buys an established restaurant with a name that is well-known locally. Consideration may specify that the original owner cannot open a restaurant with a similar name in the area for a specified time.

Courts usually do not decide the relative fairness of consideration. A restaurant may rent a banquet room for $25, $250, or $2,500 per night; a guest can agree or not agree to rent the room. As long as both parties to a legitimate contract agree, the amount of consideration is generally not disputable in court. It is the agreement to exchange payment that establishes consideration and the contract's enforceability—not the amount of the payment.

Acceptance

It takes at least two parties to create a contract. A legal offer and its consideration must be clearly accepted by a second party before the contract exists. An **acceptance** must exactly mirror the offer's terms for the acceptance to make the contract enforceable. If it doesn't, it is considered to be a counteroffer rather than an acceptance.

> **ACCEPTANCE** Unconditional agreement to the precise terms and conditions of an offer.

When an acceptance mirroring the offer is made, an **express contract** is created.

> **EXPRESS CONTRACT** A contract in which the components of the agreement are explicitly stated—either orally or written.

Sue was offered a restaurant manager's position. She received a written employment offer on the first of the month with a stipulation that the offer would be in effect for 14 days. If she accepted the offer, she would have to sign and return the contract to the property's owner before the offer expired.

She thought that the specified salary was too low, adjusted it upward by $5,000, and initialed her change on the contract. She mailed the offer letter with a cover letter, stating she was pleased to accept the position as detailed in the contract. The owner called Sue to express his regret that she had rejected the employment offer. During the call, Sue realized that the owner would not accept her revised salary proposal, so she orally accepted the position at the original pay, but the 14-day deadline had passed at that point.

If you were the owner, what would you do?

An offer may be accepted orally or in writing unless it specifies the manner of acceptance. It must be clear that the offer's terms are accepted. It would not be fair (or ethical) for a wine steward to ask whether a diner desires an expensive bottle of wine and then, because the guest does not say "No," assume the lack of response indicates an acceptance of the offer. If that occurs, the diner should not have to pay for the wine. Similarly, a contractor who offers to change the light-bulbs on an outdoor sign cannot quote a price to the manager and then do the work without the manager's clear acceptance.

Legal acceptance may be established several ways, which generally include:

- Written or oral agreement—The acceptance of an offer can be done orally, with a handshake, or even just nodding of the head. A guest in a lounge who orders drinks for the table is orally agreeing to an unspoken but valid offer to sell drinks at a specific price. After consumption, guests who are asked about another round and who nod their head affirmatively are considered to have accepted the offer of a second round.

- Acceptance by conduct—Assume that a guest stands in a take-out line to order coffee and sees muffins clearly marked for sale. If the guest unwraps a muffin and begins to eat it while waiting in line, these actions imply the acceptance of an offer to sell the muffin.

- Acceptance of a deposit—A restaurant may require a nonrefundable deposit to accompany and affirm the acceptance of an offer. This may occur when a deposit on a banquet room rental is required.

- Acceptance of partial or full payment—The concept of payment prior to enjoying the benefits of a contract is exemplified when a restaurant requires prepayment of table d' hôte dinners at a busy New Year's Eve party.

- Agreement in writing—Often the best way to indicate acceptance of an offer is by agreeing in writing. This generally occurs when the sum of money involved is substantial. A written confirmation of an offer provides more than just proof of acceptance; most people are cautious when their promises are committed to paper. Because a written contract acceptance often includes a summary of contract terms, it also helps prevent confusion.

Today, a written agreement can take several forms. The fax machine allows rapid confirmation and revision of contract terms and can be an indispensable tool for a manager. Electronic mail (E-mail) is also a quick and effective way to accept contract terms in writing and allows both parties to revise documents directly as they are passed back and forth. The U.S. mail service has traditionally been recognized as a legally binding method of providing written acceptance of contracts, as has the use of overnight delivery services.

CONTRACT DETAILS ARE IMPORTANT

A supplier promotes a sale on hams by faxing a flyer to customers. The sale's offer includes a 20 percent price reduction if orders exceed $2,000 and if payment is made by November 1. A manager decides to purchase, completes the order form, and mails it along with a check for the full purchase amount. The envelope is postmarked on November 1, so the manager will have met the contract terms and responded within time limitations. However, if the supplier had stated, "Acceptance must be received in our offices by November 1," the manager's reply would not have been timely. Clarity and specificity are important when agreeing to a contract's terms.

WWW: Internet Assistant

Log onto the Internet and enter: http://www.yahoo.com

Under "Search," enter: Hospitality Contracts

Select: Related News

Search for stories related to contracts and contract negotiations making news headlines.

A CLOSE LOOK AT RESTAURANT CONTRACTS

Many restaurant contracts are similar to contracts used in other industries, including those for employment, facility maintenance, equipment purchases, employee insurance, and accounting services. There are, however, some unique contracts and contractual relationships that restaurant managers will encounter. Several deserve special explanation.

Franchise Agreements

FRANCHISEE A person or business that has purchased and/or received a franchise.

FRANCHISE The right given by a franchisor to a franchisee to sell a product or service within a specific geographic area.

FRANCHISOR A person or business that has sold and/or granted a franchise.

In a franchise agreement, the restaurant owner (**franchisee**) agrees to operate the property in a specific manner in exchange for a **franchise.** A franchise can take many forms but generally includes the right to use the **franchisor's** name, trademark, and procedures for the sale of a product or service in a specific geographic area.

Typically, the franchisee gives up some freedom to make operational decisions in exchange for the expertise and marketing power of the franchisor's brand name.

Franchise agreements are very common but are also quite complex. Agreements and operating relationships associated with franchises are reviewed in Chapter 3. A franchise agreement is simply a variation of a normal contract, and although complicated, it is governed by the same legal system governing all contracts.

Meeting Space Contracts

Some restaurants contract with guests to reserve banquet or meeting rooms. The price of the space may be tied to the number of guests who will be attending the banquet. A sample meeting space contract is shown in Appendix B.

Purchase Agreements

Employees, including managers, who purchase can bind employers to contracts valued at thousands of dollars or more. Agreements can cover simple purchases such as the daily delivery of milk, bread, or produce. A manager may agree, either orally or in writing, to buy a certain product at the market (current) price from a supplier. In other situations, the contract may involve the delivery of many products at agreed-upon prices to several outlets. Purchase agreements may have an expiration date or, as in the case of contracts for services (trash removal, grounds maintenance, etc.), may continue until changed by one of the parties. When practical, purchase agreements are best committed to writing and then reviewed regularly, or at least annually.

Uniform Commercial Code (UCC)

A special code of laws helps facilitate business transactions carried out with sales contracts. The **Uniform Commercial Code (UCC)** simplifies, modernizes, and ensures consistency in laws regulating the buying and selling of personal property (not land), loans granted to expedite those sales, and the interests of sellers and lenders. UCC rules were designed to add fairness to the transfer of property and to promote honesty in business transactions. In addition, they balance the philosophy of **caveat emptor** by giving buyers, sellers, and lenders some legal protection.

> **UNIFORM COMMERCIAL CODE (UCC)** A model statute covering such things as the sale of goods, credit, and bank transactions. All states except Louisiana have adopted the UCC.

> **CAVEAT EMPTOR** Latin for, "Let the buyer beware," a phrase implying that the burden of determining the relative quality and price of a product rests with the buyer—not the seller.

The UCC applies to the selling of food and drink, the buying and selling of goods (personal property), and borrowing and repaying money. In purchasing goods under contract, there are three basic requirements:

1. Sales of $500 or more must be in writing and agreed to by both parties.
2. The seller is obligated to provide goods that are not defective and that meet the criteria and terms in the contract.

3. The buyer must inspect purchased goods to ensure that they conform to contract terms and must notify the seller immediately about discrepancies.

The UCC requires a manager to fulfill any promises made in a purchase or sales contract. For example, if a manager contracts to buy four cases of lettuce from a supplier on or before a specified date and the supplier delivers the order on time, the manager must pay for it.

The UCC protects buyers' interests by requiring that goods or products offered for sale be fit for use and free of known defects. The supplier who delivers cases of spoiled lettuce will not have fulfilled the terms of the contract. Likewise, the UCC protects sellers' interests by requiring that managers inspect all goods upon receiving them and inform the seller immediately about defects. (The manager cannot claim three months after receipt that the lettuce was spoiled and then refuse to pay the bill.)

The UCC is a complex law with many requirements that affect managers. Some aspects are reviewed in Chapter 4 in a discussion of the buying and selling of property. Chapter 11 discusses how the UCC regulates the wholesomeness of food and beverage products sold in restaurants.

MANAGING GUEST RESERVATIONS

Reservations are an often troublesome form of oral contract. Many restaurants accept guest reservations for specific meal periods and times. One of the manager's most difficult tasks is to forecast guest counts needed for a reservation system. A reservation, even if oral, can be a contract. Most legal experts agree that a contract is established when a reservation is accepted by the restaurant in a manner consistent with its policies. Some restaurants accept only reservations guaranteed with a deposit or a credit card number; in these cases the contract will not exist until that deposit is received or the credit card number is supplied. If a restaurant regularly accepts reservations on an **exchange of promise** basis (the guest agrees to arrive, and the facility agrees to provide space), a contract exists when the reservation is made.

EXCHANGE OF PROMISE   An oral agreement made by two or more entities meeting all requirements of a legal contract.

WHAT WOULD YOU DO?

A certain restaurant's Mother's Day brunch is the busiest meal of the year. The dining room seats 300. The average group dining on Mother's Day stays 90 minutes. The restaurant will serve its buffet from 11:00 A.M. to 2:00 P.M. Reservations are required, and currently 100 percent of the restaurant is reserved. Past records, however, indicate that about 15 percent of those making reservations will be no-shows.

What would you do if you were the restaurant manager?

Importance of Reservations

Restaurants are different from many other businesses because of the highly perishable nature of their products. A table for five at a Mother's Day brunch can be sold only once or twice on that day. If the table goes unsold, the lost revenue cannot be recovered. The cost of no-shows must eventually be passed on to other guests in the form of higher menu prices.

Reducing No-Show Reservations

Several steps can help improve the forecasting of reservations:

- Become known as a property that honors reservation times.
- Whenever possible, document all reservations in writing.
- Have all policies related to making reservations and billing no-shows put in writing. Follow them.
- When possible, reconfirm restaurant reservations prior to reservation date.
- Develop a clear and easily communicated reservation cancellation policy.
- Support staff members who are charged with collecting payment from no-shows (if applicable).
- Use good judgment and ethical principles when deciding whether circumstances require policy exceptions.

Best Practices for Reservations

When taking reservations, consider use of the following procedures:

- If a credit card is used to make a reservation, take the cardholder's account number, card expiration date, name embossed on the card, and the address. Explain to cardholders that if they fail to cancel by the agreed-upon time and the reservation time cannot be resold, their credit card will be charged at a specific rate plus applicable tax.

- Confirm the reservation date and time, number in party, smoking preference (if applicable), and any other necessary information.

- Explain the property's no-show policy.

- Remember that if a cardholder with a reservation arrives within the specified time range (for example, within 15 minutes of the reservation time), the property is obligated to provide a table.

ESSENTIAL RESTAURANT CONTRACT CLAUSES

Contracts cover a variety of offer and acceptance situations, and their form and structure vary considerably. However, all contracts should contain certain essential clauses, which should be identified and reviewed before entering into the contract. It is always better to resolve potential difficulties before agreeing to a contract than be forced to resolve them later with ill will or legal problems resulting. Effective food and beverage contracts contain important clauses.

Clauses for Providing Guest Products and Services

Length of Time Price Terms Exist. An offer should include the seller's proposed price and should clearly state how long that price will be in effect. When issuing coupons, for example, the manager of a quick-service restaurant should inform consumers about the coupon's expiration date.

Authorization to Modify Contract. Unanticipated circumstances can cause guests to change their plans. A property may have a signed banquet contract. If the guest count changes at the last minute, which staff member(s) can address the problem? It is important to identify, prior to agreeing to contract terms, exactly who has authority to modify the contract if necessary. In addition, require any contract modifications to be in writing.

Deposit and Cancellation Policies. Policies and clauses about reservation deposits and cancellation were discussed earlier in this chapter. Contract clauses that detail a property's deposit and cancellation policies are critical and must be very clear. Here is a sample cancellation clause for rental of a property's meeting room:

> *If the event is canceled in full, a fee consisting of a percentage of the total anticipated revenue outlined in this contract will be charged. The fee is determined by the length of time between written notification of the cancellation and the scheduled meeting date as follows:*
>
> | | |
> |---|---|
> | *0–31 days before event* | *100% of anticipated revenue* |
> | *32–60 days before event* | *75% of anticipated revenue* |
> | *61–120 days before event* | *50% of anticipated revenue* |
> | *121–180 days before event* | *25% of anticipated revenue* |
>
> *Anticipated revenue includes meal and gratuity charges, if applicable, and taxes due on recovered sums.*

Allowable Attrition. Allowable **attrition** refers to the amount of downward variance permitted in a contract before the guest incurs a penalty. Consider a guest planning a large holiday party at a restaurant. When planning first begins, the event may be months away. At the time of contract signing the actual number of guests is unknown. The guest planning the party may estimate 200 attendees, yet only 100 individuals may actually attend. Allowable attrition clauses inform both parties of the impact (for example, the property's right to change banquet rooms) of a reduced number of actual guests.

> **ATTRITION   Reduction in the number of projected guests.**

Many guests overestimate projected attendance, and without considering attrition, negative financial implications for the restaurant may arise.

Indemnification for Damages. To **indemnify** means to secure against loss or damage.

Clearly specify who will be responsible if damages to meeting rooms or banquet space should occur. Also specify who will be responsible if liability arises from the event held in the room. A general clause in a meeting room contract may read as follows:

> **INDEMNIFY   To make a person or entity whole; to reimburse for a loss already incurred.**

The group shall be liable for any damage to the Restaurant caused by any of the group's officers, agents, contractors, or guests. The group also indemnifies and holds harmless the restaurant for any damages that might arise from the event.

Payment Terms. Although payments and terms for payment may seem straightforward, they can sometimes be complex.

Restaurants generally require a cash, check, or credit card payment at the time of meal service. Sometimes a deposit is required when a contract for a group function is signed, with a clause stipulating that the total amount due must be paid immediately upon the conclusion of the function.

Performance Standards: Quantity. Problems of attrition and no-shows have been discussed. But what happens when numbers *exceed* original estimates? If a restaurant anticipates 200 guests but 225 people arrive, there may be space and production difficulties. Because this situation is common, many managers prepare food and set tables for more guests than the contracted number.

Although there is no industry standard, many managers find that preparing for 5 percent more than the number of guests than contracted for is a good way to balance the potential needs of the guests with the actual needs of the property. With this plan, the manager agrees to provide and the guest agrees to pay for the greater of the guarantee or the number of guests served to the 105 percent maximum.

Clauses for Purchasing/Receiving Products and Services

Just as essential contract clauses are needed in selling products, essential clauses are also needed in contracting to purchase or receive products and services. As always, everyone benefits when all arrangements are in writing.

Payment Terms. Payment terms are a significant contractual component. Consider a manager purchasing a new roof. Three bids have been obtained from contractors, all quoting a similar price. One builder wants full payment before beginning work. The second builder wants half the purchase price prior to beginning and the balance upon "substantial completion" of the work. The third builder requires payment in full within 30 days of job completion. Payment terms can make a considerable difference as to which contractor gets the bid.

Required down payments, interest rates on remaining balances, payment due date(s), and penalties for late payments should be specified in the contract and reviewed carefully.

Delivery or Start Date. Sometimes a range of times may be acceptable. For example, food deliveries may be accepted "between the hours of 8:00 A.M. and 4:00 P.M." In some cases, the delivery or start date may be unknown. Consider a contract clause written when a restaurant owner leases space in a strip mall. The time needed to get the leased store stocked and operational may be unknown, and the start date of the lease may not be easily determined. The delivery/start clause would be part of a longer contract document. Language in a section titled "Start Date" may read:

> *The initial Operating Term of this agreement commences at 12:01 A.M. on the first day the shop is open for business and terminates at 11:59 P.M. on the day preceding the second (2nd) annual anniversary thereof; provided, however, that the parties hereto may extend this agreement by mutual consent for up to two (2) terms of five (5) years each.*

Note that the actual start date is uncertain, but the language identifying precisely when the start date is to occur is clear.

Completion Date. Completion dates tell contracting parties when contract terms end. If a painter is hired to paint a banquet room, the completion date identifies the date by which the work will be finished. If the contract is written to guarantee a price for a product purchased, the completion date is the last day the price will be honored by the supplier.

It is often difficult to estimate completion dates for construction contracts when weather, labor difficulties, or material delays can affect timetables. However, completion dates should be included whenever products or services are secured.

Some contracts provide that the contract's completion or stop date is extended indefinitely unless specifically discontinued. A sample clause follows:

> *Unless otherwise noted in the contract, this participation agreement between the Restaurant and the XYZ Trash Service automatically renews on an annual basis unless written cancellation notice is received by either party 90 days prior to the end of the contract term.*

Self-renewing contracts are common but must be carefully reviewed prior to acceptance. Required action times to discontinue a self-renewing contract should be noted on a calendar so that critical dates will not be missed.

Performance Standards. Performance standards refer to the quality of products or services purchased or received. Setting such standards can be complex because some products and services are difficult to quantify. The thickness of concrete or an equipment item's brand or model can be specified. The quality of an advertising campaign or of interior design work is more difficult to evaluate.

Quantify contractual performance standards to the extent possible. With some thought and help from experts, great specificity is possible. Consider a manager who wishes to purchase canned peach halves. A purchase specification can be included as part of the purchase contract:

> *Standards for Peaches:*
> *Peaches, yellow cling halves, canned. U.S. Grade 3 (Choice), packed 6*
> *number 10 cans per case with 30–35 halves per can. Packed in heavy*
> *syrup with 19 to 24 Brix; minimum drained weight 66 ounces per*
> *number 10 can; certificate of grade required.*

Recall that the Uniform Commercial Code (discussed earlier in this chapter) requires a supplier to provide goods fit for use and free of defects. Clauses specifying performance standards give both buyers and sellers added protection; details identify the quality expectations of both parties.

Licenses and Permits. Obtaining licenses and permits required for contracted work should be the responsibility of the outside contracting party. Tradespeople such as plumbers, security guards, air-conditioning specialists, and the like, who must be licensed or certified by state or local governments should prove they have the appropriate credentials. It is the manager's responsibility to verify the existence of these licenses. Always attach a photocopy of the documents to the contract itself.

Indemnification. Accidents can happen while an agreement is being fulfilled. To protect themselves and their organizations, managers should insist that service provider contracts contain indemnification language similar to the following:

> *Contractor agrees to indemnify, defend, and hold harmless the restau-*
> *rant and its officers, directors, partners, employees, and guests from and*
> *against any losses, liabilities, claims, damages, and expenses, including*
> *without limitation attorneys' fees and expenses, that arise as a result of*

the negligence or intentional misconduct of Contractor or any of its agents, officers, employees, or subcontractors.

Consider the manager who hires a company to change the lights in a 60-foot-high road sign. While this work is being completed, the contractor's truck collides with a parked car. The car owner demands that the restaurant pay for the car's damages. Without an indemnification clause in the contract, the restaurant may incur expenses related to the accident.

Although it is a good idea to have all contracts reviewed by legal counsel, the nature of indemnification is significant and this clause should be written only by an attorney.

Nonperformance. Managers should decide what to do if contractual terms are not fulfilled. When purchasing products and services, a simple solution may be to buy from a different supplier. Language should be written into contracts that addresses the rights of the restaurant to terminate an agreement if the supplier performs unsatisfactorily.

Sometimes supplier nonperformance can have an extremely negative effect on the property. In such cases it is critical that contractual language be included to protect the property. The protection may be stated in general or specific terms. A common way to quantify nonperformance costs is to use a "dollars per day" penalty. In this situation, the supplier is assessed a penalty of an agreed-upon amount of dollars per day for each day it is late in delivering the product or service.

Entertainment is generally outsourced, and problems can arise if there is nonperformance by an entertainer. The following is a sample nonperformance clause to address this situation:

The Entertainer recognizes that failure to perform hereunder may require the restaurant to acquire replacement entertainment on short notice. Therefore, any failure to provide the agreed-upon services at the times, in the areas, and for the duration required hereunder shall constitute a default, which shall allow the Restaurant to cancel this contract immediately on oral notice. The Entertainer and/or his agent shall be liable for any damages incurred by the Restaurant, including without limitation, any costs incurred by the Restaurant to secure such replacement entertainment.

Dispute Resolution Terms. Sometimes contracting parties decide to agree on how to settle any contractual disputes that may arise. Several issues may be important. The first is the location for any litigation. This is not complicated when both parties and their businesses are in the same state. Otherwise, language such as the following can be used:

> *This agreement shall be governed by and interpreted under the laws of the State of _____ (location of restaurant).*

Additional terms may include the use of agreed-upon independent third parties to assist in problem resolution. Litigation costs can also be addressed before a contract is signed, as in the following sample language:

> *Should any legal proceedings be required to enforce any provisions of this Agreement, the prevailing party shall be entitled to recover all of its costs and expenses related thereto, including without limitation, expert witness' and consultants' fees and attorneys' fees.*

EXCULPATORY CLAUSES

EXCULPATORY CONTRACT OR CLAUSE A contract (or clause in a contract) that releases one of the parties from liability for wrongdoing.

An **exculpatory clause** can be added to a contract. It seeks to exculpate (excuse) the restaurant from blame in certain situations. An example is a coatroom sign stating, "Restaurant not responsible for missing garments." These clauses may help reduce litigation because they cause guests to exercise greater caution. Warning signs or contract language causing guests to be more careful help both guests and the restaurant. Moreover, some parties to a contract may accept the exculpatory statement as "legal truth"; they may assume they have given up their right to a claim because of the language of the clause.

Courts have not generally accepted the complete validity of exculpatory clauses. Therefore, these clauses sometimes provide a false sense of security for the operator. Although they can be useful, they should not be relied upon to absolve the manager of reasonable responsibilities to care for the safety and security of guests.

WHAT WOULD YOU DO?

The guests enjoyed the dinner but could not finish it all. A doggie bag was requested. You, the manager, were concerned about the possibility of food-borne illness occurring if a protein-rich entrée was not quickly refrigerated on this hot summer day. The following written card was presented and explained to the guests at the time the doggie bag was provided:

> *We are pleased that you have enjoyed your meal and wish to take the unconsumed portion with you. However, we are concerned about your health and well-being and wish to alert you to the possibility of foodborne illness if your meal is not quickly brought under refrigeration. Because we do not have control over the product when it leaves our property, we cannot be held responsible for any problems that occur.*

As the manager, are you relieved of responsibility by using this notice?

PREVENTIVE LEGAL MANAGEMENT OF CONTRACTS

Breach of Contract

Sometimes contractual agreements and promises are not kept. When this occurs, the party not adhering to the agreement is said to be in breach of, or to have **breached,** the contract's terms.

> **BREACH OF CONTRACT**
> **Failure to keep the promises or agreements of a contract.**

Sometimes it is impossible to fulfill a contract's obligations. Diners who stay longer than anticipated may make it difficult for the restaurant to honor later dinner reservations. Acts of God, war, government regulations, disasters, strikes, civil disorder, curtailment of transportation services, and other emergencies can make it impossible to keep contract promises. A restaurant closed because of a hurricane cannot service guests with reservations. An air traffic controller's strike closing major airports prevents guests flying to a certain city to honor reservations at a restaurant there.

Voluntary breach of contract occurs when a party decides to willfully violate contract terms. It is a poor idea to voluntarily breach a contract; this usually means the breaching party should not have initially agreed to the contract terms.

The consequences of a breach can be serious even when it is unavoidable. Consider a restaurant that contracts for a couple's wedding reception. The contract to provide dinner, a cash bar, and a room with a dance floor is agreed upon in January; the wedding will occur in June. In May the property is sold to a new owner, who immediately applies to the state's Liquor Control Board for a liquor license transfer. The Control Board requires a criminal background check that will take 60 days. As a result, the restaurant must operate for two months without a liquor license. The contract to provide a cash bar for the wedding is now breached, and the wedding party threatens litigation for the property's failure to keep its agreement. Even though the breach could not have been avoided, the negative effect on the wedding is real, as is the threat of litigation and loss of customer goodwill.

Remedies for Breaching Enforceable Contracts

REMEDY A legal means for compensation when an enforceable contract has been breached.

If an enforceable contract's terms are broken, the consequences can be significant. The plaintiff can pursue several **remedies** when the other party (the defendant) has breached a contract. Possible remedies include the following:

- *Suit for specific performance.* In this situation, the party breaking the contract is taken to court by the plaintiff, who requests the court to force the defendant to perform (or not to perform) per the specific contract. Example: A prospective franchisee meeting all terms and conditions of a franchisor has signed a franchise agreement. The individual is not granted the franchise, because the franchisor wishes to build and operate on the designated site. The potential franchisee can bring legal action to force the franchisor to keep its promise and grant the franchise.

- *Liquidated damages.* A contract often dictates a specific penalty if its terms are not completed on an agreed-upon date. Example: A building contractor agrees to complete a parking lot repaving by the beginning of the busy tourist season. Penalties may be built into the contract, to be applied if the job is not finished on time. These penalty payments are called liquidated, or specified, **damages.**

DAMAGES Losses or costs incurred as a result of another's wrongful act.

- *Economic loss.* When contractual damages are not specifically agreed upon, the party creating the breach may still be held responsible for damages. Example: A tour bus agency contracts for 50 dinners for its all-inclusive tour group. Upon arrival, the group finds that the restaurant cannot honor the group reservation. Because the restaurant has breached the contract, the tour agency may bring litigation. In addition, the tour agency may be able to recover the additional costs required to provide alternative meals for its clients. These damages, if granted, would be the restaurant's responsibility to pay as a direct result of the contract breach.

- *Alternative dispute resolution.* There can be honest disagreement over the meaning of contract terms. It may be difficult to determine which party, if either, is in breach. When this occurs, the parties (or in some cases the courts) may use dispute resolution techniques to resolve the situation. This process may also be used for personal injury, employment, labor, or other issues.

    The two most common dispute resolution techniques are **arbitration** and **mediation.** In arbitration, the arbitrator is an independent, unbiased individual who works with the contracting parties to understand their views about contract terms. The arbitrator then makes a decision binding on each party. In mediation, the mediator, who is also independent and unbiased, helps the two parties reach agreement. Mediation is voluntary (and neither party can be forced to come to an agreement), but it can be an effective way to resolve contract disputes. If an agreement is reached via mediation, the courts will usually enforce it.

    > **ARBITRATION** A neutral third party (arbitrator) renders a final and binding resolution to a dispute. The decision of the arbitrator is known as the "award."

    > **MEDIATION** A neutral third party (mediator) assists those involved in a dispute to resolve their differences. Successful results of mediation are called "settlements."

- *Statute of limitations.* If a manager intends to use the courts to enforce a contract, this must be done in a timely manner. There are laws (**statutes of limitations**) establishing

    > **STATUTES OF LIMITATIONS** Laws that set maximum time periods in which lawsuits must be initiated. If a suit is not initiated (or filed) before the expiration of the maximum period allowed, the law prohibits the use of the courts for recovery.

maximum time periods in which courts are legally permitted to enforce or settle contract disputes. Generally, the statute of limitations for written contracts is four years from the date of the breach; however, exceptions apply and state laws may vary.

Preventing Contract Breaches

Managers should avoid breaching an enforceable contract. Prevention is typically better than attempting to manage problems arising from a contract breach. In most cases a manager can avoid breaching a contract by following specific steps:

- *Get it in writing.* The single best way to avoid contract breach is to get all contracts in writing. When the relationship between contracting parties is complex, it is nearly impossible to remember all the contract requirements unless they are in writing.

  Complex contracts should be reviewed by an attorney; this is easiest if the proposed contract is written. Then an attorney can study the contract to assess modifications, if any, that might be required.

  Even though the contractual parties may change, the contract may survive. For example, the contract between a waste hauler and a restaurant may provide that the trash removal service will continue even if the restaurant is sold. The terms of the trash removal contract should be written with that in mind.

- *Read the contract thoroughly.* It is not possible for managers to fulfill all contractual terms unless they know their responsibilities. Nor is it possible to hold suppliers accountable unless contract language is known and understood. Consider a manager who plans a beach party. The manager contracts one year in advance with a talent agency to provide a popular and expensive band for the party. A fee is agreed upon, and the agent sends the manager a standard performance contract. Upon reading the contract carefully, the manager discovers the following:

  > *The agent, on behalf of himself and the entertainers, hereby authorizes the restaurant and its advertising agency to use all*

publicity information, including still pictures, and biographical sketches of any and all entertainers supplied by the agent. These pictures and information may be used in any media, including television, radio, newspaper, and Internet, that is deemed appropriate by the restaurant. Agent further agrees that all such publicity information will be made available to the Restaurant no later than 30 days before the performance.

Thirty days is not long enough to advertise the event. At least six months' lead time has been required for past events. A single sentence in a very long document can have a tremendous impact on the event's success. The talent agent will likely agree to provide publicity material within a time frame acceptable to the restaurant.

If the manager does not have time to read or the knowledge to understand a complex contract, it should be reviewed by an attorney. Many managers refer any contract exceeding a specific dollar amount or length of time to an attorney.

■ ***Keep copies of all contract documents.*** When there is a disagreement or failure by either party, contract language is critical. (It has been said, in a tongue-in-cheek manner, that "the large print giveth; the fine print taketh away.") Because it is not possible to determine whether a contract will be trouble free, keep a copy of all signed contracts. If the contract is oral, it is helpful to make notes about significant agreement points and file these notes.

Many managers keep separate files for contracts. Others place contracts with customer or supplier files; some do both. A contract must be easily available for review when clarification is needed.

■ ***Use good faith when negotiating contracts.*** Good faith is an individual's honest belief that what is being agreed to can be done. Carefully consider all contract commitments. Often, they are breached because one party finds it impossible to perform its obligations. Although circumstances can change and no one can be perfectly clear about the future, a careful, realistic assessment of contract capability and capacity can be helpful.

■ ***Note and calendar performance deadlines.*** When a contract requires specific actions by or on designated dates, list them in calendar form to know when performance is required. Create these time lines before signing a contract. Many lawsuits are initiated because one party did not do what was agreed to in a timely manner.

- *Ensure performance of third parties.* A manager often relies on others to fulfill part of a contract. Example: A restaurant hosts a meeting. To secure the contract, the manager agrees to provide audiovisual services. This property uses a third-party equipment supplier, whose failure can result in the restaurant's inability to keep its promises. When third parties are required, contract language addressing their possible failure to perform should be included.

- *Share contract information with those who need to know; educate staff about the consequences of contract breach.* Managers negotiate contracts that employees must fulfill. However, an employee's ability to honor contract terms relates to his or her knowledge of those terms. Suppose a manager agrees to opening earlier for lunch to secure a large group reservation. All affected staff must be informed so that there will be no surprises.

- *Resolve ambiguities as quickly and fairly as possible.* Despite everyone's best intentions, contractual problems can arise. It is important to deal with them promptly and ethically. Example: A tour bus company contracts to stop at a restaurant for a meal. The tour operator has a written contract. Upon leaving, the operator is surprised to find that the restaurant has added a bus parking charge to the bill. The operator protests that this charge was not part of the contract. The restaurant's manager indicates that nothing in the contract states that parking would be provided free. Honest people can "agree to disagree" about the original intent of the contracting parties. Had the issue arisen prior to signing the contract, it might have been quickly resolved. At this point, resolution is essential, because the restaurant's reputation and integrity are more important than the parking charge.

When managers place themselves in the position of the other party and try to understand its concerns, it may be possible to compromise and reduce the possibility of litigation.

MANAGER'S "TO DO" LIST

Review the following recommendations proposed in this chapter. Analyze your interest in and need for implementing these recommendations by completing the columns on the right side of the form. Remember that when task assignments are made, time requirements for completion should also be stated. Follow up, as improvement activities evolve, to ensure that your property is moving closer to the goal of minimizing litigation risks.

Recommended Procedures	In Place Now?			Needed to Implement			Assigned To	Completion Date
	Yes	No	N/A*	Policy	Training	Other		
When practical, written contracts are used.								
The manager ensures that all contracts are legally valid.								
Potential proposals are analyzed to ensure that all offers include specific information about how, where, when, and to whom the offer is made.								
Contracts are analyzed to ensure that the intended consideration is clearly identified.								
When practical, express contracts (those in which all components of the agreement are explicitly stated) are used.								
All complex contracts are reviewed by a competent attorney.								
Purchase agreements are committed to writing and are reviewed on a regular basis, at least annually.								
As required by the Uniform Commercial Code, all promises made by the manager in a purchase or sales contract are fulfilled.								
The restaurant has an effective guest reservation policy in effect, which is consistently used and always explained to guests.								
The manager discusses the implications of requiring a credit card to make a reservation with the guest when the reservation is made.								
Reservation systems incorporate practical procedures to reduce the number of no-shows.								

*N/A = Not Applicable

Recommended Procedures	In Place Now?			Needed to Implement			Assigned To	Completion Date
	Yes	No	N/A*	Policy	Training	Other		
When contracts providing products and services to guests are developed, the following essential clauses are carefully considered and utilized when applicable: • Length of time that price terms exist • Authorization to modify the contract • Deposit and cancellation policies • Allowable attrition • Indemnification for damages • Payment terms • Performance standards for quantity								
In developing contracts to purchase/receive products and services, the following essential clauses are carefully considered and utilized when applicable: • Payment terms • Delivery/start date • Completion date • Performance standards • Licenses and permits • Indemnification • Nonperformance • Dispute resolution terms								
The manager carefully studies all aspects of the operation and develops and properly advertises exculpatory clauses wherever necessary.								

*N/A = Not Applicable

Recommended Procedures	In Place Now?			Needed to Implement			Assigned To	Completion Date
	Yes	No	N/A*	Policy	Training	Other		
All contracts are read carefully in advance of signing to reduce the possibility that a contract breach will arise. Procedures include: • Contracts are in writing. • Proposed contracts are read thoroughly. • Copies of all contract documents are retained. • Good faith is used in negotiating contracts. • Calendar deadlines for performance are noted. • The performance of third parties is ensured. • Contract information is shared with those who must know about it. • Staff are educated about the consequences of a contract breach. • Ambiguities are resolved as quickly and fairly as possible.								

For more information and suggestions log onto www.hospitalitylawyer.com.

*N/A = Not Applicable

CONSULTANT'S CORNER

What Would You Do? (page 14)

Your first instinct may be to hit Vincent with one of the branches he cut down, but then you would just end up in jail for assault and battery. If, in fact, the agreement was just for trimming, then Vincent is probably right even though you believe that the removal of the trimmed branches and brush was implied in an agreement. This is why we emphasize writing down an agreement and thinking carefully through what it is you are contracting to do and contracting to receive prior to signing the agreement.

The recommendation might be different if you had contracted with Vincent's Landscaping Services previously and removal had never been discussed, yet removal had always occurred for the agreed-upon price for the trimming. That would show a pattern or a course of conduct, and you would probably be entitled to rely on that past conduct to believe that in this instance Vincent's would also remove the brush and branches.

What Would You Do? (page 18)

It is clear in this situation that Sue, rather than accepting the offer, made a counteroffer. Therefore, it is now totally up to the owner, at his sole discretion, as to whether to accept Sue's counteroffer. The owner is right when he tells Sue that she rejected the offer. When Sue made a counteroffer she rejected the first offer. In this instance, it is up to the owner to decide whether he is still interested in having Sue as the manager at the originally proposed salary.

What Would You Do? (page 23)

To overbook or not, that is the question. If you choose to overbook your capacity, you are doing so with the understanding that the guests who have made reservations are coming in with the expectation that you will honor those reservations according to their terms (i.e., time, price, and food items). And they have a legal right to expect that. You also have a legal right to expect that the guests who make reservations will show up and pay for the meals and the space they have reserved. Unfortunately, it is not common practice among restaurants to have guests guarantee their reservations as it is in the hotel business. As more restaurants charge customers for failure to have reservations and/or for not canceling those reservations it is hoped that problems with no-shows and overbooking will decrease.

What Would You Do? (page 31)

This is a situation faced by restaurateurs every day. The card that you have passed out is a very nice way to remind guests about the potential for food-borne illness. It is also an example of an exculpatory clause, particularly the last line that states, "We cannot be held responsible for any problems that occur." As you have learned in this chapter, courts are not usually inclined to enforce exculpatory clauses, so if in fact it was found that the food was contaminated prior to its being placed in the doggie bag or prior to being served to the guests, then you would more than likely be held responsible. That would, of course, be a very difficult thing to prove once the food is removed from the restaurant and it becomes the responsibility of the guests to care for it.

Using the card, however, does demonstrate the operator's sensitivity and concern for the guests, which could certainly have a positive impact on a jury or judge should a claim arise in the future.

3

RESTAURANT OPERATING STRUCTURES

MANAGER'S BRIEF

Managers reading this chapter will learn about alternative organizational business structures used by restaurants, along with the advantages and disadvantages of each. The responsibilities and obligations created by an agency relationship are explored as well. Many restaurants are owned and operated as franchises. The unique franchising business relationship is reviewed in detail. Specifically, managers will learn how franchise agreements affect the purchase, operation, and sale of a restaurant operation.

IMPORTANCE OF PROPER ORGANIZATIONAL STRUCTURE

Many people want to own their own businesses, and this is a strong factor in an ongoing interest in restaurant management.

When entrepreneurs start their businesses, they face many decisions, including location, product offerings, and financing. An important decision affecting the business's future involves organizational structure: the legal formation of the business entity. This is important because the courts and governments treat businesses and their owners differently, based on organizational structure.

Consider John, who, after years of working for a national restaurant chain, wishes to open his own restaurant. Depending on the type of organizational structure selected, the income tax he will pay on profits will vary considerably. In addition, the limits of his personal liability for business debts will be influenced by the organizational structure.

Officials in banks and other sources of capital make decisions about investing in a business venture based, in part, on its organizational structure. Equally important, a person's ability to sell or transfer ownership of a business is affected by the structure selected.

COMMON RESTAURANT ORGANIZATIONAL STRUCTURES

There are several common restaurant organizational structures, which are examined in this section.

Sole Proprietorship

A **sole proprietorship** is the simplest of all organizational structures. One individual owns all of the business and is responsible for all of its debts. The majority of small businesses in the United States are sole proprietorships.

In a sole proprietorship the owner's personal assets can be used to pay losses, taxes, or damages resulting from lawsuits. There is no personal protection

SOLE PROPRIETORSHIP A business organization in which one person owns, and often operates, the business and is responsible for all of its debts.

from any of the risks associated with owning a business. The sole proprietor has unlimited liability for business indebtedness.

Profits in a sole proprietorship are taxed at the same rate as the owner's personal income tax. Each year, the owner files a tax return listing the proprietorship's income and expenses. The profit or loss is reported on the owner's tax return. If the owner has income not directly related to the business, losses from the business can be used to reduce the overall amount of income subject to taxation.

Sole proprietorships can be started by opening a bank account to track the business's income and expenses. Because the owner will have unlimited liability, lenders evaluate the financial position of the owner carefully before providing capital. If the owner of a sole proprietorship operates under an "assumed name" (a name other than his or her own), an Assumed Name Certificate should be filed with the local government. If David Daniels began operating a diner called Davey's Diner, the term "Davey's Diner" would be the trade name. The Assumed Name Certificate filed with the local government lets others know that when they do business with Davey's Diner, they are actually doing business with David Daniels d/b/a (doing business as) Davey's Diner. Any entity operating under an assumed name—not just sole proprietorships—should file a certificate disclosing the operation's ownership and ownership structure. In many states filing this certificate is required by law.

Typically, should owners of sole proprietorships wish to sell the business or pass ownership rights to others, they can do so without requiring approval of any third party.

General Partnership

A **general partnership** is similar to a sole proprietorship, except that it consists of two or more owners who agree to share responsibility for the operation, financial performance, and liability of the business. Partnerships are formed through oral or written contracts. Generally, these agreements specify the contributions and responsibilities of each partner, including:

> **GENERAL PARTNERSHIP A business organization in which two or more owners agree to share the profits of the business and are also jointly and severally liable for its debts.**

- How much money each partner will contribute
- How much time each partner will contribute

- Who will make decisions about how the business is operated

- How profits or losses will be divided

- Procedures for ownership transfer if one (or more) partner wishes to sell part of the business or becomes unable to participate as a partner

Partnerships are occasionally used to begin small restaurant operations, but as the risk of liability increases, the operation is better served by converting to one of the limited liability structures described in the following discussions.

Like an owner of a sole proprietorship, the partners in a general partnership have unlimited liability for business indebtedness. The partners are liable for the partnership's debt jointly (they are liable as partners/owners), but they are also liable severally. This means that even if the partnership is owned on a 50-50 basis, if one partner cannot pay his or her portion of the debt, the other partner is liable for it. If loans are needed to establish the business, the assets of each partner will be evaluated by potential lenders. Business profits are distributed to the partners and taxed at the same rate as the owners' personal income tax.

Partnership agreements can be simple or complex, but because they are contracts, they are best documented in writing. This is particularly important in addressing the transfer of ownership rights by one or more partners.

Consider Greg and Mike. They have been equal partners in a restaurant for 20 years. Greg now wants to sell his portion of the partnership to his daughter. If there is nothing in the partnership agreement prohibiting this sale, he can transfer his half of the business. If, however, there is language in the partnership agreement allowing the remaining partner the right of first refusal, Mike can purchase the other half of the business before Greg can sell it to someone else.

LIMITED PARTNERSHIP A business organization with two classes of owners. The limited partner invests in the business, but in return for protection from liability, may not exercise control over its operation. The managing partner assumes full control of the business operation and can be held liable for any debts incurred.

Limited Partnership (LP)

A **limited partnership** (LP) consists of two classes of owners, the **limited partner** and the **general partner.** The limited partner invests money in the partnership. The general partner may or may not be an investor, but is the business's operating and financial manager.

A limited partnership is so named because of the limits placed on the potential liability of a particular

class of partners. As a general rule, liability will be limited if a partner is not directly involved in the daily
managerial decision making. The legal principle involves control. The general partner exercises control
over daily operations and, as a result, bears unlimited
liability for debts or damages incurred. A limited partner risks only his or her investment in the business but
must give up control of that investment in exchange
for a limited amount of liability. If a limited partner
becomes actively involved in the business's decision
making, the state may revoke the limited partnership's
protected status. This would subject all limited partners to potential unlimited liability for business debts.

LIMITED PARTNER The entity in a limited partnership who is liable only to the extent of personal investment. Limited partners have no right to manage the partnership.

GENERAL PARTNER The entity in a limited partnership who makes management decisions and can be held responsible for all debts and legal claims against the business.

The taxation on a limited partnership's profits is subject to the taxation requirements of general partnerships. The profits are distributed to the partners
and taxed at the same rates as the owners' personal income tax.

The limited partnership is a special type of business arrangement provided for by state law. Most states require specific forms to be filed with the
Secretary of State, or another agency, for a business to be granted limited partnership status. A limited partnership is closely regulated by the state, and most
states also require a written Limited Partnership Agreement to be filed. Even
where not required, an attorney should draw up an agreement prior to business
start-up.

WHAT WOULD YOU DO?

Nick formed a limited partnership with Ray to open a French restaurant. Nick was designated the managing partner and owned 75 percent of the business. Ray, with 25
percent ownership, was the limited partner and invested $100,000. After one year,
difficulties in the operation caused business to drop off, and Nick called Ray for advice.

Concerned about his investment, Ray visited the restaurant. After observing the
operation, the two partners decided to launch an expensive television ad campaign.
Ray designed the campaign with the help of a local advertising agency.

After a brief sales increase, revenues continued to decline, and three months after the campaign was launched, the restaurant closed. Total debts equaled $400,000,

with partnership assets of only $200,000. Included in the debt was $150,000 owed to the advertising agency. The agency sought payment directly from Ray, who claimed his liability was limited to the $100,000 previously invested in the business and refused to pay additional money. The agency sued the limited partnership, as well as Nick and Ray individually.

What would you do if you were Ray?

C Corporation

CORPORATION   An entity granted a charter legally recognizing it as a separate entity having rights and liabilities distinct from those of its shareholders.

A **corporation** has an identity separate from its shareholders. It is empowered with legal rights usually reserved only for individuals, including the right to sue and be sued, own property, hire employees, and lend and borrow money. Corporations differ from sole proprietorships and partnerships in that the corporation, not individual owners, is liable for debts incurred. This is a powerful advantage. Accordingly, as an operation becomes complex and liability risk is greater, incorporating becomes a sound business practice. Today many restaurant companies are incorporated.

The corporation owners are called shareholders because they own "shares" of the business. Legally, shareholders have the power to determine a corporation's direction and the way it is managed. In reality, shareholders may have little influence on how a corporation is run. Shareholders elect directors, who oversee the business and hire managers for daily operations (although many of these directors and managers may be shareholders). A shareholder is not liable for the corporation's debts or other obligations except to the extent of any commitment made to buy shares. Shareholders may also participate in any residual assets of the corporation if it is dissolved, after liabilities have been paid. The two most common types of corporations are "C" and "S" corporations.

A C corporation (referred to simply as a corporation) gets its name from Chapter C of the United States Internal Revenue Code. Although C corporations

DIVIDEND   A portion of profits received by shareholders, usually in relation to their ownership of a corporation.

shield shareholders individual liability, they also have a significant disadvantage. Profits from a C corporation are taxed twice. The first tax is levied on the profits of the corporation. Then the remaining profits may be distributed to the shareholders as **dividends.** Shareholders will then pay taxes on those dividends. The corporation must pay corporate taxes on profits even if the profits are not distributed to the corporation's owners.

Corporations are taxed at different rates from those applied to individuals, and the taxes paid may be affected by special rules allowing certain business expenses to be deducted from revenues prior to establishing the corporation's taxable income.

WHAT WOULD YOU DO?

Michelle wishes to start a restaurant. She has an inheritance of $1 million held in her name in a bank account. She wants to use $100,000 to begin the business. Because of concern for potential liability, she selects her business structure carefully. A sole proprietorship or a general partnership provides no liability protection. A limited partnership would also be ineffective because, as the business manager, she would have to take on the general partner's role and her liability would still be unlimited. If she selects a C corporation structure, her liability will be limited to the corporation's assets. If the restaurant is successful, however, it will pay a corporate tax at a higher rate than she pays as an individual on the profits. Then she must pay her own individual tax on profits removed from the business.

If you were Michelle, what would you do?

Corporations are more costly to establish and administer than sole proprietorships and general partnerships, but their ability to limit liability makes them popular. To establish a corporation, the business officers must file a document, "Articles of Incorporation," with either the Secretary of State or a Corporate Registrar's office in the state where the business will be incorporated. These Articles will disclose the corporation's officers and board of directors and the number of shares the company is authorized to sell initially.

> **S CORPORATION** A type of business entity offering liability protection to its owners, which is exempt from corporate taxation on profits. There are some restrictions that limit the circumstances under which an S corporation can be formed.

S Corporation

An **S corporation,** which avoids the double taxation of a C corporation, gets its name from the tax code. (An S corporation is also known as a "Sub-Chapter S" corporation.)

This structure makes good sense for many restaurants, including family-owned operations. Requirements for establishing and maintaining an S corporation status include:

- There must be no more than 35 shareholders.

- Only one class of stock may be issued.

- All shareholders must be U.S. citizens.

- All shareholders must be individuals—not corporations.

- The business operates on a calendar-year financial basis.

An S corporation provides the same liability protection offered by a C corporation, but must be established with all shareholders' agreement. This is done by filing a form with the Internal Revenue Service (IRS) signed by all corporation shareholders signifying agreement to elect S status.

In an S corporation, any business profits are distributed directly to shareholders in proportion to their ownership of the corporation. The profits are reported on the individuals' tax returns and are taxed at the individuals' taxable rates. This is similar to the favorable taxation treatment of a partnership, yet shareholders also receive the liability protection of a corporation.

Profits from an S corporation are taxable even if not distributed. For example, two brothers open a restaurant and select the S corporation structure. Profits in the first year are $50,000. They decide to use all profits from the first year to expand marketing efforts in the second year. The brothers must still pay individual taxes on the first year's profits in proportion to their ownership in the S corporation.

In addition, the requirement to file the S election form with the federal government, sometimes the state government also requires notification. Some states do not recognize the S corporation for state income tax purposes but do recognize it for liability purposes. Generally, S corporation restrictions make it most suitable for smaller companies, especially when the owners are also the employees and managers.

LIMITED LIABILITY COMPANY (LLC) A type of business organization that limits owners' liability for debts incurred by the business without some formal incorporation requirements.

Limited Liability Company (LLC)

A **limited liability company** (LLC) is a form of corporation created under state law. This is a fairly new structure created by some states to combine the best features of a corporation with the simplicity of a partnership. Under the typical LLC statute, the members (similar to shareholders in a corporation or partners in a partnership) are protected from the company's debts unless they undertake personal responsibility for a debt (such as a loan for the business). A member can serve as the owner or manager, yet still protect personal assets from liability.

An LLC is governed by an operating agreement similar to that of a partnership. It establishes rules for managing the company, as well as the rights and responsibilities of members. Depending on the state, the LLC may have to pay a filing or annual registration fee.

If it is developed properly, the IRS treats an LLC as a partnership for tax purposes, so there is no double taxation. However, in some states an LLC must pay state income taxes on profits. If an LLC is not properly organized within state guidelines, the IRS may consider the LLC a corporation for tax purposes.

This structure may become the preferred organizational structure for many restaurants, but, like all organizational structures, an LLC should be selected only after seeking the advice of a business attorney and tax advisor.

Important differences between each type of organizational structure are summarized as follows:

Sole Proprietorship

Liability	Owner has unlimited liability
Tax liability	Owner pays
Tax rate	Individual
To transfer ownership	No restrictions

General Partnership

Liability	Partners liable
Tax liability	Partners pay even if profits not distributed
Tax rate	Individual rate
To transfer ownership	Per partnership agreement

Limited Partnership (LP)

Liability	General partner has unlimited liability
	Limited partners liable only to extent of investment
Tax liability	Partners pay even if profits not distributed
Tax rate	Individual rate
To transfer ownership	Per limited partnership agreement

C Corporation

Liability	Shareholders protected from personal liability
Tax liability	Corporation taxed on profits
	Shareholders taxed on dividends
Tax rate	Corporate rate on profits; individual rate on dividends
To transfer ownership	Shares are transferable but can sometimes be restricted

S Corporation

Liability	Shareholders protected from personal liability
Tax liability	Shareholders pay even if profits not distributed
Tax rate	Individual rate
To transfer ownership	Limitations covered in shareholder's agreement

Limited Liability Company (LLC)

Liability	Members protected from personal liability
Tax liability	Members pay even if profits not distributed
Tax rate	Individual rate
To transfer ownership	Can require consent of all members unless organizational agreement states otherwise

THE AGENCY RELATIONSHIP

Sole proprietorships, partnerships, and corporations are subject to federal and state laws governing employer–employee relationships. The actions of employees directly affect the organization's liability (or potential liability). Owners must consider employee relationships when deciding their businesses' organizational structure and should select the one that best permits the absorption of liabilities incurred by employees.

In the United States, regardless of organizational structure selected, the relationship between businesses and employees usually takes the form of one of the following:

- Master–servant (also called employer–employee)

- Agent–principal

- Employer–independent contractor

To illustrate each relationship consider this scenario: John wants to start a restaurant but cannot operate it by himself. He must hire bartenders, waitstaff, and kitchen help. When hiring for these positions, he is creating an employer–employee relationship. John is the employer; those he hires are employees. The employer–employee relationship implies that the employee is under the employer's direct control. Therefore, employers are generally held responsible for an employee's behavior at work.

John may hire someone to act as general manager. If so, some of the manager's work may be directly controlled by John, but the manager may be empowered to make decisions for and to enter into contracts on behalf of the restaurant. Employees who act on behalf of the principal are referred to as **agents** of the principal. The agent would be the general manager, and the **principal** would be John and/or the restaurant itself.

> **AGENT** A person authorized to act for or to represent another, usually referred to as the principal.

The distinction between agent–principal and employer–employee is often blurred. As empowerment becomes more commonplace, the distinction may fade altogether. Employees who are given more discretion and authority may be categorized as agents. The distinction becomes important in trying to assess an employer's responsibility for an employee's acts. Suppose a customer becomes violently ill from foodborne pathogens linked to unsanitary practices by a kitchen employee. In an employer–employee relationship, John is held legally responsible for the guest's injuries under the concept of **respondeat superior.** However, it would be rare for a court to hold John responsible if the employee made any contracts or

> **PRINCIPAL** The person from whom an agent receives instructions and for whom the agent is expected to perform and make beneficial decisions; the agent's employer.

> **RESPONDEAT SUPERIOR** Literally, "Let the master respond." A legal theory holding the employer (master) responsible for the acts of employees.

promises on behalf of the restaurant with third parties. The employee in the employer–employee relationship cannot bind John or the restaurant. In an agent–principal relationship, the principal is responsible for the promises or obligations undertaken by the agent on behalf of the principal or the restaurant. If the manager of the restaurant (the agent) enters into a long-term contract to purchase meat, the principal and the restaurant will be responsible for fulfilling the obligations of the contract (assuming the contract meets the requirements discussed in Chapter 2).

Because they may be held responsible for the acts of their employees, managers must carefully select and train employees. A manager is responsible for hiring employees who will represent or make decisions on behalf of the operation. The manager must trust the capability of those individuals, as well as their integrity to act in the business's best interests when making decisions and/or entering into contracts. Chapters 7 and 8 will discuss how to minimize liability risk by selecting and managing employees properly under current federal and state employment laws.

INDEPENDENT CONTRACTOR
A person or entity that contracts with another to perform a particular task but whose work is not directed or controlled by the hiring party.

John may also have to hire individuals or companies to perform specialized tasks. For instance, he may need to repaint the exterior walls. John can hire an individual painter or a company that provides painting services. This suggests an **independent contractor** relationship.

Employers are usually not liable for the behavior of independent contractors. The general rule is that the more control the worker retains, the more likely the worker will be characterized as an independent contractor.

The following factors help to establish the existence of an independent contractor relationship:

- Degree of control or direction over the worker (the greater control the higher the probability that an independent contractor relationship does *not* exist).

- Amount of worker investment in the enterprise. (For example, does the worker provide personal tools and materials [independent contractor] or are they provided by the employer?)

- Opportunity for profit and loss. (Employees are ordinarily guaranteed a wage or salary; independent contractors usually bid a job for a set amount and must then perform efficiently to make a profit.)

- Permanency of the work relationship. (Most employees have a permanent, consistent relationship, full- or part-time, with one employer; independent contractors randomly work with different employers.)

- Whether worker's services are integral to the operation. (A plumber making a repair every few months is different from a dishwasher needed daily.)

A summary of characteristics used by courts and government agencies to help determine the type of relationship that exists is shown in the following chart.

RELATIONSHIP	CHARACTERISTICS
Employer–employee	The employees performance is controlled by the employer.
Agent–principal	An agent is empowered to act on behalf of or for the principal with some personal discretion. The principal is ordinarily responsible for the agent's conduct and obligations.
Employer–independent contractor	The employer has very little, if any, control over the conduct of the independent contractor, who is not an employee and usually not an agent. One could hire an independent contractor specifically to be an agent—examples include a real estate agent and an attorney.

RESTAURANT FRANCHISES

Regardless of the organizational structure selected, there are essentially two alternatives in owning a restaurant: independent ownership and **franchise**.

Definitions of Terms

A franchise exists when one party allows another to use its name, logo, and systems to operate a business.

FRANCHISE   A contract between a developing business (franchisor) and an operating company (franchisee) allowing the franchisee to run a business with the brand name of the developing business as long as contractual terms are followed.

WHAT WOULD YOU DO?

Suppose you develop a unique style of roasting pork that becomes popular. You own and operate five units selling this product. Each unit costs $175,000 to develop. Total unit revenues average $600,000, with a net profit margin of 10 percent per unit.

You discuss your success with a friend who wants to open some stores. He wants to know what you would charge to sell your recipe and your Standard Operating Procedures (SOP) manual, as well as the use of the same business name.

What would you do?

Owners who decide to operate a franchise can gain the marketing support of an established trademarked name; credibility with potential investors, lenders, customers, and supporters; and, often, assistance with operational problems. These advantages come with a price. Typically, the franchisor charges an initial fee plus a percentage of gross revenue. In addition, both parties sign a franchise agreement outlining the duties and responsibilities of each. This is referred to as a **"licensing" agreement,** because the franchise company (**licensor**) is granting the right (**license**) to operate as one of its franchisees (**licensee**).

LICENSING AGREEMENT A legal document detailing the specifics of a license.

LICENSOR One who grants a license.

LICENSE Legal permission to do a certain thing or operate in a certain way.

LICENSEE One who is granted a license.

DISCLOSURE To reveal in a full and honest way.

Franchise Disclosure

Evaluating and purchasing a franchise is a very complex undertaking. It is more difficult when franchisors are not open and honest about their offerings. Some franchisors have been fraudulent or deceptive in their claims. Therefore, regulations and laws have been enacted to specify **disclosure** requirements for franchisors in describing their product offerings.

The Federal Trade Commission (FTC) is mandated to regulate unfair or deceptive trade practices and franchise offerings. The FTC requires franchisors to supply information necessary for a potential franchisee to make an informed decision. However, it does not verify information accuracy.

The FTC has developed "Disclosure Requirements and Prohibitions Concerning Franchising and Business Opportunity Ventures." Commonly called the Franchise Rule, it establishes very detailed disclosure requirements for franchisors.

WWW: Internet Assistant

Log onto the Internet and enter: http://www.ftc.gov

Select: Business Guidance

Select: Franchise and Business Opportunities

Select: Franchise Rule Text

The Franchise Rule imposes six requirements applicable to "advertising, offering, licensing, contracting, sale or other promotion" of a franchise, as described in the following paragraphs.

Basic Disclosures. Franchisors must give potential investors a basic disclosure document at the earlier of the first face-to-face meeting or ten business days before any money is paid or an agreement is signed relative to investment (Part 436.1(a)).

Earnings Claims. If a franchisor makes historical or forecasted earnings claims, there must be a reasonable basis for those claims. Written evidence supporting claims must be given to potential investors at the same time as basic disclosures (Parts 436.1(b)–(d)).

Advertised Claims. The Rule affects only promotional ads that include an earnings claim. Ads must disclose the number and percentage of existing franchisees that have achieved the claimed results, along with cautionary language. The use of earnings claims in promotional ads also triggers required compliance with the Rule's earnings claim disclosure requirements (Part 436.1(e)).

Franchise Agreements. The franchisor must give investors a copy of the standard-form franchise agreement and related agreements at the same time as the basic disclosures, and final copies intended to be executed must be provided at least five business days before they are signed (Part 436.1(g)).

Refunds. Franchisors are required to make deposit refunds and initial payments to potential investors subject to refund conditions stated in the disclosure document (Part 436.1(h)).

Contradictory Claims. Although franchisors can supply investors with any promotional or other materials, no written or oral claims may contradict information provided in the required disclosure document (Part 436.1(f)).

Franchise Offering Circular

Some states have franchise investment laws requiring franchisors to provide a presale disclosure called a "Franchise Offering Circular" (FOC) to potential franchisees. These states treat a franchise sale like the sale of a security. They typically prohibit the offer or sale of a franchise within their state until a company's FOC has been filed as public record with, and registered by, a designated state agency.

States with disclosure laws give franchise purchasers important legal rights, including the right to bring private lawsuits for violation of the state disclosure requirements. The FTC tracks states that require franchisors to provide FOCs. Potential franchise purchasers residing in a state with these requirements should contact their state's franchise law administrator for additional information about the protection these laws provide.

The purpose of an FOC is to encourage a franchise purchase, and therefore it must be read carefully. The following information must be included under FTC guidelines:

- A description of the franchisor and the type of license being offered
- The business experience of the franchise company's owners and/or managers
- Initial fees, continuing fees, and royalties, if required
- Initial investment estimates
- The licensee's obligations
- The licensor's obligations
- Policies about the geographic territory protected by the license agreement
- Restrictions on what the licensee may sell and how it may be sold
- Renewal and termination policies
- Transfer of ownership policies
- Claims regarding average earnings or profitability of current franchisees
- Locations of current franchisees
- A sample franchise (license) agreement
- Any state-specific information
- The name and address of the franchisor's legal representative

Additional items may be needed as mandated by state law, FTC requirements, and the specific nature of the franchise. As with any disclosure, those preparing it should be honest; otherwise, they may face possible litigation for deception. Those that read the document should try to verify, to the greatest extent possible, the information it contains.

Purchasing a Franchise

After reviewing the FOC, the owner may elect to execute a contract with a franchisor. If so, a Franchise Agreement will be signed. This document regulates the relationship between franchisee and franchisor. Ensure that information in the FOC is consistent with that found in the Franchise Agreement.

Franchise Agreement. The franchise agreement details the rights and responsibilities of the franchisor and franchisee. The document will detail the following:

- The license granted
- Franchisee responsibilities
- Franchisor responsibilities
- Proprietary rights
- Audit requirements
- Indemnification and insurance requirements
- Transfer of ownership policies
- Termination policies
- Renewal options
- Relationship of parties to the contract
- Areas of protection
- Terms of the agreement (start and stop dates)

The franchise agreement is critical because it details the responsibilities of the franchisor and the franchisee. It should be carefully examined by an attorney. The manager with franchise responsibilities, either as an owner or as an employee hired by the owner, must carefully follow the contract terms. If not, the franchisor may have the right to terminate the contract.

Advantages of a Franchise. The purchase of a franchise license can have a tremendous impact upon the success of the restaurant. For a price competitive with that spent on a start-up venture, the buyer may obtain a proven concept with local or national name recognition. In addition, operating manuals, training assistance, and national advertising support may be supplied by the franchisor as part of the franchise contract.

Further benefits are gained when research and development is part of the franchisor's responsibilities. Most small business owners are too busy with day-to-day operations to research industry trends and develop new products or services to meet customers' needs.

Disadvantages. Although consumers often prefer the consistency offered by franchised properties, managers may be hampered by franchisor rules and regulations that ignore local needs. (Offering grits on a breakfast menu may be important in the South, but makes less sense elsewhere.) The best franchisors allow franchisees to make adjustments for local conditions while maintaining the integrity of the franchise concept.

Before Signing a Franchise Agreement. Franchisors are generally in the stronger bargaining position, so the franchise agreement is often heavily weighted in their favor. Like any contract, this agreement is negotiable. Up-front application fees, monthly royalties, areas of protection, required purchases, and facility renovations are contract areas that can be negotiated before signing the agreement. It is a good idea to seek the advice of a franchise attorney before signing a franchise agreement.

Franchisor/Franchisee Disagreements

Difficulties and misunderstandings can arise between franchisors and franchisees even when details seem to be clearly spelled out. Some glaring areas of tension center on specific ways of operating the business and balancing the franchisee's needs with those of the franchisor.

Encroachment/ Impact. Franchisors desire growth, and franchisees desire profitable units. Although these two interests often coincide, sometimes they do not.

Consider a certain owner who opens a franchise unit. The franchise agreement prohibits the franchisor from granting additional franchises of the same brand in a proximity that will damage the original franchisee. What constitutes damage, and who makes that determination? An unscrupulous franchisor may claim that no damage will result and grant competing franchises simply to maximize short-term revenue from franchise fees.

Franchisors may grant franchises to individuals who then develop strong sales. This sometimes prompts the franchisor to build company units nearby that compete with the franchisee. Granting additional franchises in an area already served by a franchisee can be cause for litigation.

Robert signs a franchise agreement to operate a restaurant. His agreement prevents the franchisor from granting additional franchises in his market area without an impact study. Three years later, the franchisor buys a second restaurant brand that targets the same customers. Robert learns that a franchisor-owned restaurant will be built across the street from his property. He believes that many of his customers will like the new restaurant and protests that his franchisor is violating franchise agreement terms. He requests a copy of the impact study he feels should have been produced. The franchisor maintains that Robert has protection only against other restaurants of the same brand. Therefore, no protection exists nor should an impact study have been performed.

What would you do if you were Robert?

Some franchisors grant franchisees a geographic territory that cannot be entered by the company or additional franchisees without the original franchisee's consent.

Purchasing Requirements. Franchisors often establish standards for products to be sold or supplies to be used. Sometimes a product is so specialized that it may be purchased only from the franchisor. When this is true, it is reasonable for the franchisor to dictate the supply source. Problems can arise, however, when franchisors dictate product specifications for standard items and try to designate "sole source" vendors. This practice, called a **tying arrangement**, usually violates antitrust law.

> **TYING ARRANGEMENT** An often illegal agreement requiring that as a precondition of purchasing or obtaining services, other services must be purchased through the seller.

Some franchisors come close to violating the tying arrangement prohibition by using "preferred suppliers" to provide a specific product to all franchisees. The preferred supplier may be charged a fee, kept by the franchisor, to participate in the program. Instead of creating a mandated specification, the franchisor dictates the supply source. This practice eliminates opportunities to accept bids from local suppliers that could be lower. Although franchisors may take reasonable steps to ensure product conformity, the courts have not supported their efforts to force franchisees into tying arrangements.

Operations Manual Changes. Before a franchisee purchases a franchise, he or she should examine the franchisor's Standard Operating Procedures (SOP) manual. This may specify details about product and service offerings, guest relations policies, and even opening/closing times. SOP manuals can be hundreds of pages long. Franchisors generally require franchisees to follow the manual and any subsequent changes that are made.

Franchisors continually review their policies and procedures manuals. Ideally, franchisors seek operators' input prior to making changes in their manuals. However, franchisees are generally required to follow any new policies and procedures even if they were not in place when the original agreement was signed.

Renewal Clauses. The duration of a franchise agreement can be established for any time agreeable to both parties; ten years is common. When the agreement expires, the franchisee generally wants a renewal because if the operation is still in business after ten years, the venture has been successful. Unfortunately, the franchisee typically is not able to renew the existing agreement but is asked to sign a new agreement with terms that may be very different from the original ones.

NONCOMPETE AGREEMENT A contractual agreement between two parties in which one party, upon termination of the business relationship, agrees not to compete within a designated geographic area for a designated period of time.

Noncompete Clauses. Franchisors often write **noncompete** clauses into the franchise agreement. The intent is to prevent a franchisee from learning trade secrets and then using them to run a competitive operation in the same market. The franchisee may argue that these clauses prevent the legitimate practice of a learned profession.

WHAT WOULD YOU DO?

Lo Vin Do is an immigrant who spent ten years operating a small restaurant serving lunches, dinners, and carry-out baked goods. Later, he bought a franchise operation that sold European-style fresh baked breads. A clause in the franchise agreement prohibited, "the operation, by Mr. Do, of a Similar Business" within a ten-mile radius for five years if the franchise agreement were terminated for any reason.

Mr. Do established the franchise as a limited partnership. The limited partnership declared bankruptcy two years later. Mr. Do closed the operation and returned all confidential operating materials to the franchisor.

Mr. Do, operating as a sole proprietor, again opened a small table-service restaurant serving Vietnamese foods and French pastry products. This restaurant was located approximately three miles from his previous site. The franchisor contacted Mr. Do, stating that he must cease operation of the restaurant/bakery or face litigation.

What would you do if you were Mr. Do?

Franchisees may assume, when signing the franchise agreement, that a non-compete clause is a minor item. It seems fair to agree not to compete in a similar business. Difficulties can arise, however, if relationships dissolve; franchisors may use their generally stronger legal capabilities to diligently enforce the non-compete clause.

Selling the Franchise

Selling a franchise can be very difficult, because the sale generally requires the franchisor's approval. The rationale is clear: It is in the franchisor's best interest to ensure that any new owner meets the requirements set for all franchisees. This is a legitimate concern, which can result in a situation that places restrictions on the seller.

In some cases, the franchisor retains the **right of first refusal** in a franchise sale.

In other cases, the franchise agreement requires the franchisor to be notified about a pending sale. Should the new buyer not renew the franchise, the franchisee may have to pay a termination fee to the franchisor.

> **RIGHT OF FIRST REFUSAL A clause in a contractual agreement between two parties whereby one party, upon termination of the business relationship, can exercise the right to buy the interest of the other party before those rights can be offered for sale to another.**

An independent owner can determine a suggested selling price, advertise the business for sale, and sell the business as desired. A franchisor, however, often requires the buyer to sign the then-current franchise agreement, which probably contains significantly different financial terms than those which are contained in the selling franchisee's agreement. (What the buyer is buying is often different from what the seller is selling!)

Legal Responsibilities of Managers

The manager of a franchise operation must satisfy both the owners and the franchisor. When conflicts occur, an agency relationship clause in the franchise agreement will be clear about that issue. Language similar to the following will be included:

> *The franchisee is an independent contractor. Neither the franchisee nor the franchisor is the legal representative or agent of the other. No partnership, affiliate, agency, fiduciary responsibility, or employment relationship is created by this agreement.*

In reality, however, the courts may hold a franchisor responsible for the acts of its franchisee operators/managers.

MANAGER'S "TO DO" LIST

Review the following recommendations proposed in this chapter. Analyze your interest in and need for implementing these recommendations by completing the columns on the right side of the form. Remember that when task assignments are made, time requirements for completion should also be stated. Follow up, as improvement activities evolve, to ensure that your property is moving closer to the goal of minimizing litigation risks.

Recommended Procedures	In Place Now?			Needed to Implement			Assigned To	Completion Date
	Yes	No	N/A*	Policy	Training	Other		
The owner has sought the advice of competent legal and tax advisors about the best organizational structure for the restaurant. (If this was not done when the business was initially organized, the owner will seek this assistance now.)								
All agreements about organizational structure are in writing and are closely examined by an attorney before being signed.								
All documents required by the state and federal governments about organizational structure are completed and filed.								
Job descriptions and other human resource tools make it very clear whether a staff member is in an employee–employer or agency relationship with the principal.								
Managers address all factors to ensure that independent contractors are truly independent and cannot make the business responsible for independent contractor actions.								
Owners carefully review and seek advice from attorneys regarding all information in a franchise disclosure, including: • Basic disclosure • Earnings claims • Advertised claims • Franchise agreement • Refunds • Contradictory claims								

*N/A = Not Applicable

Recommended Procedures	In Place Now?			Needed to Implement			Assigned To	Completion Date
	Yes	No	N/A*	Policy	Training	Other		
If the manager lives in a state requiring franchise offering circulars, this information is carefully reviewed by the prospective franchisee and by an attorney.								
Before purchasing a franchise, the owner carefully reviews the proposed franchise agreement and seeks advice from an attorney about every detail of this document.								
When reviewing a proposed franchise agreement, the potential owner considers every area in which negotiation can help the prospective franchisee operation.								
Among the areas of a proposed franchise agreement to be carefully studied are: • Encroachment • Purchasing requirements, including tying arrangements • Operations manual changes • Renewal clauses • Noncompete clauses • Proposed restrictions relating to sale of the franchise								

For more information and suggestions
log onto www.hospitalitylawyer.com.

*N/A = Not Applicable

CONSULTANT'S CORNER

What Would You Do? (page 48)

Ray should contact an attorney immediately. From the facts presented, it does appear that he has crossed the line from the status of a passive limited partner to an active managing partner by making significant decisions about the operation itself. The outcome of this situation will depend on whether the advertising agency believed that it was dealing with the limited partnership or Ray individually, and whether Ray is found to have violated the limited partner management restrictions by his active participation in the day-to-day operations of the business.

What Would You Do? (page 49)

This scenario emphasizes the value of the S corporation to the small businessperson. If Michelle incorporates and elects S status, she will then receive the tax benefits of a sole proprietorship or partnership as well as the liability shield provided by the corporate structure.

What Would You Do? (page 55)

Even though the situation sounds fairly simple and you are dealing with a friend, the best advice is to seek legal counsel that deals in protecting intangible property rights such as recipes, procedures, and names (trademarks/service marks). Moreover, in most states the sale of a "franchise" such as this is normally subject to very specific disclosure requirements. In addition, the Federal Trade Commission governs the sale of franchises, so one must use extreme caution in order to comply appropriately with all of the applicable rules and laws.

By using caution and complying with all applicable laws, you would reap the benefits of your sale if the friend is successful in using the concept; if your friend is not successful, it will be very difficult for you to be held responsible for his business failure.

What Would You Do? (page 61)

This is a very complicated situation that is totally dependent on the terms of the franchise agreement and/or the interpretation of the intent of the agreement by the court. If the franchise agreement specifically precludes additional franchises from being placed in the geographic area, then Robert is probably on the losing end of a very expensive battle. If, however, the franchise agreement uses language such as "additional franchises or similar food service operations," then the similarity of the two restaurants would have to be assessed. It would probably be in Roberts's best interest to seek an attorney who is well versed in franchise agreements and litigation surrounding franchises.

What Would You Do? *(page 62)*

It does appear from the specs that Mr. Do has violated the noncompete agreement that was included in the franchise agreement. In many states, courts have been reluctant to enforce broad noncompetes because they did not want to deprive a person the opportunity of making a living or practicing a trade. However, they are sensitive to the fact that noncompetes are an important part of commerce and the sharing of proprietary information.

There are usually two significant issues in a noncompete agreement: distance, or geographic area, and length of time the agreement will be in effect. In this case, it appears that Mr. Do has violated both major restrictions, and it is likely that the court will enforce the agreement. Accordingly, Mr. Do may have to move his operation outside the ten-mile radius or request that the court refine the noncompete because his small operation is not affecting the franchisor's operations that it was designed to protect.

4

LEGAL RESPONSIBILITIES
OF MANAGERS

MANAGER'S BRIEF

Managers reading this chapter will understand the difference between real and personal property. They will understand components of a bill of sale form, know the difference between a bill of sale and deed, and realize when each should be used. Managers will understand the difference between an express and an implied warranty. A discussion of leasing includes the components of a lease agreement necessary for adequate protection. Managers will learn the difference between trademarks, patents, copyrights, and concept rights and will know when they are in compliance with the laws governing them. Finally, they will understand the legal aspects involved in the public broadcasting of music and videotapes.

PROPERTY BASICS

When managers are away from the restaurant, they are said to be "off-property." "Property," in this sense, refers to the restaurant's grounds and buildings. We all hope that guests do not leave with fancy stemware glasses, because these are the property of the restaurant. In this case, "property" refers to a physical asset owned by the restaurant. The concept of **property** and its legal characteristics are important for a manager to understand.

> **PROPERTY** Includes money, tangible items, and intangible rights that have a value or are a source of revenue.

There are two types of property of concern to a manager: real property and personal property.

Laws affect property ownership disputes and claims and an individual's right to use property. The law treats real property differently from personal property, and the distinctions between the two must be well understood.

Real Property

Real estate, a related term, is frequently used when referring to **real property.**

> **REAL PROPERTY** Land and all the things permanently attached to it.

Trees and grasses on a restaurant's land are part of its real estate. **Improvements** are features such as fences, sewer lines, and the like, which are changes or additions to land that make it more valuable.

> **REAL ESTATE** Land, including soil and water, buildings, trees, crops, improvements, and the rights to the air above and minerals below the land.

Personal Property

Any property that is not real property is **personal property.** This includes anything that isn't attached, dug, or built into the land. A restaurant on an acre of ground is real property, but the tables and chairs in the dining room are not. A restaurant building permanently attached to a plot of land is real property. However, a catering van parked in the restaurant's parking lot is not.

> **IMPROVEMENTS** Additions to real estate that enhance its value.

> **PERSONAL PROPERTY** Any property that is not real property.

Personal property can be **tangible** or **intangible.**

Tangible personal property is the type we most often think of when referring to something owned by a company or an individual. Tangible property includes items easily moved between locations, such as autos, furniture, and equipment.

Intangible personal property can be just as valuable as real estate or tangible personal property. It includes items such as franchise rights, trademarks, stocks, bonds, and interests in securities.

To appreciate the importance of intangible personal property, consider Stanley who uses a personally blended seasoning salt for beef, which he also sells at his restaurant. He creates a small, stylized cartoon drawing of a cow for the seasoning's label. An attorney helps him apply for and receive the exclusive right to use this drawing in the business. Stanley's product is successful, and soon the stylized cow is associated with creativity, good taste, and uncompromising quality. "Everyone" recognizes the cow drawing. Stanley is approached by a multinational seasoning company that would like to use the drawing on its products.

> **TANGIBLE PERSONAL PROPERTY** Personal property that has physical substance and can be held or touched. Examples include furniture, equipment, and food inventories.

> **INTANGIBLE PERSONAL PROPERTY** Personal property that cannot be held or touched. Examples include patent rights, copyrights, and concept rights.

The right to use the stylized drawing of the cow is an example of an intangible property right. Although the drawing itself may be easily duplicated and worth only pennies, what it represents and the right to use it are valuable and may not be taken from Stanley without his consent. He has the right to determine how this property can be legally used.

A partnership or company can also own personal property. In this context, the word "personal" designates only that the property is not "real" property or real estate.

Fixtures: Can Personal Property Become Real Property?

Although it appears simple to determine what is real and what is personal property, the solution can be complex. The difficulty comes from distinguishing between items intended as improvements that are "permanently attached" to the land and others simply placed on the land.

A chimney built into a restaurant is considered permanently attached to the building. What about a fan placed on the floor of the dining room? Would a fan affixed to the chimney to improve heat circulation be considered real property? Would it matter exactly how the fan was attached?

> **CHATTEL** Personal property, easily removable, not considered real property.

The answer to these questions comes with an understanding of the terms **chattel** and **fixture.**

FIXTURE   An article that was once a chattel but has now become a part of the real property because it is permanently attached to the soil or to something attached to the soil.

A fan on the floor of a dining room is not considered real property. Because it is clearly removable, it would be classified as chattel.

Fixtures include all things that are permanently attached to property, such as ceiling lights, awnings, window shades, doors, and doorknobs. A fan that has been permanently installed in the fireplace itself would be a fixture. One can remove an item that has been permanently attached to real property; for example, a ceiling fan that has been permanently installed in a dining room can be removed. However, legally, an item that is to remain with the property and is not removable without doing damage to the property is ordinarily a fixture.

WHAT WOULD YOU DO?

Jay purchased a small building from Tom. The two individuals agreed on a fair price, and both signed the sales contract. Jay was to take possession of the property on March 1.

On February 28, he arrived at the property to take some exterior measurements and observed Tom removing a window air-conditioning unit from the office at the rear of the building. Jay protested that the air conditioner should not be removed because it was part of the sale. Tom replied that the unit was his personal property, was never intended to be sold with the building, and was not specifically mentioned in the contract.

What would you do if you were Jay?

Questions often arise about whether certain fixtures and/or improvements are considered real property or should be treated as personal property. The general rule is: If an item can be removed without damaging any real property, it is considered personal property. When the issue is not clear, consult with an attorney.

PURCHASING PROPERTY

Purchasing Real Property (Deeds)

To sell property legally, the seller must have a legal **title** to it. It is the buyer's responsibility to verify this, otherwise, after the purchase the buyer may learn that he or she does not legally own the property.

Whether real or personal property is purchased, the establishment of its title is the manager's responsibility. Although title to land and real estate may seem simple to verify, the process can be complex.

Deeds. Title to real property can be transferred from an owner in a variety of ways, including marriage, divorce, death, an act of the courts, bankruptcy, gift giving, or sale. A **deed** is used to transfer ownership of real property from one person or entity to another. It consists of the date, names, and descriptions of the parties involved in the transfer, the consideration given for the property, a full description of the property, and any exceptions to the transfer.

Deeds may be either **warranty deeds** or **quitclaim deeds.** The laws governing deeds vary from state to state, so it is important to ensure that legal title to the real property is provided in the deed.

When there is any doubt as to the legitimacy of the title to a property, it is sometimes necessary to conduct a **title search.**

Title Insurance. Even when the ownership of a piece of property is well established by a title search, it is advisable for a buyer to purchase title insurance. This is a critical part of any commercial or private purchase of real estate. Title insurance helps protect the buyer's interests should someone else claim ownership of a

> **TITLE** The sum total of all legally recognized rights to the possession and ownership of property.

> **DEED** A written document used to transfer land or other real property from one person to another.

> **WARRANTY DEED** A deed that provides that the person granting the deed agrees to defend the title from claims of others. In general, the seller is representing full ownership of the property and that he or she will stand behind this representation.

> **QUITCLAIM DEED** A quitclaim deed conveys only those rights that the grantor has. This type of deed transfers the owner's interest to a buyer, but does not guarantee that there are no other claims against the property or that the property is, indeed, legally owned by the seller.

> **TITLE SEARCH** A review of real estate records to determine the ownership and description of a piece of real property.

property after the buyer has completed the sale. Title insurance covers any losses as the result of these claims.

Common instances in which title insurance has protected a buyer include:

- Forgery
- Improper court proceedings
- Survey mistakes
- Missing heirs
- Unfiled liens

Some managers may confuse title insurance with a lender's title policy. The latter (lender's policy) protects a lender (such as a bank) from claims against the title to the real property, and title insurance protects the buyer.

To illustrate the importance of title insurance, consider Kimberly's case. When her father dies, she inherits land outside a city. Her father does not leave a will, but his house and the land on which it rested is passed on to Kimberly (his only living heir) by state law. Thirty years later, Kimberly sells the land to Brian, who builds a restaurant on the site. Five years later, Joshua produces a lien and a will that, he claims, was signed by Kimberly's father. The will states the father's wishes to leave the land to Joshua to settle a debt. In this case, Brian's claim to the land may be questionable. Title insurance will protect Brian if the newly produced will is proved valid.

Purchasing Personal Property (Bill of Sale)

Managers must have a thorough understanding of the law and practices surrounding the transfer of ownership of personal property.

BILL OF SALE A document under which personal property is transferred from a seller to a buyer.

Bill of Sale. This is the formal document used to transfer ownership of personal property from one individual or entity to another. The following items are included in a bill of sale:

- Name of seller
- Name of buyer
- Consideration
- Description of the property

- Statement of ownership by seller

- Date of sale

A bill of sale is a contract and can take many forms. For example, buyers commonly agree to buy a certain product from a supplier on a regular basis. Consider Renee, the manager of a large restaurant. She knows she will need a large quantity of ground beef throughout the year but wants to take delivery on a daily basis. To negotiate the best price, she places her entire order with the same wholesaler and executes a Contract for Sale of Goods to ensure that the quality, price, and terms agreed upon are maintained throughout the year. (See Sample Contract for Sale of Goods in Appendix C.)

A contract developed to transfer ownership of personal property is common when the property cannot be viewed at the time of sale or when it has not yet been manufactured. For example, if a restaurant orders custom-made furniture, it may not be manufactured by the seller until a contract has been signed by both parties. As with all contracts, the contract for the sale of goods should be carefully examined by both the buyer and the seller.

One must determine exactly when the transfer of ownership occurs in a sale of personal property. Generally, goods are shipped FOB (free on board). This term refers to shippers being responsible for the care and safety of goods until they are delivered to the buyer's designated location. Transfer of ownership occurs not at the time of sale in this case, but upon delivery.

Neither the bill of sale or the more formal contract for the sale of goods requires the seller to provide a title when transferring ownership. This is different from the sale of real property, where a title (deed) is required. Unlike real property, ownership of personal property is generally assumed by its possession, and it is not customary for the seller to prove ownership rights. (An exception involves the sale of motor vehicles.)

Purchasing Stolen Property

When property is stolen, its possession does not equate to the lawful right to sell. There is no criminal penalty if a buyer innocently purchases stolen goods from a seller who indicates ownership. However, if the rightful owner reclaims the goods, the innocent buyer's only recourse is the thief. (The buyer can file a lawsuit against the thief for the return of any money paid.) In reality, the buyer's ability to identify and help prosecute the thief is minimal, and it is in a manager's best interest to buy only from reputable sellers.

Managers may be punished if they have knowingly purchased stolen goods. Although it may be easy to trace stolen goods, it is more difficult to determine whether a buyer knew the goods were stolen.

WHAT WOULD YOU DO?

Your friend tells you about a purchase of 50 full-sized stainless steel pans for $2 each from a passing "liquidator." He jumped at the chance to buy them because, when new, the pans cost over $75 each.

When you ask about the seller, he says that two men simply arrived at his restaurant in a small pickup truck full of small food service equipment.

"Best of all," he says, "as soon as I washed them and put them in with my regular stock, there was no way anyone could tell the difference between the ones I just purchased from the ones I already had!"

What would you do if you needed pans?

A buyer is violating federal law if he or she knowingly purchases stolen goods, and those goods:

- Have a value of more than $5,000 and
- Have been a part of interstate commerce

The term "interstate commerce" refers to the movement of property from one state into another.

Because severe penalties are involved, wise managers avoid purchasing any property that is sold at far below its real value, is sold at odd times or by questionable salespersons, or if there is doubt about its origin. If something appears too good to be true, it generally is, and should be avoided.

Warranties

WARRANTY A promise about a product, made by either a manufacturer or a seller, that is a part of the sales contract.

Those who sell property often find that the promises they make about the property can help to sell it. For example, if a manager decides to purchase a copy machine, the promises, or **warranties,** made by the machine's manufacturer may influence the selection of a machine. If two machines cost approximately the same, but the manufacturer of one warrants free repairs during the first two years, whereas the other manufacturer does not, the first manufacturer's warranty may be influential in the selection of that machine.

Before signing any contract to purchase goods, a manager should determine what warranties, if any, are included in the purchase. When purchasing real property, a deed helps explain exactly what is included. Similarly, a warranty helps explain exactly what rights are included when personal property is purchased. Remember that a warranty is part of the sales contract, and the intangible rights it offers the buyer are just as real and significant as the property itself.

Make sure that any warranties offered orally are documented in the sales contract. Warranties can be either expressed or implied.

An **express warranty** is created when a manufacturer makes a statement of fact about the capabilities and qualities of a product or service. These statements can be made by a salesperson or in promotional literature. For example: "This copier will make 35 copies per minute" or "This dishwasher uses six gallons of water for each rinse cycle."

> **EXPRESS WARRANTY   A statement of fact made by a seller about a product or service being sold.**

A seller who makes claims about the capabilities of a product or service offered is obligated under law to deliver a product or service meeting all described capabilities.

Express warranties are considered part of the sales contract. The law enforcing the truthfulness of warranties is the Uniform Commercial Code (UCC; see Chapter 2). When a buyer relies on facts to purchase a product or service that later prove to be false, a breach of the sales contract has occurred. Under the UCC, the buyer may be entitled to recover damages from the seller.

The UCC requires that personal property being sold conform to two **implied warranties.** One is that the item is fit to be used for a particular purpose (an implied warranty of fitness). The second is that the item will be in good working order and will adequately meet the purposes for which it was purchased (an implied warranty of merchantability).

> **IMPLIED WARRANTY   The unwritten expectation that a product or service being sold is fit for use, free of defects, and suitable for its stated purpose.**

In many states consumers can enforce their rights with respect to implied warranties up to four years after purchase, during which time the seller is liable for product defects or breakdowns, including implied warranties established by the UCC.

The seller may disclaim (negate) an express or implied warranty by inserting certain language in the sales contract. The UCC has drafted standard contract clauses that can be used for these situations. As with any sales contract, the disclaimer must be in writing and agreed to by both parties.

Just as price is negotiable, so are warranties. Try to negotiate additional warranties before making a purchase. Before buying personal property, understand the warranty offer and compare warranties from competing brands. Seek to negotiate the longest, strongest, most comprehensive warranty possible and insist that it be in writing.

When evaluating a warranty offer, ask the following questions:

- How long is the warranty?

- When does the warranty begin?

- Will it include charges for the parts and/or labor to make the repairs?

- What parts of the purchase are covered by the warranty?

- Can you lose the warranty if you do not follow manufacturer's guidelines for routine service and maintenance? (Who is permitted to perform these tasks?)

- Where is authorized service to be performed?

- Who pays to deliver the defective product to the repair area?

FINANCING PROPERTY PURCHASES

The buying and selling of property is fairly straightforward when the buyer pays the entire purchase price all at once. It is more complicated when the buyer decides to extend payments over time. Consider Bill, who operates a large restaurant. He determines that his dish washing machine must be replaced. The cost will be in excess of $8,000. He cannot afford to purchase a machine for cash but can afford a monthly payment. He secures a bank loan to purchase the machine.

What if he cannot make the loan payments? What rights would the bank have? (Can it repossess the machine?) These and other complications can arise when personal property is financed.

Debtor and Creditor Relationship

A **lien** is a person's right to retain a lawful interest in another's property until the owner fulfills a legal duty. If a manager purchases new tables and pays one half of the purchase price when they are delivered and the other half over six months, the seller would retain a lien on the furniture. That is, the seller maintains a lawful ownership interest until the furniture is completely paid for. Because the tables are housed in the restaurant, the buyer (restaurant) would also have partial ownership and rights to the property. In this example, two parties have legitimate and legal claims to the ownership of the furniture. This dual ownership involves liens and collateral.

> **LIEN** A claim against property that gives the creditor (lien holder) the right to repossess and/or sell that property if the debtor does not repay the debt in a timely manner.

Collateral is an asset a person agrees to give up if a loan is not repaid. A lien is a claim against the asset used to ensure payment of a debt—the collateral. Liens can be recognized by contract, in general trade practices, or implied by law.

> **COLLATERAL** Property pledged to secure the repayment of a debt.

The process of legally recording a contractual lien is called making the lien **perfect,** or "perfecting" the lien. The possessor of a lien who files appropriate records with the proper public office is a secured creditor. This creditor has a superior right to possession of the collateral or any proceeds if the collateral is sold.

> **PERFECT (lien)** To make a public record of a lien or take possession of the collateral.

Perfecting a lien implied by law is done by taking possession of the property. If an air-conditioning unit is taken to a repair facility, the repaired unit normally stays in possession of the service facility until payment for repairs has been made.

Other liens include judgment liens ordered by the courts and landlord liens whereby a landlord can secure rent payment by taking a tenant's property if necessary. In most states, mechanics and persons who furnish building materials are entitled to a lien. In some states, these claims must be filed in the appropriate government office or established by a suit brought within a limited period of time. Upon the subsequent sale of the property, these liens, if properly filed, are paid.

Mortgages and Deeds of Trust

When financing the sale of real property, creditors generally insist on securing the debt with a lien backed by collateral. Usually, the lien will be filed on the real property being purchased. For example, if Marion wishes to purchase land and a building to house a restaurant, he might secure funding from a bank. Marion would actually buy the real property with money lent by the bank, and the bank would file for a **mortgage** lien on the property; the land and building would serve as loan collateral. In some states, a **deed of trust** serves as a substitute for a mortgage lien.

> **MORTGAGE** The pledging of real property by a debtor to a creditor to secure debt payment.

If Marion decides to sell the property before the mortgage is completely repaid, a buyer cannot obtain a clear title until the lien is removed.

> **DEED OF TRUST** Used in some states instead of a mortgage. A deed of trust places legal title to real property in the hands of a trustee until the debtor has paid for the property.

Security Agreements

When creditors retain some legal rights of ownership in personal property, they have a **security interest** in that property.

> **SECURITY INTEREST** A legal ownership right to personal property.

When personal property is involved, creditors protect and establish their interest with a **security agreement,** which is similar to a mortgage or deed of trust. In such a contract, the creditor makes a loan and the debtor agrees to pay back the loan or forfeit the personal property described in the security agreement.

> **SECURITY AGREEMENT** A contract between a lender and a borrower stating that the lender can repossess personal property offered as collateral if a loan is not paid as agreed.

The UCC regulates purchases made using security agreements. It gives a creditor the right to take back property a debtor either cannot or will not pay for. The UCC requires debtors and lenders to follow specific procedures to finance the purchase of property so that it is legally binding and will be upheld by the courts. Because it is a contract, a security agreement must include a written description of the property being purchased and must be signed by both parties.

Financing Statements

> **FINANCING STATEMENT** A formal notice of a lien's being on personal property. It is required under the UCC in most cases and is also called a "UCC-1," because this is its form number.

Under UCC rules, for a security agreement to fully protect the creditor of personal property, it must be recorded (perfected). This is generally done by preparing and filing a **financing statement** with the Secretary of State's office or the local county recorder of liens. To perfect the lien, the creditor files a financing statement or UCC-1 form. The document filing publicly states that a lien exists on the personal property.

Typically, the financing statement remains in effect for five years. When the loan has been paid, the debtor can request a termination statement to clear the financing statement from public records.

Creditors using personal property as collateral for a loan can review the financing statements on file at the office of the applicable governmental agency. If no previous liens have been recorded against the property, they will have perfected their interest in the property when they file a UCC-1 on that property.

In Review

Restaurateurs often buy personal property with a loan from a third-party creditor such as a bank or have the purchase price financed by the seller. If a manager wishes to purchase equipment for a restaurant, there are three options:

1. Pay the seller the purchase price in full; no security agreement or UCC-1 required.

2. Borrow the purchase price from a third-party lender (such as a bank) and pay the seller in full; the third-party lender enters into a security agreement with the debtor (restaurant) and files a UCC-1 on the equipment to evidence its lien on it.

3. The seller agrees to finance the purchase price over time; the seller enters into a security agreement with the debtor (restaurant) and files a UCC-1 on the equipment to evidence a lien against it.

LEASING PROPERTY

Both real and personal property can be leased.

A **lease** is a type of contract and must clearly indicate the item to be leased, the price or rent to be paid, and the consent of the two parties (**lessor** and **lessee**) to the lease. A lease is different from a property purchase because it transfers possession rather than ownership. Managers must understand the essential terms of their leases and the differences between leasing and owning property.

> **LEASE** A contract that establishes the rights and obligations of each party with respect to property owned by one entity but occupied or used by another.

Essential Lease Terms: Lessor's Concerns

A restaurant serves as a **landlord** if it designates specific space at its property to be operated by a **tenant.** For example, a parking lot operator may lease part of a restaurant's parking spaces, or the restaurant owner may also own a strip mall with nonrestaurant space available for lease.

LESSOR The entity that owns the property covered in a lease.

LESSEE The entity that occupies or uses the property covered in a lease.

LANDLORD The lessor in a real property lease.

TENANT The lessee in a real property lease.

When restaurant owners become landlords, their lease contracts should always be reviewed by an attorney before signing. This will help to ensure that landlord and tenant duties are clearly identified and that, in case of a breach, appropriate remedies are available to the landlord. Consider Michael's case. He is a restaurant owner who leases a second building at the property to an elderly couple for a small business. Because of illness, the couple's business fails, and the exterior of the building begins to deteriorate, which creates an eyesore for the restaurant. The rights of Michael and the tenant in a situation like this must be clearly documented to remedy the problem.

The following aspects of a lease agreement deserve special attention when a manager assumes the role of the lessor (or landlord).

Length of Lease. Landlords prefer long leases to minimize vacancies and guarantee a steady revenue. (Tenants also prefer long leases to avoid rent increases that often occur when leases are re-signed.) However, a lease period that is too long may prevent a landlord from raising the rent when necessary (and may prevent a tenant whose business is growing from moving to a required larger space). The lease length should meet both the short-term and long-term interests of both parties.

Lease start dates (occupation dates) should be clearly established in the agreement. A lessee often wants early access to the space to install fixtures and make improvements. The time required for this work can be lengthy, and the party responsible for rent, if it is to be paid during this period, should be spelled out.

Rent Amount. Lease payments on real property are typically of four types, based on the payment responsibilities of the lessee.

1. In a "net" lease, the lessee pays some or all of the taxes due on real property in addition to the base rent amount.

2. In a "net net" lease, the lessee pays for taxes and insurance as required by the lessor.

3. In a "net net net" (triple net) lease—the most common type for restaurants—the lessee pays all of the costs associated with occupying the property, including building repairs and maintenance.

4. In a "percentage" lease, tenants pay a fixed percentage of their gross revenue as part of the lease payment. Although some fixed charges may also apply, the unique feature of this lease is its variability. A manager or owner may charge a monthly rent based on revenues. In this case, rent payments are lower when business in the leased space is slow but increase as the business succeeds.

The landlord and the tenant must understand all costs for which they will be responsible.

Tenant's Subleasing Rights. A lessee may want to **sublet** (transfer or assign to another) an interest in a lease. The owner's concern is that a new lessee must meet the requirements of the lease. Before approving the sublease, the lessor (owner) should insist that any sublessee demonstrate financial strength and integrity.

> **SUBLET To rent property one possesses by a lease to another; also called subleasing.**

Although it would not be reasonable for the lessor to have complete control over the selection of a sublessee, it is also not reasonable for the choice of sublessee to be left solely with the original tenant. Leases should address this issue with a clause acknowledging the right of the lessee to sublease, but only with the landlord's written consent.

Insurance. Landlords are targets for litigation. If a tenant is careless and injury results, the lessor must be protected. The size and types of policies lessors should require vary, but in all cases the lessor should insist that:

- The lessee's insurance carriers are acceptable to the lessor.
- Copies of insurance policies are given to the lessor when the lease is signed.

■ Lessees and their insurance companies give prior notice to the lessor if the policies are to be canceled, withdrawn, or not renewed.

Landlords may insert exculpatory clauses seeking to limit their liability. Although these clauses may not provide complete protection, they can sometimes be helpful. A commercial insurance agent or attorney experienced in insurance should review lease provisions and insurance policies to ensure that both parties have adequate insurance coverage.

Termination Rights. A lease may be terminated for certain reasons, which must be spelled out in the lease. If a tenant is delinquent in paying rent, the lessor can require that the premises be vacated. However, most landlords allow a payment to be made within a few days without penalty. This grace period should be identified in the lease, as should penalties to be assessed if payment is tendered beyond the grace period.

> **EVICTION The procedure a lessor uses to remove a lessee from physical possession of leased real property, usually for violation of a significant lease provision such as nonpayment of rent.**

Disturbances, violation of operating hours, significant property damage, and failure to follow lease terms may all be justification for termination. However, these reasons will not ordinarily justify an **eviction** unless they are distinctly identified in the lease.

Essential Lease Terms: Lessor's Concerns

When a manager becomes involved in a lease, the lease may be for either real or personal property. When Mike decided to open a steakhouse, the owner of the existing property agreed to lease the land, building, and equipment in exchange for a percentage of the restaurant's gross revenues. This provided Mike with a lower-cost entry into the business and gave the landlord continued ownership of the property.

Whether the land, buildings, or equipment is leased, an attorney should review the lease provisions before signing. Several items deserve special attention.

Landlord Representation and Default. When a tenant leases real property or an individual leases personal property, it is generally assumed that the lessor has the legal right to lease the property for its intended purpose.

The issue of landlord representation and truthfulness can become complex. Consider the restaurateur who wanted a property for use as a restaurant.

The landlord stated in the lease that the space could lawfully be operated as a "restaurant." After the lease was signed, the restaurateur found that its proximity to a school prevented the obtaining of a liquor license. (Community zoning laws prohibited selling alcohol near a school.) The landlord's representation that the space could be used as a "restaurant" was true, but only if no alcohol was served. A prospective tenant should verify all landlord representations about the fitness of property for its intended purpose.

What are a lessee's rights if the landlord loses possession of the property through default? The lessee's rights should be addressed in the lease, which should protect the lessee if, for example, he or she pays the rent on time but the landlord defaults on loans for which the property serves as collateral. A clause can be inserted that guarantees that the tenant's lease will be undisturbed. This area of a lease should be carefully reviewed by legal counsel.

Expenses Paid by Landlord. Whether the lease is a net, net net, triple net, percentage lease, or a combination thereof, the payment of expenses is a common source of disagreement. If electricity is to be paid by the landlord, this should be addressed directly by the lease. In both a net and a net net lease, the repair and maintenance of heating, ventilation, and air-conditioning (HVAC) are part of the lease and are ordinarily paid for by the landlord. The services provided for HVAC maintenance and repair should be included in the lease along with a schedule of times when the services are available.

WHAT WOULD YOU DO?

Sandy leased space in a shopping center to operate her "Olde Style Buffet." Kathy was the shopping center's landlord. She and Sandy signed a net net lease clearly stating that maintenance and repair of the HVAC system would be the responsibility of the shopping center's commercial real estate company.

On Easter Sunday (the operation's busiest day of the year) the overhead exhaust system in the kitchen went out, and the kitchen was becoming unbearably hot, smoky, and humid. Sandy called the landlord's leasing office and heard a recorded message stating that the office was closed. Sandy then contacted an emergency HVAC repair service, which sent a representative to replace a broken belt on the exhaust fan.

Sandy submitted the bill (including a triple-time labor charge for holiday service) to Kathy's company for payment. Kathy refused to pay the bill, stating that the authorized HVAC service company was not used and that the lease did not specifically state that HVAC service would be provided on holidays.

What would you do if you were Sandy?

Cleaning services, if provided as part of the lease payment, should be clearly identified, and a schedule of cleaning times should be attached to the lease.

Renewal Terms. The terms under which a tenant may renew a lease are important. Consider Ron, the district real estate manager for a chain of restaurants. One of Ron's prime concerns when negotiating a lease is the renewal provision. If he selects a successful site, he will want to renew the lease with as little upward change in rent as possible. If the site is less successful, he may not want to renew the lease or will do so only with a reduction in lease payments.

A landlord has no obligation to continue an expired lease. Therefore, Ron encounters landlords wanting to dramatically increase the rent payments for spaces where the restaurants have shown success. To prevent this, Ron insists that renewal formulas limiting rent increases be written into each lease when originally signed.

Normally, leases are extended only with written notice from the lessee. They can, however, be written so as to renew automatically unless terminated in writing by the lessor.

Landlord Rights. Landlords have the right to periodically inspect their properties, but this should occur at reasonable hours and with reasonable notice.

Of even more importance to most tenants is a landlord's right to lease to a competing business. Consider a landlord with a 30-store shopping center. The landlord wants to fill all the space with quality tenants. The space may be large enough to house more than one restaurant. If the landlord rents space to an upscale pizzeria, should the landlord also rent space in the same shopping center to a second upscale pizzeria? Unless the first pizzeria's lease expressly prohibits it, the landlord can lease to a direct competitor. It is reasonable to expect a landlord to tightly define competitors to help ensure a tenant's success.

Deposits, Damages, and Normal Wear and Tear. Landlords generally require a deposit payment when leasing real property. Landlords leasing personal property may also require deposits to ensure return of the leased item in good condition. The amount of the deposit should be clearly stated.

Tenants must be held responsible for damages they inflict on leased property. They should not be responsible for normal wear and tear associated with the use of a piece of property. Difficulties arise when the definition of "normal wear and tear" varies between landlord and tenant. The more detail included in the lease, the less likely it is that litigation will result. The date by which a landlord must return a deposit upon lease termination, and the appropriate method of resolving disputes about owed amounts, should also be included.

Legal clashes between landlord and tenant are common but can be reduced if both parties consider the essential lease terms most directly affecting their relationship. When vacancies are high, landlords may negotiate on terms they would otherwise reject. If space is in short supply, tenants may be in a weaker negotiating position. A careful review of all lease terms is essential, and the manager is advised to do this with the aid of an attorney.

THE BUY OR LEASE DECISION

The decision as to whether to purchase or lease a piece of property is an important one. Numerous business issues are affected, such as those shown in the following chart:

Issue	Purchase	Lease
Right to use	Unlimited use in any legal manner decided by the owner.	Use strictly limited to lease terms.
Treatment of cost	Property is depreciable according to federal and state tax laws.	Lease payments are a deductible business expense according to federal and state tax laws.
Ability to finance	Property can be used as collateral.	Property may not generally be used for collateral.
Liability	Owner liable.	Lessee and/or lessor liable.

Improvements	As desired by owner.	Limited to those allowed by lease terms.
Termination	Ownership passes to estate holders.	Right to possess concludes with lease termination.
Default	Lender retains down payment and/or may foreclose on the property.	Lessor retains deposit and/or may evict. With personal property, the lessor may reclaim the leased item.

Often, the decision to lease rather than purchase is an economic one. A new dishwasher may cost more than $20,000. If it is purchased, the restaurant has undertaken a **capital improvement.** Principle payments for the dishwasher are not deductible as a business expense on the monthly income statement. The value of the dishwasher, however, may be **depreciated** over a period of time fixed by law.

CAPITAL IMPROVEMENT The purchase or upgrade of real or personal property resulting in an increased depreciable asset base.

DEPRECIATION The decrease in value of a piece of property due to age and/or wear and tear.

If a manager does off-site catering four times a year, it makes little sense to purchase a truck that can be leased on a daily basis. Alternatively, a manager desiring to open a restaurant in a prime location in a mall's food court may have no option other than leasing. (The mall is not likely to sell the space but will lease it under a **commercial lease.**)

COMMERCIAL LEASE A lease applying to business property.

A property owner has rights a lessee does not enjoy. Sometimes, however, a manager finds it desirable to lease property. Either way, it is important to know and protect the rights associated with buying and leasing.

INTELLECTUAL PROPERTY RIGHTS

Some important personal property rights protected by law relate to **intellectual property,** which is both intangible and conceptual.

Some managers violate intellectual property rights by using, without payment, the intellectual property of others. Good managers avoid infringing on others' property rights and pay for those intellectual items legitimately used to assist their business.

> **INTELLECTUAL PROPERTY** Personal property created through the intellectual efforts of its original owner.

Individuals creating something unique and valuable enjoy the financial proceeds of that creation, a right afforded by laws related to trademarks, patents, copyrights, or trade dress. Intellectual property maintains its status even after the death of the person creating the property.

Trademarks

A **trademark** identifies the producer, manufacturer, or source of a product; trademarks are frequently used in the restaurant industry. Guests like to see name brand products. Well-established trademarks (also called marks) let consumers know what product is being used. For example, many restaurants serve ketchup directly from the bottle. A bottle labeled "Heinz" elicits a much different response than one labeled "Bob's." When consumers see the Heinz name, they associate the ketchup with a specific quality. An unscrupulous food service manager who buys Bob's ketchup and puts it in a Heinz bottle violates not only food safety laws but also trademark property right laws.

> **TRADEMARK** A word, name, symbol, or combination of these, indicating the source or producer of an item.

A trademark owner has the right to prevent others from using that mark if the owner was the first to use it in the marketplace. When a trademark has been properly applied for and received, no other person may manufacture or sell any article using the same or similar sign, mark, wrapper, or label.

Trademark law protects the public by helping consumers identify brands for purchase without being confused or misled. It also protects managers by ensuring that they are getting the quality they are paying for.

Patents

Inventors creating something new may apply for a **patent.** If a manager invents a device to peel and remove centers from large Spanish onions, that manager would be able to quickly produce a popular appetizer. Another manager should not be allowed to manufacture that device if the first manager has applied for and received a patent on it.

> **PATENT** A grant issued by the government ensuring an inventor the right to exclusive production and sale of an invention for a fixed period of time.

The U.S. Patent and Trademark Office is the federal entity responsible for granting patents. An inventor, as a patent owner, has the right to exclude any other person from making, using, or selling the invention covered by the patent anywhere in the United States for 17 years from the date of patent issue. Inventors who have applied for, but not received, a patent may use the term "patent pending" or "patent applied for."

Copyrights

A **copyright** governs the rights to reproduce and use intellectual property. For example, a songwriter, holding a copyright on a song, has a right to compensation when that song is performed. If a singer records it and sells the recording, copyright law requires the singer to fairly compensate the songwriter for creating the song's music and lyrics.

> **COPYRIGHT** The legal and exclusive right to use, publish, or reproduce intellectual property.

A copyright owner has the right to prevent another person from reproducing, distributing, performing, or displaying the work for a specific time. The Copyright Act of 1976 states that copyrighted work includes literary, musical, and dramatic work and motion pictures, audiovisual work, sound recordings, and computer programs. Most items found on the Internet are also copyrighted, including Web page text, E-mail contents, and sound and graphic files.

An individual who has been granted a copyright is said to be the **copyright owner.** Copyright laws exist in foreign countries as well as in the United States.

> **COPYRIGHT OWNER** A person or entity that legally holds a right to intellectual property under the copyright laws.

In the hospitality industry, copyrighted works should be used only when appropriate authorization has been received, particularly when the use of a copyrighted work—such as the broadcasting of a football game—will provide an economic benefit to the operation. Generally, the courts are aggressive enforcers of copyright laws.

Trade Dress

Rights related to trade dress are actually a part of those rights related to trademarks, but they merit special discussion. A **trade dress** is a very special and unique visual image.

> **TRADE DRESS** A distinct visual image created for and identified with a specific product.

Trade dress includes color schemes, textures, sizes, designs, shapes, and placements of words, graphics, and decorations on a product or its packag-

---

WWW: Internet Assistant

Log onto the Internet and enter: http://www.law.com

Select: Self-Help Law Guide

Select: Restaurant Law from the "Choose Topics" menu

Select: The state and nearest city of your restaurant; click on "Go"

Select: Helpful Web sites

Select: U.S. Hotel and Restaurant Law

Select: U.S. Supreme Court Recent Decisions

---

ing. An entire restaurant may be created in a way so as to be protected under laws related to trade dress. No restaurant chain has an exclusive right to operate with a "down-home" theme. A trade dress question arises, however, when one restaurant uses the same items to create that atmosphere as does its competition.

Italian, Mexican, French, and American restaurants all have unique characteristics associated not only with the products served but also with the feel and visual image of the establishment. Trade dress protection allows the creative restaurateur to protect aesthetic ideas in an industry that highly rewards innovation and creativity.

Preventing Infringement of Intellectual Property Rights

To prevent infringement on the rights of intellectual property owners, the United States Patent and Trademark Office maintains a database of registered patents and trademarks. That database should be consulted if there is a question about whether a mark or an invention is in the **public domain.**

PUBLIC DOMAIN Property that is owned by all citizens—not by an individual.

If a company does not take precautions, its trademarks can become part of the public domain. The word "aspirin" began as a trademarked term but later passed into such common usage that the courts no longer enforce the property rights of the word's creator. A common word used frequently by society cannot become trademark protected.

Although most managers can avoid infringing on patent and trademark rights, copyright issues are more complex. Restaurants are not free to reproduce any music desired as background music for dining or in a lounge unless they are in compliance with U.S. copyright laws.

U.S. copyright laws give songwriters and publishers rights to collect royalties on their intellectual property whenever their songs are played in public. The law allows copyright owners to recover profits made by any group unlawfully using copyrighted material.

Whether a manager plays songs on CDs, television, tape, or in a live performance, the song owners have a right to royalties because federal copyright laws state that playing copyrighted music in a public place constitutes a performance. When copyrighted music is performed in public, managers violate the law if they do not pay royalties to owners of music that has been played.

It would be impossible for a manager to know the ownership rights to all music. Most songs played in the United States are licensed for use by either Broadcast Music, Inc. (BMI) or the American Society of Composers, Authors, and Publishers (ASCAP). To play a given piece of music, a fee must be paid to the licensor that holds the right to license the music in question. Fee structures are based on a variety of factors, but the average restaurant, playing background music seven days a week, would expect to pay several hundred dollars annually for the right to broadcast most music available for play. Managers who refuse or neglect to pay the fees rightfully due a licensing group can be subject to fines or prosecution.

Congress has determined that any facility playing background music on a piece of equipment that could normally be found in a home will not be held to the normal copyright infringement rules if the facility does not charge admission to hear the music. It is not the intent of the copyright laws to prohibit turning on a simple radio or television in a public place. The Fairness in Music Licensing Amendment allows small restaurants an exemption from some licensing fees.

Specific provisions of the amendment permitting free broadcasting of music and video are clear. Restaurants of less than 3,750 square feet can play as many televisions and radios as desired without paying royalty fees. There is no restriction on the size of the television set that may be installed in these restaurants.

For restaurants larger than 3,750 square feet, owners can apply for and receive an exemption to play up to four television sets (no more than one per room) and use up to six speakers (no more than four per room); the television sets cannot be larger than 55 inches.

Some restaurants utilize jukeboxes. Ordinarily, jukebox providers must pay royalties for the music in the jukeboxes. This should be stated in the agreement prior to installation of a jukebox.

Copyright laws also address broadcasts of groups like the National Football League (NFL), Major League Baseball (MLB), the National Basketball Association (NBA), National Collegiate Athletic Association (NCAA), and others. The right to air these broadcasts is reserved by the group creating the programming, and managers who violate their copyrights do so at risk.

Managers concerned about the legality of an intended broadcast should contact the broadcast company (e.g., cable operator) or the owner of the broadcasted product (NFL, MLB, etc.) to clarify circumstances under which a broadcast is possible; they should obtain written permission for such broadcasting.

WHAT WOULD YOU DO?

Suppose you manage a restaurant in a town with an NFL team that will be playing in the Super Bowl. You want to hold an event in your largest meeting room, which holds 300 people. The festivities will begin at 3:00 P.M. on Super Bowl Sunday with the televised pregame show, a darts tournament, and a Mexican buffet. At 6:30 P.M. the game will be shown on five 60-inch TV screens placed around the ballroom. The evening will conclude with a postgame "Victory Party."

Part of your planning involves the admission price. The issue of reserved seating is raised by another manager, who believes guests will be more inclined to attend if they have seats near the large-screen televisions.

What would you do if you were the manager?

MANAGER'S "TO DO" LIST

Review the following recommendations proposed in this chapter. Analyze your interest in and need for implementing these recommendations by completing the columns on the right side of the form. Remember, when task assignments are made, time requirements for completion should also be stated. Follow up, as improvement activities evolve, to ensure that your property is moving closer to the goal of minimizing litigation risks.

Recommended Procedures	In Place Now?			Needed to Implement			Assigned To	Completion Date
	Yes	No	N/A*	Policy	Training	Other		
The manager consults with an attorney anytime there is a question about whether something is real or personal property.								
Managers verify that sellers have legal title to any property that is purchased.								
Managers carefully consider the need for title insurance when purchasing real property.								
Managers require a bill of sale whenever personal property is purchased.								
Concerns about the transfer of ownership when personal property is purchased are addressed in the contract for sale of the personal property.								
Managers take precautions to ensure that stolen property is never purchased.								
Managers carefully consider the need for and topics to be addressed in warranties for equipment to be purchased.								
Before personal property is purchased, comparisons between warranties of alternative items are made.								
Managers understand differences between mortgages, deeds of trusts, and security agreements and recognize the impact they have on property being purchased.								
When loans have been repaid, managers request a termination statement to clear any financing statement from the public record.								

*N/A = Not Applicable

Recommended Procedures	In Place Now?			Needed to Implement			Assigned To	Completion Date
	Yes	No	N/A*	Policy	Training	Other		
Careful analysis involving input from an attorney and an accountant is undertaken before decisions about leasing or purchasing equipment are made.								
Any purchase or lease contract is reviewed by an attorney before signing.								
When managers negotiate leases as landlords (lessors), they pay special attention to: • Length of lease • Rent amount • Tenant's subleasing rights • Insurance • Termination								
When managers negotiate leases as lessees they pay special attention to: • Landlord representations and default • Landlord expenses • Renewal terms • Landlord's rights • Deposit, damage, and normal wear and tear								
When managers make buy or lease decisions, they carefully evaluate the following factors: • Right to use • Treatment of costs • Ability to finance • Liability • Improvements • Termination • Default								
Managers understand the difference between trademarks, patents, copyrights, and trade dress and are careful to ensure that the intellectual property rights of original owners are not violated.								

*N/A = Not Applicable

Recommended Procedures	In Place Now?			Needed to Implement			Assigned To	Completion Date
	Yes	No	N/A*	Policy	Training	Other		
Managers pay fees as applicable to Broadcast Music, Inc. (BMI) and/or the American Society of Composers, Authors, and Publishers (ASCAP) to minimize the possibility of being subject to fines or prosecution.								
Managers understand the impact of the Fairness in Music and Licensing Amendment as it applies to their property.								
Managers are aware of copyright laws applicable to broadcast of groups such as the National Football League (NFL), the National Basketball Association (NBA), and others.								
The broadcast company (cable operator) or owner of the broadcast product is contacted to clarify circumstances under which charging viewers for watching broadcasts is allowed.								

For more information and suggestions log onto www.hospitalitylawyer.com.

*N/A = Not Applicable

CONSULTANT'S CORNER

What Would You Do? (page 72)

This situation is another reminder that assumptions are often the root of trouble. Jay just assumed that the window air-conditioning unit was a fixture and that it was included in the sale of the building. It is just as obvious that Tom thought that the window air-conditioning unit was his personal property, and because it was not included in the description of the property to be sold, that Jay was not buying it.

In this particular situation Tom would probably prevail unless the sales agreement included "any and all personal property that was located on the described real estate" to be sold; if so, then an inventory of the personal property that is agreed upon to be sold with the land is usually attached to the sales contract.

What Would You Do? (page 76)

It is pretty obvious that your friend realizes that these were stolen pans. It may sound like a good deal, but the best way to keep things from being stolen is to eliminate the market for stolen goods. So, by purchasing items that are stolen, even though in the short term it may seem like a good deal, what you are really doing is perpetuating the stolen goods market, and it is just a matter of time before you become a victim.

Remember, if the rightful owner ever traces the stolen property to you, you will likely lose the property. If you are shopping for a good price for pans, look for a good used-equipment supplier or check out auctions, which are great places to purchase used equipment at better prices. Always get a bill of sale when you purchase personal property.

What Would You Do? (page 85)

First, Sandy must be sure that she has a copy of the lease agreement and that she is interpreting it correctly. Second, she has to follow very carefully the notice provisions in the lease agreement regarding reimbursements.

If, in fact, there was a certain ventilation company specified in the lease to do the repairs, Sandy would have to explain why she did not use that particular company, or if it was unavailable, at least to demonstrate her attempts to reach that company.

This example also points out that the restaurant business is much different from most other businesses in that its operation ordinarily includes holidays, early mornings, and late nights, and that emergencies during these time periods must be considered and discussed in agreements between the parties.

What Would You Do? (page 93)

This scenario points out the concern that arises when you consider broadcasting a licensed product such as NFL football games or boxing matches that in some cases, although not in this instance, may even be pay-per-view situations. In such cases, the requirement is clear—you must contract with your cable company or the pay-per-view provider in order to purchase the broadcasting rights and to be able to rebroadcast it to your audience. If an event is not pay-per-view and it is broadcast over normal cable channels or network television, the best approach is to seek permission from the license holder or the broadcast company (the NFL or cable operator or network) to show it in your venue. It is much better, as many small operations have found out, to strike an agreement up front, rather than to be on the opposite side of litigation with the NFL, NBA, or Time Warner Cable.

5

MANAGING WITHIN REGULATORY
AND ADMINISTRATIVE REQUIREMENTS

MANAGER'S BRIEF

Managers reading this chapter will learn about a wide range of regulatory and administrative controls required by federal, state, and local agencies. They will learn how the industry is regulated by these agencies, including the filing of forms, submitting to inspections and applying for licenses, operating their businesses in a specified manner, and maintaining facilities and equipment in good working order. Additional topics include managing conflicting regulations, responding to an inquiry made by a regulatory or administrative agency, and monitoring regulatory modifications to keep current with ever-changing requirements.

Restaurants are regulated by numerous federal, state, and local governmental entities. Managers must interact with these agencies and follow all of the applicable procedures and regulations they impose. This includes filling out forms and paperwork, obtaining licenses, maintaining the property to specified codes and standards, providing a safe working environment, and opening facilities for periodic inspection.

It is not possible for managers to be completely knowledgeable about all requirements that may be applicable to their operations. They must, however:

- Be aware of the major regulatory agencies
- Understand how to resolve conflicting regulations
- Know how to respond to an inquiry or complaint
- Keep current with regulatory changes that affect their operations

FEDERAL REGULATORY AND ADMINISTRATIVE AGENCIES

Internal Revenue Service (IRS)
(http://www.irs.gov/)

The IRS is part of the U.S. Department of the Treasury. Its ability to charge a person with a criminal act makes it an agency that deserves a manager's thoughtful attention. Managers interact with the IRS because a manager is both a taxpayer (who pays income tax on compensation and/or business profits) and a tax collector (who withholds employee taxes on income). The IRS requires businesses, including restaurants, to:

- File quarterly income tax returns (Form 941) and make payments on profits earned from business operations. Taxes must be filed on or before the last day of the month following the end of each calendar quarter.
- File an Income and Tax Statement (Form W-3) with the Social Security Administration on or before the last day of February.
- Withhold income taxes from the wages of all employees (as specified in Circular E) and deposit these taxes (Form 8109) with the IRS at regu-

lar intervals. Employee withholding taxes must be paid quarterly if the period's total withheld tax is less than $500, once a month if the total withheld tax is between $500 and $3,000, or within three working days of a payroll if the withheld amount is greater than $3,000.

- Report all employee tip income (Form 8027) and withhold taxes on it.

- Record the value of employee meals when they are considered part of an employee's income.

- Record all payments to independent contractors (Forms 1096 and 1099) and file forms listing those payments.

- Furnish a record of withheld taxes (Form W-2) to employees on or before January 31 and maintain these records for four years.

The IRS conducts periodic audits of a business's financial accounts and tax records. A manager must respond if notified by the IRS of a forthcoming audit. The manager should also consult a Certified Public Accountant (CPA) or an attorney specializing in tax audits to ensure that the appropriate documents are properly prepared.

Federal tax laws are very complex. Managers may be responsible for submitting or filing business taxes and must understand their role in ensuring a company's compliance with federal tax laws. For a complete list of a business's tax responsibilities and to obtain copies of various tax forms, visit the IRS Web site.

WWW: Internet Assistant

Log onto the Internet and visit the IRS Web site.

Enter: http://www.irs.gov/

Select: Enter

Select: Small Business Corner

Select: Employment Taxes

Select: Critical Forms and Publications

Select: Publication 15 Employers Tax Guide

Review the portion of Publication 15 referring to Employer's Responsibilities.

Occupational Safety and Health Administration (OSHA)
(http://www.osha.gov/)

OSHA is an agency of the Department of Labor and works "to assure, so far as possible, every working man and woman in the nation safe and healthful working conditions."

All businesses, including restaurants, must comply with OSHA's extensive safety practices, equipment specifications, and employee communication procedures. Specifically, they must:

- Provide a safe employee workplace by maintaining facilities and providing protective clothing in compliance with OSHA's safety and health standards.

- Purchase equipment that meets OSHA's health and safety specifications.

- Establish safety checklists and training programs, especially for employees who operate equipment that may cause injury.

- Report to OSHA within 48 hours any workplace accidents that result in a fatality or require hospitalization of five or more employees.

- Maintain a record (OSHA Log 200) of work-related injuries or illnesses and file that record annually; employers must also post an annual summary of the prior year's injuries and illnesses.

- Schedule at least one employee trained in first aid for each work shift.

- Display OSHA notices about employee rights and safety in places where they are easily read.

- Provide all employees access to information about toxic or harmful substances used in the workplace and keep records certifying that employees have reviewed it.

- Offer hepatitis B vaccinations for employees who may come in contact with blood or body fluids.

OSHA monitors workplace safety with compliance officers who perform unannounced inspections during regular business hours. These officers also investigate complaints of unsafe business practices.

A manager should accompany the OSHA compliance officer during an inspection for two reasons. First, the manager may answer questions or clarify procedures. Second, the manager should know what happened during the inspection, should discuss its results, and should request a copy of the inspection report. Although such an inspection is not announced, the compliance officer must state a reason for it.

Penalties for violating OSHA regulations can be severe and costly. As always, the best way to avoid accidents, lawsuits, and penalties is to adopt a philosophy of preventive management. For worker safety, this may be as simple as providing information or as time-consuming as developing a comprehensive employee training program.

OSHA requires that Material Safety Data Sheets (MSDSs) be provided for all chemicals used by workers. These are manufacturer's statements detailing the potential hazards and proper methods of using a chemical or toxic substance. MSDSs inform workers about the hazards of the materials they work with so they can protect themselves and respond to emergencies (see Figure 5.1, for example). Employees must have access to MSDSs and receive assistance to read

---

ECONOMICS LABORATORY—JET DRY (934984)
MATERIAL SAFETY DATA SHEET

FSC: 6850.   NIIN: 00F000893

Manufacturer's CAGE: 85884

Part No. Indicator: A

Part Number/Trade Name: JET DRY (934984)

General Information

Company's Name: ECONOMICS LABORATORY, INC.

Company's Emergency Phone #: (612) 293-2233

Record No. for Safety Entry: 001

Total Safety Entries This Stock #: 001

Date MSDS Prepared: 01JANXX

Safety Data Review Date: 22JANXX

MSDS Serial Number: BBHKT

Figure 5.1   Sample MSDS.

Ingredients/Identity Information
Proprietary: YES
Ingredient: PROPRIETARY
Ingredient Sequence Number: 01

Physical/Chemical Characteristics
Appearance and Odor: CLEAR GREEN LIQUID—NO SPECIFIC ODOR
Boiling Point: 212°F
Specific Gravity: 1.022
Solubility in Water: COMPLETE
Percent Volatiles by Volume: 90%

Fire and Explosion Hazard Data
Flash Point: NONFLAMMABLE
Extinguishing Media: ALL RECOGNIZED METHODS ARE ACCEPTABLE.

Reactivity Data
Stability: YES
Hazardous Decomp Products: OXIDES OF CARBON
Hazardous Poly Occur: NO

Health Hazard Data
Signs/Symptoms of Overexp: MAY CAUSE MINOR EYE IRRITATION—
BURNING SENSATION.
Emergency/First Aid Proc: FLUSH EYES WITH PLENTY OF WATER.
INGESTION: DO NOT INDUCE VOMITING. DRINK LARGE QUANTITIES
OF WATER OR MILK.

Precautions for Safe Handling and Use
Steps If Matl Released/Spill: MOP UP SPILL. WASH AREA WITH WATER.
Waste Disposal Method: CONSULT LOCAL REGULATIONS.
Precautions—Handling/Storing: KEEP FROM FREEZING.
Label Emergency Number: (XXX) XXX-XXXX

Figure 5.1 *(Continued)*

and understand them. OSHA officers ensure that MSDSs are placed in worker-accessible areas.

WHAT WOULD YOU DO?

Carlos was a Spanish-speaking custodian who worked for Bert, the manager of a restaurant. Bert asked Carlos to clean the grout between the quarry kitchen tiles with a powerful cleaner. Bert, who did not speak Spanish, demonstrated how Carlos should pour the chemical directly from the bottle and then brush the grout with a wire brush until it was white.

The cleaner was strong, and Carlos did not wear protective gloves. His hands became seriously irritated, and in an effort to lessen the pain, Carlos diluted the chemical with water. He did not realize that this would cause toxic fumes. Carlos inhaled the fumes and later suffered serious lung damage.

Bert was contacted by OSHA, which cited and fined the property for an MSDS violation. Bert maintained that MSDS sheets, including the one for the cleaner in question, were available for employee inspection.

What would you do if you were Bert?

According to OSHA's Hazard Communication Standards, an MSDS must include:

- The material's identity, including chemical and common names
- Hazardous ingredients (in parts as small as 1 percent)
- Cancer-causing ingredients (in parts as small as 0.1 percent)
- Physical and chemical hazards (stability, reactivity, etc.) and characteristics (flammable, explosive, corrosive, etc.)
- Health hazards, including:
  Acute effects, such as burns or unconsciousness, which occur immediately
  Chronic effects, such as allergic sensitization, skin problems, or respiratory disease, which build up over a period of time
- Whether the material is a known carcinogen

- Limits of worker exposure, specific target organs likely to sustain damage, and medical problems aggravated by exposure

- Precautions, safety equipment, and emergency/first-aid procedures

- Fire fighting information

- Safe handling and use precautions, including personal hygiene

- Identity of the organization creating the MSDS, date of issue, and emergency phone number

Environmental Protection Agency (EPA)
(http://www.epa.gov/)

The EPA is an independent federal agency that regulates pesticides and water and air pollution. Restaurants must be careful when discharging waste, particularly toxic waste such as pesticides or cleaning chemicals. The EPA also monitors indoor air quality issues (such as smoking).

Many EPA directives, such as recycling laws and ordinances for trash disposal, are implemented by state and local governments. Although managers may have little contact with this federal agency, they must be aware of applicable laws.

Food and Drug Administration (FDA)
(http://www.fda.gov/)

The FDA is responsible for ensuring the proper labeling and safety of food. Managers encounter the results of the FDA's efforts when they purchase food with a mandatory FDA nutrition label. In addition, the FDA's Model Food Service Sanitation Ordinance is used by many state and community health departments as a basis for their food service inspection programs.

Food service operators should be aware of the FDA's definitions governing the use of nutritional and health-related terms. Managers using menu phrases such as *low calorie, light,* or *cholesterol free* must ensure that recipes for those dishes meet the FDA's requirements. These and other health claim requirements are discussed in Chapter 11.

Equal Employment Opportunity Commission (EEOC)
(http://www.eeoc.gov/)

The EEOC enforces laws against discrimination in employment, which relate to the following general areas:

- Sexual harassment

- Race/color discrimination

- Age discrimination

- National origin discrimination

- Pregnancy discrimination

- Religious discrimination

- Portions of the Americans with Disabilities Act

Some of these areas are discussed in Chapter 8.

The EEOC's impact on a manager's daily work is significant. Consider the manager scheduling a Christian worker on Christmas Day. Do the needs of the manager take precedence over those of workers who desire a day off because of religious convictions?

The Civil Rights Act prohibits discriminating against individuals because of religious beliefs when hiring and firing. It also requires employers to reasonably accommodate their employees' religious practices unless this creates an undue hardship. Flexible scheduling, voluntary substitutions, job reassignments, and lateral transfers may help accommodate religious beliefs. Whether a manager can "reasonably" accommodate the request of a Christian worker to be off schedule on Christmas Day is a complex question. Managers cannot act in any manner they desire. The EEOC investigates complaints of employees who think they have been discriminated against. Businesses can be ordered to compensate employees for damages such as lost wages and attorney fees and may also be ordered to pay punitive damages.

Bureau of Alcohol, Tobacco, and Firearms (ATF) (http://www.atf.treas.gov/)

The ATF is housed within the U.S. Department of the Treasury and enforces all federal laws and regulations governing the manufacture and sale of alcohol, tobacco, firearms, and explosives. It also investigates incidents of arson and enforces the payment of federal taxes on the production and sale of alcoholic beverages.

Managers interact with the ATF in several ways:

- Retail sellers of alcohol, including bars and restaurants, must pay a special federal liquor tax each year (IRS Form 11, Special Tax Return).

They receive a Special Tax Stamp showing proof of payment and must keep this stamp on-site for inspection.

- Alcohol vendors cannot mix cocktails in advance of a sale, must properly dispose of empty liquor bottles, and may not reuse or sell them.

- Operators must keep records, invoices, and receipts of all alcohol purchased.

ATF officers enforce regulations by conducting inspections during regular business hours. Additional information about the sale of alcohol is included in Chapter 11.

Department of Labor (DOL)
(http://www.dol.gov/)

The DOL works to "foster, promote, and develop the welfare of the wage earners of the United States, to improve their working conditions, and to advance their opportunities for profitable employment."

The DOL helps prepare the workforce for new and better jobs and ensures the adequacy of America's workplaces. It administers more than 180 federal laws relating to workers' wages, health and safety, employment, pension rights, equal employment opportunity, job training, unemployment insurance, and workers' compensation programs, and collective bargaining and collects, analyzes, and publishes labor and economic statistics.

Several federal labor-related regulations commonly apply to restaurants.

Wages and Hours. The Fair Labor Standards Act (FLSA) prescribes standards for wages and overtime pay affecting most private and public employment. Employers must pay covered employees the federal minimum wage and overtime of one and one-half times the regular wage. The FLSA restricts the hours that children under 16 can work and forbids their employment in certain dangerous jobs. It also establishes guidelines for tip and meal credits and uniform purchases. (See Chapter 8.)

Pensions and Welfare Benefits. The Employee Retirement Income Security Act (ERISA) regulates employers who offer pension or welfare benefit plans for employees. It also details reporting requirements for the continuation of health care provisions required under the Comprehensive Omnibus Budget Reconciliation Act (COBRA).

Employee Polygraph Protection. Most employers are prohibited from using lie detectors (polygraphs) to test present or prospective employees under most circumstances. Employers can request that employees take a test as part of an incident investigation resulting in a loss to the employer. Lie detector test results cannot be shared with anyone except the examiner, the employer, or those ordered by the courts.

Family and Medical Leave. Employers with 50 or more employees must grant up to 12 weeks of unpaid leave to an employee for the birth or adoption of a child or because of a serious illness of the employee or a family member. Other provisions of the Family and Medical Leave Act are discussed in Chapter 8.

Department of Justice
(http://www.usdoj.gov/)

The Department of Justice, headed by the U.S. attorney general, investigates and prosecutes federal crimes, represents the federal government in court, manages federal prisons, and enforces immigration laws.

Many managers interact with the Department of Justice relative to immigration laws. The Immigration and Naturalization Service (INS) requires managers to obtain identification documents from all whom they hire. Precise methods of verifying employment eligibility are discussed in Chapter 7. Penalties for noncompliance can be severe.

The Department of Justice also enforces Title III of the Americans with Disabilities Act (ADA), which requires restaurants to remove barriers that can restrict access or the full enjoyment of their amenities by people with disabilities. Requirements for compliance are discussed in Chapter 10.

STATE REGULATORY AND ADMINISTRATIVE AGENCIES

States serve regulatory roles that are both complementary to and distinct from those of the federal government. The roles are complementary because they support federal efforts, but they are distinct because they regulate areas in which they have sole responsibility. The administrative structure and the specific name of the entity vary by state, but the regulatory processes are similar. State and/ or local regulations may affect a manager's actions even more than federal regulations. State and local codes and ordinances can be strict and may require investment in equipment or extra management diligence. Penalties for violation can be just as severe as those at the federal level.

Employment Security Agency

Each state regulates employment and employee–employer relationships, including work-related unemployment benefits, worker safety issues, and injury compensation. The entity regulating the workplace is also responsible for employment assistance for employees and employers.

Consider Virgil. He works in a restaurant purchased by a new owner, who states that Virgil's position is no longer needed. In the state where this restaurant is located, an employer is not required to pay **unemployment compensation** if an employee is terminated because of staff reductions. However, Virgil believes he has been terminated for other reasons, none of which relate to work performance. The state's Employment Security Agency will determine what, if any, unemployment compensation benefits Virgil should receive.

UNEMPLOYMENT COMPENSATION A benefit paid to an employee who involuntarily loses employment without just cause.

Workers' compensation is of great concern to managers because the safety of their workers is important. Employee injuries are also expensive in terms of money and workplace disruption. Managers must know and follow state regulations about workplace safety, including methods for properly documenting and reporting work-related injuries. Worker safety is monitored by a workers' compensation agency, commission, or subdivision of the employment security agency.

WORKERS' COMPENSATION A benefit paid to an employee suffering a work-related injury or illness.

Alcohol Beverage Commission

Alcohol and its consumption subjects a manager to intense regulation at both the state and local levels. The agency regulating the sale of alcoholic beverages is responsible for the following areas of control:

- License issuing and revocation
- Permitted hours of sales
- Advertising and promotion policies
- Methods of operation
- Reporting sales for tax purposes

Managers who fail to follow alcoholic beverage regulations may be subject to criminal prosecution, as well as an administrative hearing before the state's ABC. In addition, **Dram Shop Act** legislation may make a manager or the business itself liable to guests or third parties and their families if violations of regulations result in injury to an intoxicated guest or to persons harmed by an individual who was illegally served. In other words, managers can be held responsible for the acts of their intoxicated patrons if they

> **DRAM SHOP ACT** Legislation passed in a variety of forms and in many states that imposes liability for the acts of others on those who serve alcohol negligently, recklessly, or illegally.

were illegally served. Specific techniques related to the proper selling of alcoholic beverages are fully discussed in Chapter 11.

States are careful when granting licenses to sell liquor, and they are generally aggressive in revoking licenses of operations that do not follow required procedures. In most states, license revocation can result from:

- Frequent incidents of fighting, disorderly conduct, or creating a public nuisance
- Allowing prostitution or solicitation on-site
- Drug and narcotic sales or use
- Illegal adult entertainment
- Failure to maintain required records
- Sale of alcohol to minors

WHAT WOULD YOU DO?

Chantel managed a bar near a college campus. She was active in her business community and served on the college's Advisory Board for Responsible Drinking. All servers and bartenders in her facility underwent a mandatory four-hour alcohol service training program before their employment and took a required refresher course each year. Each server was certified in responsible alcohol service by a national trade association program.

On a busy night, a server approached a table with four female patrons. Because all appeared to be nearly 21 years old and well under the 35-year-old limit Chantel had established for a mandatory identification (ID) check, the server asked to see each guest's picture ID.

The server checked each ID, verifying the age, hair color, general likeness, and absence of alterations to the ID card, and then requested—in a feature unique to the bar—the mandatory recitation of the birthdate and address printed on the ID. All four guests passed their ID checks, and the employee served each guest three glasses of wine in 90 minutes.

The next day Chantel was contacted by the state ABC agency which regulated the sale of alcoholic beverages and by an attorney for the parents of a teenager whose car was in an accident with one of the guests served the night before. In fact, one guest, whose ID had been professionally altered, was 20 years old—not 21—and was involved in the auto accident after she left the bar. The state agency began an investigation into the sale of alcohol to minors, and the attorney scheduled an appointment with Chantel's attorney to discuss a settlement based on potential liability arising from Dram Shop Act legislation in Chantel's state.

What would you do if you were Chantel?

Managers must report all sales of alcohol to the state Alcohol Beverage Commission, which will perform random audits to determine the accuracy of the information received. Other enforcement tools of the ABC include unannounced inspections and/or intentionally sending minors (à la mystery shoppers) into an establishment to see whether they will be served.

Treasury Department

A state's Treasury Department collects taxes levied by that state. These include liquor sales and various use taxes.

Attorney General

The Attorney General is the chief legal officer of the state. One responsibility of this office is to specify the franchise information required for disclosure in the state. If, for example, an entrepreneur wanted to purchase a franchise, the Attorney General's office (in conjunction with a state securities office, if in existence) would regulate the franchisor–franchisee relationship in that state.

Public Health Department

The Public Health Department is responsible for the inspection and licensing of facilities serving food. It may be autonomous, but is often housed in a state's Department of Agriculture.

Managers must comply with a variety of health codes and regulations. The most common areas of state health regulation include:

- Standards for cleanliness of and proper procedures for storing, handling, preparing, and serving food and supplies

- Mandated health procedures for employees working with food

- Standards for the proper care and washing of food equipment, utensils, and serviceware

- Standards for the supply and use of water for cleaning and dishwashing, including sewage discharge

- Display of procedures to save choking victims

- Regulations for smoking in public places

Penalties for violating state health ordinances vary from a fine to the closing of a business. In minor cases, if an operator can correct the violation within a specified time, no penalty is imposed. However, the inspector will return to verify that appropriate corrections have been made.

Some state and local health departments furnish a list of health violators to local newspapers or television stations, which can result in negative publicity. This is an added incentive to ensure that operations are in compliance with the various ordinances.

Department of Transportation (DOT)

The state DOT is responsible for several areas directly affecting managers of restaurants. Consider the owner of a property on a busy street that is maintained by the DOT. During lunchtime, guests have difficulty turning into the parking lot from the opposite side of the street because there are few breaks in traffic. Vehicles travel this street at a high speed, so crossing can be dangerous. This manager should request the DOT to develop a solution. Perhaps a reduced speed limit or a turn lane could be justified. Typically, DOTs also regulate driveways, exits and approaches, and traffic signage, including highway billboards. Issues relating to these concerns should be discussed with DOT officials.

LOCAL REGULATORY AND ADMINISTRATIVE AGENCIES

Many regulatory processes confronting managers occur at the local level.

Health and Sanitation Department

Food and beverage operations are often inspected and licensed by local Health and Sanitation Department personnel. Inspectors may ensure compliance with state codes and municipal ordinances. In addition, local officials may undertake mandatory certification of employees and managers, issue and revoke licenses, establish standards for rest rooms, and ensure a safe water supply.

Building and Zoning Department

Building and zoning personnel issue building permits and inspect new buildings before, during, and after construction. They also regulate building additions and renovations and ensure that all building code requirements are met. Standards for lighting, ventilation, rest rooms, elevators, and public corridors and entryways may be established by local agencies. (Insurance companies may have additional requirements for lighting levels and ventilation systems.) Local zoning ordinances may regulate outside land use, such as parking spaces, and permits for sidewalk or patio dining.

These departments often regulate the type of businesses that can be located in specified areas. Many citizens agree, for example, that a bar or nightclub should not be operated in a building adjacent to school or church grounds.

Zoning officials regulate land use to benefit managers by prohibiting some businesses from locating next to land reserved for restaurants and other commercial use. Imagine a manager's concern, for example, when a landfill operator purchases a vacant lot next to the restaurant.

Local building and zoning officials are typically responsible for the construction and placement of outside signage. There can be extensive regulations controlling the size and number of signs and the construction materials required.

Inspectors randomly visit businesses to ensure compliance with building and safety codes. Violators can be fined, and if a customer or employee is injured because of a violation, a lawsuit may result.

AGENCY(IES)

In most communities, an agency of the court (sometimes called a "friend" of the court) assists creditors in securing payment for legally owed debts, including numerous court-ordered payments, such as child support. In these cases, **garnishment** of an employee's wages may be ordered. A garnishment order requires the restaurant to withhold money from an employee's paycheck and forward it to the court.

> **GARNISHMENT** A court-ordered method of debt collection whereby a portion of a person's wage or salary is withheld and paid to a creditor.

Historical Preservation Commission

Sometimes the use and renovation of historical buildings is regulated. If a restaurant is located in a historical building, city zone, or community, a manager may face regulations dealing with preserving the property's historical integrity. This may limit the types of alterations or improvements that can be made and/or may require maintenance of the property in a manner consistent with the area's historical nature.

Fire Department

Dependable fire departments assist managers in limiting potential liability through careful adherence to all local fire codes and procedures. Fire department personnel normally conduct routine property inspections, assist building departments in reviewing plans for new or renovated buildings, ensure that emergency lighting and sprinklers are installed and properly maintained, and offer fire safety training. Managers should know the local fire codes and be certain that the operation always has the required number of fire extinguishers, smoke detectors, sprinklers, fans and ventilation ducts, emergency lights, and emergency exit signs. Equipment should be tested periodically to ensure that it is in good working order. The National Fire Protection Association has established national standards for ventilation systems and automatic fire protection systems in commercial kitchens. Insurance company regulations detail the type and amount of fire protection equipment needed for an operation.

Fire departments also regulate the number of individuals allowed in a particular space at a given time. The capacity of bars and dining and banquet rooms are examples of areas regulated by fire departments. Signs indicating the maximum number of people permitted in a public space must be prominently displayed.

Law Enforcement Agencies

In most communities, some laws or codes are enforced by the police department (in a city) or by the sheriff's department (in a rural community). Liquor laws, for example, may be enforced by the local police. Parking enforcement and the removal of disorderly guests may also be police responsibilities.

Tax Assessment/Collection

Local municipalities may levy taxes on the basis of property value, revenue, or a combination of both.

MANAGING REGULATIONS THAT CONFLICT

Given the large number of legislative bodies creating new policies daily, there are surprisingly few instances in which regulations directly conflict. As a rule, local legislators and public officials review state and federal guidelines prior to implementing new regulations, just as state regulators review federal guidelines. In fact, where there are agencies at each governmental level, the federal agency may create model regulations that will be adopted in whole or in part at the state level, just as the state may create model regulations for possible use at the local level.

Consider A. J. Patel, a regional food & beverage manager for a hotel company operating properties that provide a free continental breakfast to all registered guests. His properties operate in three different states. Patel must be familiar with the public health codes of three different state and local governments, so he must stay current with changing health code regulations of all six entities. His task has been made easier, however, because the federal Food and Drug Administration (FDA) has created a model Food Service Sanitation Ordinance (found at www.foodsafety.org) that is followed, with varying degrees of specificity, by many state and local communities.

There will be times when requirements that must be met by a manager are in conflict. A federal requirement may conflict with a local one, for example. Although this can be frustrating, managers should know what to do in such a situation.

A conflict of regulatory restriction occurs when one entity sets a standard higher or lower than another. If, for example, a local sanitation code requires all kitchen shelving to be 12 inches above the floor and the state code allows shelving to be within 6 inches of the floor, the more restrictive regulation will prevail. In this case, a shelf 12 inches above the floor satisfies *both* regulatory bodies. The principle to remember is this: When regulatory demands conflict, the most restrictive regulation should be followed.

WHAT WOULD YOU DO?

Sharon operated a restaurant. Employees were permitted to eat one meal per shift. For those who voluntarily ate this meal, Sharon deducted 25 cents per hour ($2.00 per eight-hour shift) from the federal minimum wage rate she paid her entry-level dishwashers, which reflected a reasonable meal cost.

Sharon relied on the Fair Labor Standards Act (FLSA), Section 3(m), which states that employers can consider as wages "reasonable costs . . . to the employer of furnishing such employees with board, lodging, or other facilities if such board, lodging, or other facilities are customarily furnished by such employer to his employees." Sharon interpreted this to mean that she could pay the dishwashers a rate which, when added to the $0.25 per hour meal deduction, equaled the federal minimum wage.

Sharon was contacted by her state Department of Employment, charging that she was in violation of the state minimum wage law, which stated, "Total voluntary deductions for meals and uniforms may not decrease an employee's wages below the Federal minimum wage on an hourly basis." Sharon maintained that because she was in compliance with the federal law, she was allowed to take the meal credit against the wages paid to her entry-level dishwashers.

What would you do if you were Sharon?

RESPONDING TO AN INQUIRY

Despite a manager's best efforts, a property may be found to violate a regulation. Consider Gerry who, for many years, heavily decorated the public areas of his restaurant during the Christmas season. This year, Gerry has received a letter from the local fire chief citing the property for three violations of the fire code. Some holiday lights are illuminated with the use of extension cords, which are not allowed, by ordinance, in the township where the restaurant is located. In this case, the problem can be quickly resolved by replacing the extension cords with surge protector cords allowed by local ordinance.

At the other extreme, consider a manager notified that the IRS will be conducting an audit of tip reporting compliance. The auditors plan to study the last three years to verify that the required employment taxes were paid on those tips. The manager assembles three years of paperwork and discovers that some taxes were not paid during the first year before she became manager. A penalty may still be assessed.

Some regulatory violations can be very serious. Managers should follow standard procedures anytime a governmental agency suggests that there has been regulatory noncompliance. The recommended steps for responding to inquiries and complaints by government agencies include the following:

- *Upon notification of a complaint or violation, document the date and time that all paperwork was received; check all correspondence for required deadlines.* This can be done manually or with a small mechanical stamping device. Include the day, month, and year of receipt; many agencies require a response within a specified time from the date correspondence is received.

  Check due dates for responses. Some are measured from the date of receipt; others are measured from the date mailed. A letter may state, "If you do not respond within ten days of receipt of this correspondence, we will assume that the claimant's position is true and act accordingly." (This is known as an automatic default provision; it is imperative that you respond within the time frame specified. There is rarely a remedy to a missed deadline for an initial response.)

- *Assess the severity of the complaint; determine whether legal consultation is necessary.* In addition, decide whether the issue should be referred to your insurance carrier. (Consider faxing the correspondence to your insurance agent for an additional opinion and about whether there is coverage for the concern that is raised.) If the carrier determines that there is coverage, the carrier will ordinarily provide an attorney to defend the claim. If coverage is denied, the operation's own counsel may be needed; it may be necessary to engage an administrative law specialist (an attorney who spends significant time handling complaints for alleged violations of government regulations and/or government prosecutions).

- *Develop a plan of action.* How a manager responds differs according to whether legal assistance is needed.

Without an attorney. Calendar all response dates; allow enough time for mailing. Identify all who must be involved in the response; contact them in a timely fashion for input. Keep clear, legible copies of anything forwarded as a response to a complaint. Do not state anything that is not true or that you cannot prove. Follow correspondence instructions exactly. (If instructions say to use only one page and/or that the response must be typed, make sure that the response is typed and on one page. If your response must be signed and your signature notarized, be certain to sign and notarize it. Make sure that you retain copies of your signed and notarized responses.)

With an attorney. Forward all correspondence immediately to your attorney, along with any supporting documentation that can clarify the situation completely. Provide a list of people, along with contact information, who may have knowledge of the situation. Stay in direct communication with your attorney until the matter is resolved. It is crucial to meet deadlines and to be aware of potential witness schedules. (If you know certain people (including yourself) who will be unavailable, inform the attorney so plans can be made in case additional information or statements are needed.)

Managers should never willingly violate a legitimate regulation. Usually, noncompliance is unintentional, and the government agency has the duty to inform managers of violations.

MONITORING REGULATORY CHANGES

It is not possible to know every governmental regulation affecting restaurants, and some laws change regularly. Changes in major federal laws may be well publicized, but a manager cannot know about all policies of all governmental agencies. Reading about the industry will make you a better manager and will help you keep up with changing regulations as well. Appendix D lists helpful publications. For managers employed by a national chain or management company, the parent company can provide information about changing regulations. A valuable service provided by franchisors to franchisees is regular updates on governmental agencies and regulations that they issue.

The federal government plays a large role in regulating the hospitality industry, and a manager should have current and rapid access to actions taken by each federal regulatory agency. (The Web sites noted in this chapter can help managers to keep up-to-date on changes in the law.)

Managers should stay involved in the trade association(s) representing their industry segment. The National Restaurant Association (NRA) and others regularly provide legislative updates. Many of these organizations have state, regional, or local chapters.

Locally, chambers of commerce, business trade associations and personal relationships with local police, fire, and building officials can help keep managers up-to-date with municipal changes.

Managers should take an active role in shaping the regulations affecting the industry. Governments attempt to pass regulations that are in the best interests of their constituencies. The problem arises when costs or infringement on individual rights exceeds the societal value of a proposed regulation.

WHAT WOULD YOU DO?

After the highly publicized death of a college student, a local sports bar lost its liquor license for 60 days. The student had consumed 21 shots of alcohol on his birthday at the bar and died from alcohol poisoning. The bar was crowded that night, and because shots were purchased by many of the victim's friends, the bar manager and staff were unaware of the problem. The college newspaper published editorials warning against the perils of binge drinking and accusing the manager of negligence or indifference.

Sorrow in the community and outrage in the press caused the city's mayor to propose a local ordinance banning the sale of more than three drinks per day to any individual. (A drink, under the ordinance, would be defined as either a 12-ounce beer, a 4-ounce glass of table wine, or a 1½-ounce shot of liquor.) Violators would face a fine of $5,000 per incident. Enforcement would be the responsibility of the local police. The mayor, generally a strong promoter of business, is a nondrinker. Support for the ordinance is strong because of the incident.

The president of the local restaurant association has been asked to address the proposed ordinance at the next meeting of the city council.

If you were the president of the association, what would you do?

MANAGERS "TO DO" LIST

Review the following recommendations proposed in this section. Analyze your interest in and need for implementing these recommendations by completing the columns on the right side of the form. Remember, when task assignments are made, time requirements for completion should also be stated. Follow up, as improvement activities evolve, to ensure that your property is moving closer to the goal of minimizing litigation risks.

Recommended Procedures	In Place Now?			Needed to Implement			Assigned To	Completion Date
	Yes	No	N/A*	Policy	Training	Other		
File quarterly income tax returns and make payments on business profits on a timely basis.								
File an income and tax statement with the Social Security Administration on a timely basis.								
Use proper procedures to withhold income taxes from employees' wages and pay these to the IRS on a timely basis.								
Properly report all employee tip income and withhold taxes on it.								
Correctly record the value of employee meals when considered part of an employee's income.								
Record all payments to independent contractors and file forms listing these payments on a timely basis.								
Furnish a record of withheld taxes to all employees on a timely basis.								
Consult a Certified Public Accountant or an attorney specializing in tax audits if an IRS audit has been scheduled.								
Maintain facilities and provide clothing in compliance with OSHA standards.								
Purchase equipment meeting OSHA's health and safety specifications.								
Establish and use safety checklists and training programs relating to potentially dangerous equipment.								
Report workplace accidents to OSHA on a timely basis.								

*N/A = Not Applicable

Recommended Procedures	In Place Now?			Needed to Implement			Assigned To	Completion Date
	Yes	No	N/A*	Policy	Training	Other		
Maintain a log of work-related illnesses and injuries and file on a timely basis.								
Schedule one employee trained in first aid for each work shift.								
Appropriately display OSHA's notices about employee rights and safety.								
Ensure that Material Safety Data Sheets for all required chemicals are available to employees.								
Offer hepatitis B vaccinations to employees coming in contact with blood or bodily fluids.								
Accompany OSHA compliance officers during any inspections.								
Comply with all aspects of OSHA's Hazard Communication standards.								
Apply for and properly display proof of payment of special taxes for retail sellers of alcohol.								
Know and consistently follow all state regulations applicable to workers' compensation.								
Know and follow all aspects of state health department regulations regarding sanitary food-handling procedures.								
Know and carefully follow all applicable requirements relating to health and sanitation imposed by applicable local agencies.								
Carefully follow requirements imposed by local building and zoning departments and the property's insurance company, if applicable.								

*N/A = Not Applicable

Recommended Procedures	In Place Now?			Needed to Implement			Assigned To	Completion Date
	Yes	No	N/A*	Policy	Training	Other		
Know and consistently comply with all local fire codes applicable to the property and facility.								
When regulatory demands conflict, always know and follow the most restrictive regulation.								
Use a well-thought-out process when responding to an inquiry made by a regulatory agency. (Procedures are spelled out under "Responding to an Inquiry.")								
Keep up with special reading, become active in national, state, and/or local hospitality-related associations, and be active in the local Chamber of Commerce and related organizations.								

For more information and suggestions log onto www.hospitalitylawyer.com.

*N/A = Not Applicable

CONSULTANT'S CORNER

What Would You Do? (page 105)

This situation raises two issues:

1. MSDS sheets should not only be available, but they should be reviewed with the worker prior to the task being performed.

2. Managers must understand the reading and language skills of their employees to ensure a thorough understanding of the potential dangers of interacting with certain chemicals or machinery. In most instances, MSDS sheets are available from the manufacturer in several languages. A Spanish-language sheet would certainly have been helpful in this situation.

If it had been the common custom and practice to review the MSDS sheet with the worker prior to the task, Bert, if he had not already known, would have discovered that Carlos did not understand English and perhaps could have located a Spanish version of the MSDS sheet. This is an accident that should have been prevented.

What Would You Do? (page 111)

This is a difficult situation, because it appears from the facts presented that Chantel's organization was well trained and followed through on its responsibilities. Nevertheless, there are two concerns:

1. The fact that a minor was served. The courts recognize that a server of alcohol can only do so much to prevent the use of fraudulent identification to procure alcoholic beverages for minors. This particular situation demonstrates excellent procedures that can be used to demonstrate diligence by the server to ensure that minors are not served via fraudulent identification. It is unlikely that liability will result from the fact that the minor was served alcohol.

2. The other issue that will need to be defended is the decision to serve three glasses of wine in 90 minutes. Most people become somewhat impaired when they consume two alcoholic beverages within a one-to-two-hour period. The question is, Were the patrons demonstrating any physical signs of intoxication during the time they were served? If so, and if the attorney for the injured patron can demonstrate that alcohol played a role in the accident, then the bar may have some concerns.

It appears that Chantel has contacted her attorney. Her next step, if she has not already done so, would be to make her insurance company aware of the claim and begin to request statements from her employees regarding the incident.

Finally, it may be a good idea to implement a policy used by some restaurants and clubs: When a patron orders a third drink, prior to that drink's being served to him or her, or any other drink during the evening, a manager must visit with that patron for a few minutes to determine whether service is still appropriate.

What Would You Do? (page 117)

It appears that Sharon's business is in compliance with the federal law but in violation of the more restrictive state law. When there is a conflict between laws, it is the obligation of the operator to comply with the more onerous or strict law.

Unfortunately for Sharon, in this situation she must be in compliance with both the federal and state laws as well as any local laws. Accordingly, just because she is in compliance with the federal law does not excuse her noncompliance with the state law.

Sharon probably needs to negotiate a settlement with the Department of Employment for the underpayments that have occurred with her employees to date.

This situation certainly points out the severe cost to a business for noncompliance with administrative laws. If an issue like this comes up, be sure to contact the state agency and request clarification prior to implementing your decision.

What Would You Do? (page 120)

Anti-alcohol sentiment seems to be growing daily. With the efforts of organizations such as Mothers Against Drunk Driving (MADD) and Students Against Drunk Driving (SADD), the dangers of the irresponsible service of alcohol are constantly communicated to the public. When a terrible incident occurs, like the one described here, it heightens the concerns of the public and the pressure on community leaders to address those concerns.

This is a delicate situation. The restaurant association may be able to challenge the ordinance in court; however, it may cause further outrage in the community. This approach could be devastating from a public relations standpoint.

Another approach may be to ask the owners of the local sports bar to offer a very public, sincere apology to the parents, the college, and the general community. Then ask them to outline the steps that they have taken to ensure that an incident like this never happens again.

The next step would be to meet with community leaders to express the association's concern about the ordinance and how it may negatively affect responsible operators. Provide information to the leaders about the diligence used by your members to serve alcohol responsibly. If, and it is to be hoped that they do, local statistics support the argument that the incident described was an isolated one, suggest that the ordinance may be a too severe reaction.

It would be appropriate to tell them of the association's support for all of the federal, state, and local ordinances that members are required to comply with and/or enforce. This particular ordinance, however, raises difficult questions about enforcement, and perhaps there are better ways to address the concerns of the public. Finally, the argument can be made that better enforcement of the laws and ordinances already in force may have the same safety impact but result in a far less negative economic impact on the members, and thus on the community (this position must be expressed extremely sensitively, because you never want to take the position that profits are more important than the public's safety and personal welfare).

6

MANAGING INSURANCE

MANAGER'S BRIEF

Managers reading this chapter will learn details about six of the most common types of insurance coverage needed by all restaurants: property/casualty, liability, employee liability, dram shop, health/dental/vision, and workers' compensation. Managers will also obtain a foundation of information helpful in selecting an insurance carrier and policy and will be able to analyze an insurance policy to assess what is and is not covered.

BACKGROUND

Everyone faces the risk of illness, accidents, the acts of others, and even death. Restaurants also face the possibility of floods, fire, the acts of customers and employees and more. To protect against the financial loss of these risks, individuals and businesses need **insurance** to spread risk from one person or business to a larger group.

INSURE (INSURANCE)   To protect from risk.

Restaurants seek insurance (risk protection) for two reasons. First, it makes good financial sense. Second, some types of insurance coverage are required either by law (such as workers' compensation) or by lenders to protect their collateral. Consider the restaurateur who owns a business that provides her a salary of $100,000 annually. The restaurant is the sole source of income. If it burned down, she would lose all income. To protect her business and her income, she buys a fire insurance policy that pays for the replacement of the restaurant if there was a fire. Failure to buy the insurance places her and her family at great financial risk. Buying the insurance provides her with financial security in the event of a fire and the peace of mind that security brings.

The insurance industry is built upon four fundamental premises:

ACTUARY   A mathematician or statistician who computes insurance risks and establishes premium rates.

1. The type of hazard the insurance company underwrites is faced by a sufficient number of individuals or businesses that statisticians can use actuarial (**actuary**) methods to predict the average frequency of loss involved in the risk.

PREMIUM   The amount paid for insurance coverage; can be paid in one lump sum or over time, such as monthly.

2. The monetary value of the loss can be determined against an accepted standard. For example, if a restaurant seeks coverage for broken windows caused by vandals, it must be possible for the insurer to determine the cost of window replacement.

INSURED   The individual or business that purchases insurance against a risk.

3. The insurance **premiums** (fees) must be low enough to attract those who seek to be **insured,** but high enough to support the number of losses that will be incurred by the **insurer.**

INSURER   The entity that provides insurance.

4. Losses must not occur so frequently during a specific period that the insurer cannot pay all

legitimate claims. Insurance companies spend millions of dollars annually to determine the risk factors in providing insurance for a specific industry. Obviously, the fewer casualty losses, workers injured, lawsuits, and so on, the lower the risk that the insurance company will have to pay claims. Logically, then, the safer the operation and the safer the industry as a whole, the lower the insurance cost.

The insurance contract between an insurer and an insured is called a **policy.** There are numerous policy types, but they can be grouped in three categories:

> **POLICY (INSURANCE) The contract for insurance agreed upon by an insurer and an insured.**

1. Life insurance

2. Health insurance

3. Property/casualty (often called "property/liability") insurance

Life insurance policies are generally written to pay proceeds when an insured person dies or to pay the insured an **annuity** upon reaching a specified age. Health insurance generally pays hospital and doctor bills and annuity payments for those who are disabled. (It is common for a restaurant manager to receive some level of life and health insurance as part of a compensation package.)

> **ANNUITY Fixed payments made on a regular basis for an agreed-upon time or until the recipient's death.**

Property liability insurance provides financial protection (**indemnification**) when events such as floods, fire, lawsuits, and automobile accidents occur.

> **INDEMNIFICATION Protection to insure against possible liability and loss and/or to compensate for losses incurred.**

Insurance companies, like restaurants, are in business to make a profit. In the insurance industry, profits result from increasing premium amounts, increasing returns from premium investments, and reducing costs, including the payment of insurance claims. Therefore, insurers are careful to pay only legitimate **claims** within the terms of an insurance policy.

> **CLAIM Demand for money, property, or property repairs.**

Because insurance protects against risk at an agreed-upon price, managers must know:

- The risks against which they are insuring
- The amount of coverage they will receive

- Exceptions to coverage written into the policy

- The cost of the insurance

- The likelihood that the insurance company will pay if it becomes necessary

To purchase insurance, a potential buyer must demonstrate an insurable interest in the premises to be insured (that is, that a loss would affect him or her in a material way). This concept is fundamental and helps protect against possible intentional acts of destruction or fraud. Moreover, an insured must honestly divulge information needed by the insurer to establish appropriate premium rates.

WHAT WOULD YOU DO?

Samuel authorized the purchase of a $2 million fidelity insurance policy for the purpose of protecting the restaurant he managed in the event of employee theft or fraud. When discussing the purchase with the insurance agent, he assured the agent that the restaurant's accountant had been through a thorough background check before being hired.

The insurance policy was purchased and went into effect on January 1. On June 1 of that year, Samuel took over the management of another restaurant. The same accountant managed the books of both properties. A few months later Samuel discovered that the accountant had been creating and submitting false invoices for payment, which, over five years, had resulted in losses of more than $500,000.

The accountant resigned, and it was discovered that, in fact, no background check had ever been undertaken. For this reason, the insurance agent maintained that the insurance company was not liable for any losses. Samuel countered that although his background had not been checked, the accountant had no criminal record, so an investigation would not have prevented him from being hired.

What would you do if you were Samuel? The insurance company?

As with any significant purchase, careful comparison shopping for insurance is important. Because insurance is a contract between the insurer and the insured, it is also necessary to read the contract carefully or to have an expert evaluate it. All insurance policies must be kept in a safe, secure location.

Purchasing insurance, often complex and confusing, is a three-step process:

- Step One—determining the type of insurance coverage needed. (Look at your operation to decide which risks to protect against.)

- Step Two—determining the ideal amount of insurance coverage and the type of policy required. (Remember, as the dollar value of coverage increases, so will the premiums.)

- Step Three—selecting a specific insurance company from which to buy the policy.

TYPES OF COVERAGE

The insurance needs of restaurants vary considerably. The insurance policy should reflect the unique characteristics of the business, including its location. A restaurant on the Gulf Coast may think that hurricane insurance makes sense; an operation in South Dakota will not.

Insurance companies offer a wide variety of products. Managers must carefully select the proper coverage. With too much or unnecessary coverage, restaurant profits are reduced because premium payments are too high. With too little or no insurance of the right type, the economic survival of the restaurant is at risk.

Many states require businesses to carry certain types of insurance, at specified minimum amounts, to conduct business. In addition, when restaurants lease space, the lease agreement may require minimum amounts of insurance.

Property/Casualty Insurance

Property/casualty insurance protects against property loss from fire, flood, or storms. This is the most common type of business insurance; it can be purchased in policies covering losses of as little as a few hundred or as much as many millions of dollars. Insurance companies classify property threats in different ways, but property/casualty insurance always protects property and its contents. The determination of risks to insure against must be made on the basis of each property's circumstances.

Consider Ralph, who operates a seafood restaurant on a ship permanently docked on a lake. Unlike many other restaurateurs, he must insure the operation against water-related events that could destroy his business, including accidentally being hit by another boat, high- or low-water damage, and seasonal storms. Ralph must select casualty insurance to reimburse him for the cost of repairs and any potential business loss.

Liability Insurance

General liability insurance protects against injuries to other people resulting from a restaurant's operation. For example, Diane's restaurant serves flamed desserts. One evening, a server accidentally spills flaming alcohol from the flambé pan onto a diner's suit. The diner suffers minor burns and is upset. Should the diner bring a lawsuit against Diane, general liability insurance will help cover expenses and any potential damages that may be awarded.

There are several popular types of liability insurance available:

- Property damage liability coverage protects against claims resulting from damage to the property of others.

- Personal injury liability coverage provides protection for offenses such as false arrest, libel, slander, invasion of privacy, food-borne illnesses, slips, and falls etc.

- Advertising injury liability coverage covers liability for problems arising from advertising of the restaurant's goods and services.

Insurance companies have the right and obligation to defend lawsuits made by customers seeking damages for bodily injury or property damage even if the allegations are groundless, false, or fraudulent. An insurance company can also enter into any settlement agreement it wishes. The company is not obligated to pay any claim or judgment or to defend any suit after the applicable limit of liability has been reached.

Consider Roger, who owns a restaurant in which a banquet customer accidentally discharges a pistol. The shot passes through the room's wall and injures a customer in the dining room, who sues Robert and the person responsible for the accidental shooting. Roger's insurance company defends the restaurant in the lawsuit. In the jury trial, Roger's restaurant is deemed partially responsible for the accident and must pay the victim $3 million. The restaurant's insurance policy provides only $1 million in coverage; Roger's property is responsible for paying the remaining $2 million.

With the increasing value of litigation awards today, managers must ensure that they have sufficient liability coverage. This is not easy, as one weighs the cost of coverage (premium payments) with the risk (possible damages) to assess the operation's ability to absorb and/or pass costs onto customers.

Employee Liability Insurance

An employee liability policy supplements general liability coverage with additional coverage for harmful acts of employees committed during their employment. Areas of coverage include those related to:

- Wrongful termination

- Workplace harassment

- Sexual harassment

- Breach of employment contract

- Discrimination

- Failure to employ or promote

- Deprivation of a career opportunity

- Negligent evaluation

- Employment-related misrepresentation

- Defamation

Dram Shop (Liquor Liability) Insurance

Dram shop (liquor liability) insurance provides properties selling alcohol with coverage for bodily injury or property damage resulting from any or all of the following acts:

- Causing or contributing to a person's intoxication

- Serving alcoholic beverages to a person under the legal drinking age

- Serving alcohol to an intoxicated person

- Violating any statute, ordinance, or regulation relating to the sale, gift, distribution, or use of alcoholic beverages

Serving alcoholic beverages today creates great risk. Dram shop insurance is a necessity, and some states require it as a condition for granting a liquor license.

Health/Dental/Vision Insurance

The cost of employee medical insurance continues to rise. Although providing health insurance is not required, the degree to which this insurance is offered can affect a manager's ability to retain and maintain a quality workforce.

The variety of medical insurance coverage available is great. The cost is generally split between the employer and the employee. Employers can elect to contribute 100 percent—or any percentage of the premiums or can simply make coverage available on a voluntary basis. Employees often depend on the coverage for their families and can maintain their insurance even if they lose their jobs.

The federal Consolidated Omnibus Budget Reconciliation Act (COBRA) requires employers to continue providing health, dental, and optical coverage benefits to employees who have resigned or have been terminated and to family members of employees who have lost health insurance because of death, divorce, or dropping out of school. COBRA participants may continue their benefits for as long as 18 months following the loss of their insurance, but they are responsible for paying the entire premium cost during this period.

Workers' Compensation Insurance

All states require public- and private-sector employers to provide some form of workers' compensation insurance.

Workers' compensation policies provide payments to workers or their families in the event of an employee's injury or death. Coverage normally includes medical expenses and a significant portion of the wages lost by the employee who cannot work because of injury. In more serious cases, lump sum payments can be made to partially or permanently disabled workers. In addition, if a worker is killed on the job, payments may be made to the family. The injury must have happened in the **course and scope** of employment. The courts have broadly defined "course and scope" to sometimes include commuting to and from work or to mealtimes on or off the work site.

COURSE AND SCOPE The sum total of all common, job-related employee activities dictated or allowed by the employer.

Injured employees are generally prohibited from suing their employers for damages beyond those awarded by workers' compensation. Only in the cases of gross negligence or an intentional act will employers potentially be required to pay greater damages than those imposed by workers' compensation.

Some states, in an effort to hold down premium costs and reduce incidents of fraud, designate specific doctors to examine employees claiming to be injured. Employers cannot claim worker negligence as a defense for a work-related injury. It is usually only where the worker has been proven to be under the influence of drugs or alcohol when injured that an employer can make a legally valid defense against a workers' compensation claim (assuming an actual injury occurred in the course and scope of employment).

When another employee or third party has caused a worker injury or when the employer challenges the legality of a worker's compensation claim, a hearing is held before the state workers' compensation board. A judge determines whether the claim has merit and how much, if any, compensation the worker should receive. Either party can appeal the judge's decision.

A manager's failure to provide workers' compensation insurance is punishable by fines and/or imprisonment. Employers are also required to accurately report on-the-job accidents to the state agency overseeing the workers' compensation program. This information is significant, because the insurance cost varies, based on the employer's safety history and the potential risk of injury to employees working for a specific employer. A manager who does not encourage the immediate cleanup of kitchen spills and who experiences a greater-than-average number of employee injuries due to slips and falls will pay a higher premium than a similar employer who does not have these accidents. Many state workers' compensation boards use experience ratings, which categorize businesses by the number of paid injury claims, to determine the amount of insurance premiums.

Depending on the state, employers may provide workers' compensation insurance through a private insurance company, a state agency, or themselves. If the state allows self-insurance, the required security deposit can be substantial, inasmuch as an employer may be solely responsible for the payment of large awards when there is a serious accident.

WHAT WOULD YOU DO?

Christina was 16 years old when she was hired to work as a busser. On her first day of work, the supervisor detailed the job's requirements during their 15-minute training session. Christina was to remove soiled dishes, take them to a side station, and scrape any leftover food into a garbage receptacle. Periodically, she was to bring the dishes to the kitchen and take the garbage receptacle to a designated area, where she would remove the plastic trash bag and replace it with an empty one. The bags with garbage were left in the designated area until they could be taken out to a dumpster by a dishwasher. The garbage receptacles were often heavy, and all buspersons were instructed to replace the plastic bags when they were half full.

Halfway through her first shift, Christina forgot to replace one of the garbage bags until it was nearly full. She placed the garbage bag with the others in the designated location. Later, a dishwasher attempted to lift the bag that was accidentally overfilled and seriously injured his back.

The injury was deemed to be within the scope of his work, and he was awarded a monetary settlement by the workers' compensation board. However, he then threatened to sue the restaurant, claiming negligence in Christina's training and stating this negligence was the direct cause of the accident. He also stated that management had provided garbage receptacles that were too large and that this directly contributed to the accident.

What would you do if you were the manager?

SELECTING AN INSURANCE CARRIER

Almost all insurance companies sell their products through agents, rather than directly to the public. Some use agents representing them exclusively. Others use independent agents who represent several insurance companies, which can be helpful in selecting the best policy at the best price. The premium rate, or charge for the insurance, however, is set by the insurance company and cannot generally be changed by an agent.

An insurance agent does not provide insurance but merely represents the company that **underwrites** the actual insurance policy. When managers buy an insurance policy, they must purchase it from a credible insurance company—not just from an agent who is an effective salesperson.

UNDERWRITE To assume agreed-upon maximum levels of liability in the event of a loss or damage.

For an insurance company to protect against risk, it must have the financial capability to pay all claims for which it is held responsible during the cover-

---

WWW: Internet Assistant

Log onto the Internet and enter: http://www. insure.com

Select: Company Ratings

Select: Standard & Poor's insurance company financial-strength ratings

Select: What the Ratings Mean; read the definitions of AAA through B insurance ratings.

Return to the www.insure.com home page and follow the path required to find the rating of your own insurance company. Determine the company's rating and assess how it ranks among the insurance companies in your state.

---

age period. Managers do not want to buy an insurance policy and then discover, after a claim has been filed, that the company does not have the assets to pay the claim. If the insurance company will not, or cannot, pay a claim, the restaurant and its owner will be responsible for payment.

Insurance companies are rated on their ability to pay claims. According to analysts, the stronger the rating, the more financially solvent the company is thought to be. Rating categories of different organizations vary, but they generally use either an A+, A, A−, B+, and so on, system or an AAA, AA, A, BBB, and so on, system. It is probably unwise to purchase a policy with a rating of less than A− or AA; buy from a company that has achieved a rating of A+ or AAA.

Ratings can be verified by contacting the rating companies directly. A. M. Best and Standard & Poor's are two such companies. Alternatively, contact your state's Insurance Regulatory Department for a list of complaints filed against insurance companies that fail to pay claims in a timely fashion or to act in good faith.

SELECTING AN INSURANCE POLICY

After identifying two or three financially sound companies, the next step is to get quotes (bids) to provide coverage.

Consider Vasal, who wants to add a dental plan to his employees' health coverage. He selects three companies (all are rated AA) and requests a bid for his 240 employees. He receives the following responses:

Insurance Company	Coverage Cost per Employee
Acme	$45.00 monthly
Best	$43.25 monthly
Heritage	$17.80 monthly

At first glance it appears that Heritage Company offers the best policy price; however, is the level of dental coverage the same under all three policies? When he investigates, he finds that the annual per employee maximum benefits are $3,000 for Acme and Best, but for Heritage the per employee maximum benefits are only $1,000. The price per $1,000 of employee dental insurance provided is actually highest from Heritage Company. Vasal must decide whether to pay for higher amounts of coverage or to ask employees to contribute partial payments.

To understand how much insurance is being purchased for the premium dollar and to discover how much total insurance is in place for the time period covered by the policy, a manager must understand the terms used in marketing insurance products.

Tina owns a bagel franchise and is seeking liability coverage. She selects some potential insurance providers, based on financial ratings, and then requests quotes on a **primary** policy with a **per occurrence** amount of $500,000, an **aggregate** of $1 million, and an additional **umbrella** policy of $1 million.

If the policy selected by Tina states $500,000 of coverage per occurrence, this means that for every incident occurring when she could be held liable, her insurance company will pay up to $500,000 less any **deductible.** If the judgment exceeds that amount, she is responsible for the remainder.

If Tina's insurance policy has the term "aggregate" after an amount, this is the total amount her insurance company will pay for all incidents and dam-

PRIMARY COVERAGE The amount of insurance provided by a traditional insurance policy.

PER OCCURRENCE The maximum amount that will be paid by an insurer in the event of a single claim.

AGGREGATE The maximum amount that will be paid by an insurer for all claims during a policy period.

UMBRELLA Insurance coverage purchased to supplement primary coverage; sometimes called excess insurance.

DEDUCTIBLE The amount the insured must pay before the insurance coverage begins to pay. Accordingly, the higher the deductible, the less risk to the insurance company, which should lower premium cost.

ages incurred during the coverage period. If Tina has a $500,000 per occurrence policy and $1 million aggregate, two claims of $500,000 would wipe out her total insurance coverage (as would four claims of $250,000, etc.).

Managers should understand how a deductible affects total insurance costs. A high deductible results in lower premium payments; the manager assumes more risk by agreeing to pay a higher share of claims that are filed. Managers must factor the cost of the deductible into their insurance buying decisions and balance the needs of having a specified amount of coverage to be paid by the insurance company with the premium payments they are willing to make.

Primary coverage is also called basic coverage. Managers can also purchase an umbrella policy (commonly called excess coverage). This coverage ordinarily pays only when the primary per occurrence coverage is exhausted by one claim.

Assume the following: You have a $500,000 per occurrence policy with a $500,000 aggregate, and you also have $1 million in umbrella or excess coverage. The policy period runs from January 1 to December 31. An accident occurs on January 20, and the claim is settled for $750,000. The primary coverage pays the first $500,000 less any deductible. The umbrella policy pays the remaining $250,000. However, there is a later claim from an incident occurring on February 15. How much coverage is available? The answer is zero! The coverage under the primary policy is depleted, because there is a $500,000 aggregate. The umbrella policy is not available, because it usually pays only if the primary per occurrence amount on a given claim is exhausted. If there is no primary per occurrence coverage remaining, the conditions for coverage of the umbrella policy cannot be met unless the operation itself pays the first $500,000. A manager in this situation needs to buy additional primary coverage.

POLICY ANALYSIS

Analyzing an insurance policy consists of determining what is and what is not covered. Managers should know and understand the types and amounts of coverage written into an insurance policy. When one purchases insurance, however, a copy of the actual policy is not received immediately, because time is needed for the insurance company to organize the formal policy with its unique coverages and exclusions. Instead, a one page **face sheet** is provided, which generally states

FACE SHEET A one-page document describing the type and amount of insurance coverage in an insurance policy; sometimes called the Declarations Page.

the types and amounts of coverages without detailed information about what is specifically included and excluded from the policy's coverage. The actual policy contains this information but, usually, will not be received until 30 to 60 days from the purchase date. The face sheet, then, contains the "large print" (overview), and the actual policy contains the "fine print," which will be provided after the policy is purchased.

It is often difficult to read an insurance policy. However, the courts will hold an insured responsible for reading and understanding its policy(ies). If a manager is unclear about insurance policy coverage, an attorney should review a sample policy provided by the insurance company.

Managers must discuss any unclear issues with the insurance agent before purchasing a policy. Ask for written answers to questions and continue to request information until satisfied with the details. Once the policy arrives, the manager should read it and make sure that he or she fully understands:

- The policy's language and whether it is consistent with the agent's earlier explanations

- The policy's coverage, **exclusions, exceptions,** and clarifying language

EXCLUSIONS Liability claims not covered in an insurance policy.

EXCEPTIONS Insurance coverage that is normally included in the policy, but which will be excluded if the insured fails to comply with performance terms specifically mentioned in the policy.

Most insurance policies have both exclusions and exceptions. The insurer nearly always retains the right to exclude certain types of liability claims. (If a restaurateur has purchased fire insurance, but then intentionally sets fire to the restaurant, the insurance company would exclude [refuse to cover] the cost of replacing the restaurant.) Common exclusions include those involving intentional acts and fraud by the insured.

Exceptions are also common in insurance policies; be aware of all that apply. For example, the company may require a restaurant to have a valid license to serve food so as to protect that restaurant if a guest claims damages resulting from food-borne illness.

An insurer usually requires immediate notification if a claim is made or if the manager believes something has occurred that may lead to litigation. Moreover, if an attorney serves a notification of intent to sue, the insurance carrier must be contacted. Some insurance policies are "claims made" policies, which means that the coverage is available only if an actual claim is brought to the attention of the insurance company during the policy period. Most insurance policies, however, cover claims occurring during the policy period even if they are not brought to the insurance company's attention until after the coverage period has elapsed. This type of policy is preferable.

Even with the problems and expenses involved, insurance is not an option; it is a protection needed to operate the business. Managers can avoid unpleasant surprises by carefully selecting insurance. This includes speaking and listening to colleagues and asking questions that will make it easier to purchase the right coverage in the right amount from the right insurance company.

Most policies are issued for a one-year period, assuming there is mutual satisfaction with the coverage, the carrier's responsiveness to claims, and an agreement about the premium (cost).

Chapter 9 examines how managers can reduce insurance costs by effective staff management and training. Prevention of insurance claims, like the prevention of all legal claims, should be the goal of every manager.

WHAT WOULD YOU DO?

Suppose you are an insurance agent who sells ABIC products exclusively. Your company, rated AA, offers coverage against a variety of risks, including workers' compensation, and specializes in the restaurant industry.

You are approached by Ted, a restaurant owner. He wants to purchase workers' compensation insurance. A review of his application and claim history indicates that Ted's restaurants have experienced a large number of worker injuries in the last four years. The rate of worker injury per labor hour worked is nearly two times that of the restaurant industry average. Further investigation indicates that most of these injuries resulted from cutting meat.

As the insurance agent, what would you do?

MANAGER'S "TO DO" LIST

Review the following recommendations proposed in this section. Analyze your interest in and need for implementing these recommendations by completing the columns on the right side of the form. Remember, when task assignments are made, time requirements for completion should also be stated. Follow up, as improvement activities evolve, to ensure that your property is moving closer to the goal of minimizing litigation risks.

Recommended Procedures	In Place Now?			Needed to Implement			Assigned To	Completion Date
	Yes	No	N/A*	Policy	Training	Other		
A careful assessment of the operation and the risks against which to protect it is undertaken to determine the type of insurance coverage needed.								
The ideal amount of insurance coverage and the types of policies required are determined.								
A competent insurance agent is selected, who reviews all insurance policies and makes specific recommendations about all types of coverage needed and the amounts required. Special consideration is given to: • Property casualty insurance • Liability insurance • Employee liability insurance • Dram shop (liquor liability) insurance • Health/dental/optical insurance • Workers' compensation insurance								
The companies providing insurance coverage to the restaurant are evaluated. The manager is aware of: • Financial capability to pay the property's claims • The rating category • Rating companies' feedback • State's insurance regulatory department feedback								
For each policy held, the manager is aware of its: • Primary coverage • Per occurrence amount • Aggregate amount • Umbrella insurance (if any) • Deductible								

*N/A = Not Applicable

Recommended Procedures	In Place Now?			Needed to Implement			Assigned To	Completion Date
	Yes	No	N/A*	Policy	Training	Other		
All insurance policies are analyzed to determine what is covered.								
All insurance policies are analyzed to determine what is not covered.								

For more information and suggestions
log onto www.hospitalitylawyer.com.

*N/A = Not Applicable

CONSULTANT'S CORNER

What Would You Do? (page 132)

Samuel will argue that the insurance company should have done its own background check and if the insurance company was truly concerned about the background check, then insurance company representatives would have asked for the results.

The insurance company will argue that it relied on Samuel's assurance that the agent had passed the requirements of his company's background check and that its understanding of a background check was that it looked at much more than a criminal record, including prior employment histories to see whether there were any prior theft or embezzlement issues, or credit problems that might demonstrate a propensity to steal, and so forth.

If it does turn out that nothing would have turned up in a thorough background check, then this would be a very difficult dilemma for the courts.

What Would You Do? (page 137 & 138)

One of the advantages to enrolling in your state's worker's compensation program is that in most instances employees are precluded from suing you for negligence in the event of an on-the-job injury. Worker's compensation programs have advantages for employees as well, because they do not have to prove that the operation was negligent in order to recover benefits if they sustain an injury on the job. Ordinarily, the employee's only burden is to show that the injury was indeed an accident and that it occurred within the course and scope of his or her employment.

What Would You Do? (page 143)

It is not uncommon for insurance companies to require specialized training for employees of an operation prior to insurance coverage being provided. Ongoing training programs and the requirement to notify the carrier when the sessions occur are also not uncommon when a company is asked to write coverage for a high-risk business.

7

LEGAL ISSUES
IN SELECTING EMPLOYEES

MANAGER'S BRIEF

Managers reading this chapter will learn basic policies and procedures applicable to the use of job descriptions, job qualifications, and other applicant selection devices, including applications, interviews, testing, background checks, references, and writing classified advertisements. They will also learn how to avoid certain practices relative to civil rights, persons with disabilities, and age discrimination as they make employee selection decisions. Managers will also learn details about the verification of work eligibility relative to an applicant's eligibility to legally work in the United States and issues related to the employment of youth under 18 years of age. Information about at-will employment, interacting with labor unions, and participation in collective bargaining is also presented.

EMPLOYEE SELECTION

The procedures for legally selecting and managing staff can be challenging in today's complex world of laws and regulations. Many experienced managers say that finding, maintaining, and retaining a qualified, service-oriented staff are their most difficult tasks. The challenges of managing people are often greater than those involved in managing technology or products. People are complex individuals and are affected by many non-work-related issues.

Background

The law is very specific about what an employer can and cannot do to secure a workforce. Both managers and workers have rights affecting the employment relationship.

Employers have wide latitude in selecting the individuals thought to best benefit the business. However, employee selection procedures must also ensure fairness and compliance with the law to avoid the risk of a discrimination lawsuit.

Job Descriptions

Before employees can be selected, managers must have a thorough understand-

JOB DESCRIPTION A written and itemized list of a specific job's basic responsibilities and reporting relationships.

ing of the essential functions they will perform. These are contained in a **job description.** Legally, only those tasks necessary to effectively carry out the required responsibilities and to perform the tasks required in the job should be used in a description.

Job descriptions need not be long. One or two pages are usually sufficient to detail all required information. Appendix E shows a sample job description.

Job descriptions are important from an operational perspective because they help keep track of the changing responsibilities of workers. They are also important from a legal perspective, because they may be needed in court to demonstrate that the manager fairly established job requirements prior to selecting persons to fill those jobs.

Job Qualifications

Once managers know the kinds of tasks employees must perform in a given job, they can consider the skills or knowledge that an employee must have to successfully perform these tasks. These **job qualifications** should be written and attached to the job description. If a job applicant is not selected and elects to bring legal action, it will be critical to show how each component of the job qualification is driven by, or logically flows from, the job description.

> **JOB QUALIFICATION** The knowledge or skill(s) required to perform the responsibilities and tasks listed in a job description.

Job qualifications can include physical and mental requirements. However, they cannot violate the law or include characteristics that would unfairly prevent a class of workers from successfully competing for a position. If a dishwasher is required to be six feet or taller, this qualification would be inappropriate because some minority groups may have difficulty meeting it. The courts could interpret the qualification as unfairly limiting the potential for minority candidates to secure the job. Even though the manager could show that dish racks are normally placed on shelves most easily reached by tall persons, it is unlikely that this occupational qualification would meet court requirements unless the manager proved that a height of six feet was a **bona fide occupational qualification (BFOQ).**

> **BONA FIDE OCCUPATIONAL QUALIFICATION** A job qualification, established in good faith and fairness, that is necessary to safely or adequately perform a job.

To establish a BFOQ, a manager must prove that employees without this qualification cannot perform the job safely or adequately and that the BFOQ is reasonably necessary to operate the business. In the case of the dishwasher, relocating the dish racks or providing a short ladder or safe step stool could open the job to candidates of any height and probably prevent a discrimination lawsuit. The following are examples of BFOQs that may be appropriate where knowledge or skill is a necessary job requirement:

- Physical attributes to complete job duties, including ability to lift a specific amount of weight
- Education
- Professional certification(s) or registration(s)
- Licensing
- Language skills
- Knowledge of equipment operation
- Previous experience
- Minimum age requirement (for serving alcohol or working certain hours)

Cruz owns and manages a bar and dance club serving Cuban-style cuisine. It has a dance floor, small tables, and outstanding food.

Cruz's clientele consists mainly of 20- to 40-year-old males who like the club for its good food and young female servers. The club advertises to women, families, and young men, but the facility's reputation includes the attractiveness of the servers, which is influenced by their uniforms.

Cruz employs women and men of all races and nationalities, but all servers are female. When, in one case, Cruz does not hire a young man for a server's job, he is contacted by the man's attorney. The attorney alleges the man has been illegally denied a server's job because of his gender, which, he states, cannot be a bona fide occupational qualification for a server's position.

Cruz replies that the club employs both men and women, but one necessary job qualification for servers is that they be "attractive to men." He states that the qualification of "attractiveness to men" is legitimate, given the importance of maintaining the successful image, atmosphere, and business the club enjoys. He maintains that the servers also help advertise and market the club's unique features. Cruz says that the characteristic of attractiveness is an occupational characteristic, citing modeling agencies and TV casting agents as examples of others who routinely use attractiveness to select employees. Cruz states that his right to select employees is unconditional as long as he does not unfairly discriminate against a protected class of workers.

What would you do if you were a jury member in the discrimination trial?

Applicant Selection

When choosing applicants, managers generally use some or all of five selection devices:

1. Applications

2. Interviews

3. Testing

4. Background checks

5. References

Applications. An employment application generally requests the candidate's name, address, work experience, and related information. Requirements for a legally sound application are many; however, in all cases, questions should focus *exclusively* on job qualifications. Managers should have their employment applications reviewed by an attorney specializing in employment law.

Each applicant for a given position should fill out an identical application, and the document should be on file for each candidate selected for the position.

Interviews. A review of applications will suggest candidates for an interview. The types of questions that can be asked in the interview are restricted, because improper interviews can subject an employer to legal liability. If a candidate is not hired because of an answer to—or refusal to answer—an inappropriate question, a lawsuit may be filed.

The Equal Employment Opportunity Commission (EEOC) suggests that employers consider the following three questions in deciding whether to include a particular question on an application or in an interview:

1. Does this question tend to screen out minorities or a particular gender?

2. Is the answer needed to judge an individual's competencies for job performance?

3. Are there alternative, nondiscriminatory ways to evaluate the person's qualifications?

Managers must be careful about questions asked in an interview. Remember that the job dictates what is an allowable question. Questions should be written and should be read to the interviewee. Supervisors and/or others who participate in an interview should be trained to avoid questions that could increase the property's liability.

Generally, age is considered irrelevant in most hiring decisions, so date-of-birth questions are improper. Age is a sensitive preemployment question, because the Age Discrimination in Employment Act protects employees 40 years old and older. Managers can ask about age if an applicant appears younger than 18 years old, because minors can work only a limited number of hours weekly. Age is also important in hiring bartenders and other servers of alcohol who must be above a state's minimum age.

Questions about race, religion, and national origin are also inappropriate, as is requiring photographs of candidates to be submitted before or after an interview.

Questions about physical traits, like height and weight, often violate the law because they may eliminate disproportionate numbers of females and Asian-American and Hispanic applicants.

If a job does not require a specific education, it is improper to ask questions about educational background. Applicants can be asked about their education and credentials if these are BFOQs.

It is permissible to ask whether an applicant uses drugs or smokes, and a manager can ask whether a candidate will submit to a voluntary drug test as a condition of employment.

Questions about home ownership potentially discriminate against those who do not own homes. Questions about military discharge are improper, because a high proportion of other-than-honorable discharges are given to minorities.

Safe questions include those about a candidate's present and former employment and job references. Appendix F contains guidelines for appropriate interview questions developed by the EEOC.

Testing. Preemployment testing may improve the employee selection process, because it can help measure the relative strength of candidates. In restaurants, preemployment testing generally involves:

- Skill tests

- Psychological tests

- Drug screening tests

Skill tests can include word processing tests for a restaurant's office workers and food production tasks for cooks. Psychological testing includes tests of personality or mental ability and others designed to predict performance. For skill and psychological tests, always remember:

VALIDITY The quality of a test ensuring that it measures exactly what it is supposed to measure.

If a test does not have *documented* **validity** and **reliability,** its results should not be used in hiring decisions.

RELIABILITY The quality of a test ensuring that it is consistently valid.

Preemployment drug testing is allowable in most states and can help to reduce insurance rates and minimize worker liability issues. A drug-free environment helps attract better applicants. Some states have strict guidelines about when and how applicants can be tested.

A document similar to that found in Appendix G should be completed by an applicant before drug testing, and the signed document should be filed with the employee's application form.

Accuracy of preemployment drug testing is of special concern. Sometimes applicants whose erroneous test results have cost them a job have successfully sued the employer. Laws surrounding mandatory drug testing are complex. Before implementing a pre- or posthiring drug testing program, seek advice from an attorney specializing in labor employment law in your state. (You can find such attorneys at **www.hospitalitylawyer.com.**)

Background Checks. Increasingly, managers use background checks before hiring workers for selected positions. Estimates suggest that as many as 30 percent of all resumes and applications include some falsification. Therefore, employers are spending more time and financial resources to validate potential employee information. Common verification points include:

- Name
- Social Security number
- Address history
- Education/training
- Criminal background
- Credit reports
- Bankruptcies
- Liens
- Judgments

Background checks, like preemployment testing, can lead to litigation if the information secured is false or used in a way that violates employment law. Moreover, if the information is improperly disclosed to third parties, it may violate the employee's privacy rights. Failure to conduct background checks for some positions can subject the employer to potential litigation under the doctrine of **negligent hiring.**

NEGLIGENT HIRING An employer's failure to exercise reasonable care when selecting employees.

Using background checks for screening involves some risk and responsibility. Search only for information directly bearing on the position for which a candidate is applying. In addition, if a candidate is denied employment because of background check information, the employer should provide the candidate with a copy of that report. Sometimes candidates can help verify or explain the content of their background checks. Reporting agencies can make mistakes, and relying on false information when hiring may put your restaurant at risk.

Employment candidates should always be required to sign a consent form authorizing a background check. Appendix H shows a sample consent form to document this authorization.

References. Employment references have historically been a popular tool in the screening process. Today, however, they are much more difficult to obtain. Although many organizations still seek information from past employers, fewer companies divulge it. Some employers have been held liable for inaccurate comments made about past employees. Some companies specialize in providing confidential, comprehensive verification of employment references from former employers. Therefore, employers are more cautious about supplying information about past employees.

> **DEFAMATION   False statements causing someone to be held in contempt, to be lowered in public opinion, to lose employment status or earnings, or to otherwise suffer a damaged reputation.**

To minimize the risk of litigation, secure the applicant's permission in writing before contacting an ex-employer. Employers must be cautious as they give and receive reference information. Employers are usually protected if they give a truthful reference; however, they may still have to defend a **defamation** case brought by an ex-employee.

For example, if a reference states that an ex-employee was terminated for inability to "get along" with co-workers, the past employer may have to prove the truthfulness of the statement and that the ex-employee was solely to blame for the difficulties.

To minimize risk of lawsuits, never reply to a request for information about an ex-employee without first receiving that employee's signed release authorizing the reference check. The amount to disclose is your decision; however, your answers should be honest and defendable. Don't disclose personal information such as marital difficulties, financial problems, or serious illness, because you could be sued for invasion of privacy.

If an applicant provides letters of reference, call their authors to ensure that they did write them. When possible, put a reference request in writing and ask that the response also be written. If an oral response is given, document the conversation; write as much of the dialogue as possible, including the name of the person spoken to and the date and time of the conversation.

Even with authorization, many employers are reluctant to provide information. Simply ask whether the company would rehire that worker. The response to that question, combined with other information, can help to determine the accuracy of the applicant's information.

Employee selection is a specialized area of human resources. Restaurant managers without a Personnel Department should seek assistance from an employment law expert to initially review and continually monitor procedures for compliance.

Classified Advertisements. The wording of classified ads in newspapers or elsewhere to announce a job opening is of special concern. Make sure that the terms used do not exclude or discriminate against individuals. Federal law prohibits the use of words or phrases that may prevent certain types of people from applying. Phrases to avoid include references to age ("ages 20–30" or "retirees"), sex ("men" or "women"), national origin, and religion. Bona fide job qualifications (as described earlier in this chapter) that may limit applicants can be mentioned. Generally, managers should focus their classified ads on a description of the job and the applicable educational or background requirements needed.

DISCRIMINATION IN EMPLOYEE SELECTION

Employers may hire any employee they wish, but they are not free to unlawfully discriminate against people when employment decisions are made. Employment discrimination laws protect certain classes of people from unfair or exclusionary hiring practices.

Discrimination by employers in the private sector has become the subject of a growing body of federal and state laws, passed to recognize protections guaranteed by the U.S. Constitution. Many anti-discrimination statutes affect employee selection. Three are most significant, as described in the following sections.

Civil Rights Act

The Civil Rights Act of 1964 and its amendments apply to employers with 15 or more employees who are engaged in **interstate commerce.**

INTERSTATE COMMERCE
Commercial trading or the transportation of persons or property between or among states.

The Act prohibits discrimination based on race, color, religion, sex, or national origin. Sex, as a category, includes pregnancy, childbirth, and related medical conditions. The Act makes it illegal for employers to discriminate in hiring and in setting terms and conditions of employment. Labor organizations are also prohibited from basing membership or union classifications on race, color, religion, sex, or national origin. Managers cannot retaliate against employees or applicants who file discrimination charges against them, refuse to comply with a discriminatory policy, or who participate in an investigation of discrimination charges.

The Equal Employment Opportunity Commission (EEOC) oversees and enforces federal laws regulating employer–employee relationships and investigates employee discrimination complaints. Businesses found to have discriminated can be ordered to compensate the employee(s) for damages, including lost wages and attorney fees, and may also be ordered to pay punitive damages.

In addition to the federal Civil Rights Act, many states also have civil rights laws prohibiting discrimination. Sometimes these state laws expand protection to workers or applicants in categories not covered under the federal law, including age, marital status, sexual orientation, and certain types of physical or mental disabilities or conditions. State civil rights laws may have stricter penalties for violations, including fines and/or jail time. Managers must know the provisions of their state's civil rights laws.

WHAT WOULD YOU DO?

Jetta Wong owns and manages the Golden Dragon restaurant, which serves a diverse clientele. She places a classified ad for a table busperson in her local newspaper. The response is good, and she narrows the field of potential candidates to two. One is of the same ethnic background as Ms. Wong and the rest of the staff. The second candidate is Danielle, the daughter of a Mexican citizen and an American citizen who was born and raised in the United States.

Ms. Wong offers the position to the candidate with the same ethnic background as hers, believing that because both candidates are equal in ability, she can select the one she feels will best suit the business. Ms. Wong thinks that diners will expect to see Asian servers and buspersons in an Asian restaurant. No one was discriminated against, she maintains, because Danielle was not denied a job on the basis of race but rather on the basis of what was best for business.

Danielle maintains that she was not selected because of her Hispanic ethnic background. She threatens to file an EEOC charge unless she is offered employment. What would you do if you were Ms. Wong?

The Civil Rights Act also includes **affirmative action** requirements, which mandate a good faith effort by employers to address past and/or present discrimination through a variety of specific, results-oriented procedures. Formal affirmative action programs are required for federal, state, and local governments, and federal contractors and subcontractors with contracts of $50,000 or more.

> **AFFIRMATIVE ACTION   A federally mandated requirement that certain employers must actively seek to fairly employ recognized classes of workers.**

Americans with Disabilities Act

The Americans with Disabilities Act (ADA) prohibits discrimination against people with disabilities in public accommodations, transportation, telecommunications, and employment.

Three different groups of individuals are protected under the Act:

1. An individual with a physical or mental impairment substantially limiting a major life activity. (Examples of a "major life activity" under the Act are seeing, hearing, talking, walking, reading, learning, breathing, taking care of oneself, lifting, sitting, and standing.)

2. A person with a record of disability. People who have recovered or are recovering from an impairment that substantially limited major life activities. For example, people with a history of mental or emotional illness, heart disease, cancer, and alcoholics and drug addicts that are in active recovery.

3. A person "regarded as" having a disability. People who have a physical or mental impairment that does not substantially limit a major life activity, as well as people that do not have an impairment but are perceived by others as having an impairment. For example, severe burn victims, people with controlled diabetes or epilepsy, and individuals that use hearing aids.

Managers cannot reduce an employee's pay simply because he or she is disabled, nor can they refuse to hire an applicant because he or she is disabled if, with reasonable accommodation, the candidate can perform the essential functions of the job. Managers must post notices of the ADA and its provisions where they can be seen by all employees.

The ADA does not require a manager to hire a disabled applicant who is not qualified for a job. The manager can still select the most qualified candidate, provided that no applicant was eliminated from consideration because of a qualified disability.

ADA law is changing rapidly; the following conditions are a representative sample that currently meet the criteria for a qualified disability and are protected under the ADA:

- HIV positive
- AIDS
- Cancer
- Cerebral palsy
- Tuberculosis
- Heart disease
- Hearing or visual impairments
- Alcoholism

Examples of conditions not currently covered under ADA include:

- Kleptomania (compulsion to steal)
- Disorders caused by the use of illegal drugs
- Compulsive gambling
- Sexual behavior disorders

The ADA has changed the way employees are selected. Questions on job applications and during interviews that *cannot* be asked include:

- Have you ever been hospitalized?
- Are you taking prescription drugs?
- Have you ever been treated for drug addiction or alcoholism?
- Have you ever filed a workers' compensation insurance claim?

- Do you have any physical defects, disabilities, or impairments that may affect your performance in the position for which you are applying/ interviewing?

When a disabled person is able to perform the duties of a particular job, but some aspect of the job or the work facility would prevent the applicant from doing so, the manager may be required to make a reasonable accommodation for that worker.

Managers have provided reasonable accommodations when they have made existing facilities readily accessible to individuals with mobility impairments or other disabilities, and restructured a job in the most accommodating manner. Managers are not obligated to provide a "reasonable accommodation" if it would result in undue hardship. Generally, an undue hardship occurs when the expense of accommodating the worker is excessive or would disrupt the natural work environment.

The law in this area is vague. A manager who asserts that accommodating a worker with a disability would impose an undue hardship should be prepared to defend that decision. After an investigation, the EEOC will ultimately issue a "right to sue" letter to an employee if the employer is believed to be in violation of the ADA.

The following questions can help a manager to reduce the risk of an ADA noncompliance charge related to reasonable accommodation:

- **Question 1:** *Can the applicant perform the essential functions of the job with or without reasonable accommodation?* (Managers can ask the applicant this question.) If "no," an applicant is not qualified and, therefore, not protected by the ADA. If "yes," consider Question 2.

- **Question 2:** *Is the necessary accommodation reasonable?* (To answer this question, the manager should ask the following: Will this accommodation create an undue financial or administrative hardship on the business?) If "yes," unreasonable accommodations do not have to be provided. If "no," consider Question 3.

- **Question 3:** *Will this accommodation or the hiring of the person with the disability create a direct threat to the health or safety of other employees or guests?* If "yes," managers are not required to make the accommodation and have fulfilled their ADA obligation.

WWW: Internet Assistant

Log onto the Internet and enter: http://www.eeoc.gov

Under the section "Laws, Regulation and Policy Guidance," select: Enforcement Guidances and Related Documents

Select: Small Employers and Reasonable Accommodation. From the document displayed, think about your restaurant and:

- What must be done after receiving a request for a reasonable accommodation

- How a job could be restructured to meet the needs of a disabled person with a reasonable accommodation

For additional information on job accommodation under the ADA, log onto the Job Accommodation Network for ADA at http://www.janweb.icdi.wvu.edu.

One ADA provision concerns employees and applicants with infectious and communicable diseases. The U.S. Secretary of Health and Human Services publishes an annual list of communicable diseases that, if passed through food handling, could put a food service operation at risk. Employers have the right to not hire or assign someone carrying one of the identified diseases to a position involving food handling if there is no reasonable accommodation that can be made to eliminate such a risk.

WHAT WOULD YOU DO?

Alex is applying for the Executive Chef position at a restaurant. While interviewing him about his work history, Samuel, the manager, learns that Alex was discharged from his two previous positions for "excessive absence."

When Samuel asks about the cause of these absences, Alex offers that it was because of alcoholism. He notes his ten-year struggle, his current weekend treatments, and his weekly attendance at Alcoholics Anonymous (AA) meetings. He states he never drank at work but sometimes missed work when he overslept or was too hungover. Past employers neither confirm nor deny Alex's problem. (Both simply state that he had worked as an Executive Chef and that he is no longer employed.)

Based on his experience, Alex is the best-qualified candidate for the vacant position. However, based on his life history, his ability to overcome his alcohol dependence is, in Samuel's opinion, questionable.

If you were Samuel, what would you do?

Age Discrimination in Employment Act

The Age Discrimination in Employment Act (ADEA) protects employees and applicants 40 years of age or older from employment discrimination based on age. It applies to employers with 20 or more employees and to labor unions and governmental agencies. It is unlawful to discriminate against a person because of age regarding any term, condition, or privilege of employment—including hiring, firing, promotion, layoff, compensation, benefits, job assignments, and training.

It is unlawful to include age preferences, limitations, or specifications in job notices or advertisements. However, an age limit may be specified when it is a "bona fide occupational qualification." (For example, states may impose a minimum age qualification for bartenders and alcoholic beverage servers.)

VERIFICATION OF WORK ELIGIBILITY

Even after a manager has legally selected an applicant for employment, the law requires at least one more employer action before an employee can begin work. The manager must require the worker to establish that he or she is legally entitled to hold the job. Verification of employment status involves verifying eligibility to work and compliance with child labor laws.

Immigration Reform and Control Act

The Immigration Reform and Control Act (IRCA) prohibits employers from knowingly hiring illegal persons for work in the United States. Illegal hiring occurs when persons are in the country illegally, or when their immigration and residency status does not allow employment. The law also applies to an employer who, after the date of hire, determines that an employee is not legally authorized to work but continues to employ that individual.

All employers in organizations of any size must verify that all employees (full- and part-time) hired after November 6, 1986, are legally authorized to work in the United States. The Act requires completion of a Form I-9 when an applicant is hired. A sample form is shown in Appendix I.

Form I-9 is often misunderstood. Its purpose is to verify an employee's identity and eligibility to work. The Immigration and Naturalization Service (INS) imposes severe penalties on employers without properly completed I-9s for all employees and has issued large fines for even minor errors, such as incorrect dates.

The new employee must complete Section 1 of the form. The employer must then review it to ensure that it is fully and properly completed. Then the employer completes Section 2 of the form.

Appendix J details documents that can be used to complete an I-9. The documents used to verify eligibility and identity must be originals. To ensure compliance, managers can remind individuals to bring necessary identification documents on their first day of employment, but management cannot dictate which document an employee will use to verify his or her identity or eligibility to work. If an employee cannot provide appropriate documents within 21 days of being hired, the employer must terminate that individual.

The employer's part of Form I-9 must be completed within three business days, or at the time of hire if employment is for less than three days. Each completed Form I-9 should be retained for three years after the employment date or one year after the employee's termination, whichever is longer. All I-9 forms should be readily available and must be presented to INS within 72 hours upon request.

A manager's good-faith effort to comply with verification and record keeping requirements is necessary to ensure that the business does not knowingly and willingly hire a person not legally authorized to work. The "letter of the law" must be followed, because fines as high as $10,000 per illegal employee can be levied against the restaurant.

Fair Labor Standards Act

The Fair Labor Standards Act (FLSA) protects young workers from employment that may interfere with educational opportunities or be detrimental to their health or well-being. It covers all workers engaged in or producing goods for interstate (between states) commerce or who are employed in certain enterprises. Essentially, the law establishes that youths 18 years and older may perform any job, regardless of hazard, for unlimited hours subject to minimum wage and overtime requirements.

Youths aged 16 and 17 may work at any time for unlimited hours in all jobs not declared hazardous by the U.S. Secretary of Labor. (Hazardous occupations, which are numerous, include operating certain power-driven bakery machinery and operating power-driven meat-processing machines including saws when performed in wholesale, retail, or service establishments, and operating motor vehicles or working as outside helpers on motor vehicles.)

Children aged 14 and 15 may work in various jobs outside school hours under the following conditions:

- No more than 3 hours on a school day, limited to 18 hours in a school week.

- No more than 8 hours on a non-school day, limited to 40 hours in a non-school week.

- Not before 7:00 A.M. or after 7:00 P.M., except from June 1 through Labor Day, when the evening hour extends to 9:00 P.M.

- A break must be provided after 5 continuous hours of work.

Workers 14 and 15 years of age may be employed in a variety of restaurant jobs, including cashiering, waiting on tables, washing dishes, and preparing salads and other food (cooking is permitted only at snack bars, soda fountains, lunch counters, and cafeteria serving counters), but not in positions deemed hazardous by the U.S. Secretary of Labor.

There are stiff penalties for employers who violate the Fair Labor Standards Act. They can be fined between $1,000 for first-time violations and $3,000 for third violations. Repeat offenders can be subject to fines of $10,000 and even jail terms.

All states have child labor laws. Employers in most states must file documents and/or permits verifying the ages of their minor employees. When both state and federal child labor laws apply, the law setting the more stringent standard must be observed. State and local child labor laws can vary, so managers should confirm the specifics of the laws in their state by contacting a state employment agency.

THE EMPLOYMENT RELATIONSHIP

EMPLOYER An individual or entity that pays wages or a salary in exchange for a worker's services.

EMPLOYEE An individual who is hired to provide services to an employer in exchange for wages or a salary.

AT-WILL EMPLOYMENT An employment relationship whereby an employer has the right to hire any employee whenever he or she chooses and to dismiss an employee for or without cause at any time, and whereby an employee also has the right to work or not work for an employer and to terminate the relationship at any time.

Laws related to employment change to reflect society's view of what is "fair" and "just" for both the **employer** and the **employee.** Fifty years ago a manager could refuse to hire an individual on the basis of race or religion without fear. Today, as discussed earlier, to refuse employment on the basis of any of a number of factors subjects the manager to legal liability both to the government and to the spurned job candidate.

At-Will Employment

The right of managers to hire and terminate employees as they see fit is a fundamental right of doing business. In most states, the relationship created when a manager hires a worker is one of **at-will employment.**

The doctrine of At-Will Employment allows an employer to hire or dismiss an employee whenever the employer feels it is in the best interest of the business, subject to the anti-discrimination laws reviewed earlier in this chapter (and which are addressed further in Chapter 8). Assume that a manager has legally hired four full-time bartenders. Business slows, and the manager terminates one bartender. The doctrine of At-Will Employment allows this. Further, it allows the manager to reduce the bartender staff even without a business downturn, or if the manager believes a better bartender can be hired. Generally, any worker can be fired for cause (i.e., misconduct associated with the job). The At-Will Employment doctrine allows employers to legally dismiss a worker without cause.

A manager's actions can affect the at-will employment status of workers (for example, by explicitly entering into an employment contract or by making a promise to keep an employee for a year). To preserve maximum flexibility for the restaurant, it is important to maintain the at-will-employment status to cover all staff members. The scope of the At-Will Employment doctrine varies among different states. Managers should become familiar with the requirements in their state, which are available from the state agency responsible for monitoring employer–employee relationships.

Labor Unions and Collective Bargaining

In some restaurants, certain categories of employees belong to an organized labor union. A group of employees make one **Collective Bargaining Agreement—CBA**—(union contract) with an employer that outlines the characteristics of their job position such as wage, hourly rate of pay, or limits on the hours per day or week that can be worked. The agreement covers anyone employed in that position.

> **COLLECTIVE BARGAINING AGREEMENT (CBA)** A formal contract between an employer and a group of employees that establishes the rights and responsibilities of both parties in their employment relationship.

Generally, members of a labor union working in a specific restaurant (or local hospitality industry) elect a representative to negotiate the terms and conditions of a CBA for the entire group. The bargaining process follows rules established by the National Labor Relations Act. The National Labor Relations Board (NLRB) enforces this Act and the relationship between employees and organized labor. It performs the following questions:

- Administers secret ballot elections that permit employees to decide whether they wish to be represented by a union, and if so, by which one
- Prevents and remedies unlawful acts (unfair labor practices) by either employers or unions

Employers are forbidden to:

- Discourage or threaten employees' attempts to unionize
- Threaten to shut down an operation if employees want to form a union
- Interfere with, restrain, or question employees about their participation in a union or interfere with union activities
- Promise wage increases as a strategy to prevent union organization
- Discriminate against union members when hiring, promoting, or managing employees
- Terminate union members participating in a legal strike

Employers are also protected from unfair labor practices by union representatives, who cannot:

- Force or coerce employees to join or participate in union activities
- Manipulate or interfere as the employer designates its negotiator
- Coerce an employer to discriminate against union member employees
- Require an employer to hire or pay for more workers than necessary (featherbedding)
- Refuse to bargain collectively
- Conduct an illegal strike (one undertaken in violation of CBA terms or one not approved by the union)

The individual employer, union, or employee must request NLRB assistance in cases of unfair labor practices. A complaint must be filed within six months of the alleged unfair activity. If, after investigation, the complaint is justified and not settled or withdrawn, a hearing will be held. If an unfair labor practice has occurred, the NLRB will issue an order that it stop. It may also require the guilty party to compensate the injured party through job reinstatement, payment of back wages, or by reestablishing conditions in place before the unfair activity occurred. Either party may appeal to federal court.

Once a restaurant is unionized, new employees may have to join the union representing their new position. Many states have "right-to-work" laws stipulating that an employee is not required to join a union if hired for a specific position, even if other employees in that position are unionized. (Managers of unionized restaurants should learn about applicable state right-to-work laws.)

Managers should treat a CBA just like any other contract. Its provisions should be read, understood, and followed. Union affiliation gives employees certain freedoms, but they still are accountable for their work. Managers still must ensure that jobs are performed properly, safely, and according to the restaurant's established policies and procedures. If problems surface, the manager should consult with the property's union representative. Most CBAs provide specifics for hiring new employees in covered positions. Managers should know these contractual terms especially well.

MANAGER'S "TO DO" LIST

Review the following recommendations proposed in this chapter. Analyze your interest in and need for implementing these recommendations by completing the columns on the right side of the form. Remember, when task assignments are made, time requirements for completion should also be stated. Follow up, as improvement activities evolve, to ensure that your property is moving closer to the goal of minimizing litigation risks.

Recommended Procedures	In Place Now?			Needed to Implement			Assigned To	Completion Date
	Yes	No	N/A*	Policy	Training	Other		
Job descriptions listing only those tasks required to perform the job are available and current.								
Specific job qualifications based on job descriptions for all positions are developed and indicate the physical and mental requirements necessary to perform tasks in each job description.								
Bona fide occupational qualifications, if any, are identified for specific positions.								
The property's employment application is reviewed by an attorney specializing in employment law.								
Questions to be asked during applicant interviews are written and do not violate specific concerns of the Equal Employment Opportunity Commission.								
Supervisors and/or others who participate in applicant interviews are trained to avoid questions that could create liability.								
Any skill or psychological test used for preemployment screening is documented for validity and reliability.								
All state laws relating to preemployment drug testing are carefully and consistently followed.								
Before pre- or posthiring drug testing is implemented, an attorney specializing in labor employment is consulted.								
Applicants complete a specially designed consent form before background checks are undertaken.								

*N/A = Not Applicable

Recommended Procedures	In Place Now?			Needed to Implement			Assigned To	Completion Date
	Yes	No	N/A*	Policy	Training	Other		
Applicants are provided with a copy of any background report obtained.								
Applicants are asked for permission in writing before ex-employers are contacted.								
Replies to a request for information about an ex-employee are not made unless a copy of that employee's signed release, authorizing the reference check, is provided by the prospective employee.								
If letters of reference are provided by applicants, authors of these letters are contacted to ensure that they wrote them.								
Classified ads for employment focus on the job description and job qualifications.								
All provisions of the state's civil rights laws are consistently complied with.								
Procedures are in place to ensure that persons with the following disabilities are not discriminated against in employment: • Those with physical or mental impairments substantially limiting a major life activity • A person with a disability record • A person "regarded" as having a disability								
Notices about the Americans with Disability Act and its provisions are posted to be seen by all employees.								
Managers provide "reasonable accommodations" to make existing facilities accessible to disabled employees.								

*N/A = Not Applicable

Recommended Procedures	In Place Now?			Needed to Implement			Assigned To	Completion Date
	Yes	No	N/A*	Policy	Training	Other		
Managers use a three-question process to reduce the risk of an ADA noncompliance charge related to reasonable accommodations.								
Procedures are in place to ensure that there is no unlawful discrimination against a person because of his or her age.								
A Form I-9 is properly completed and available for all employees in their personnel files.								
Appropriate documentation is always studied to authenticate information on the Form I-9.								
Employees without appropriate Form I-9 documentation after 21 days of employment are terminated.								
The employer's part of all I-9 forms is completed within three business days (or upon hiring if employment is for less than three days).								
All I-9 forms are retained for three years after the employment date or for one year after the employee's termination, whichever is longer.								
Work tasks declared hazardous by the U.S. Secretary of Labor applicable to the property are known.								
Youths aged 16 and 17 do not work in jobs declared hazardous by the U.S. Secretary of Labor.								
Children aged 14 and 15 work only in jobs not violating requirements of the Fair Labor Standards Act.								

*N/A = Not Applicable

Recommended Procedures	In Place Now?			Needed to Implement			Assigned To	Completion Date
	Yes	No	N/A*	Policy	Training	Other		
State laws relative to child labor are known and complied with.								
Employees are informed of their at-will employment status.								
The at-will employment status covers all staff members.								
Requirements of the state's At-Will employment doctrine are known, and all requirements are complied with.								
Rules established by the National Labor Relations Act for collective bargaining are known and consistently followed where applicable.								
Activities and practices considered to be "unfair" are avoided as interaction with a prospective employee union is undertaken.								
Managers refrain from "unfair" labor practices while interacting with union representatives.								

For more information and suggestions log onto www.hospitalitylawyer.com.

*N/A = Not Applicable

CONSULTANT'S CORNER

What Would You Do? (page 150)

This situation illustrates circumstances, such as that of "Hooters," in which the courts held that, in fact a restaurant could establish guidelines for servers that obviously excluded men because exclusive employment of women servers was part of the concept of the restaurant. Reaction to this set of facts can provide a great opportunity for significant discussion about bona fide occupational and gender-based discrimination, as the selection criteria were clearly based on gender.

What Would You Do? (page 156)

Ms. Wong would maintain that Danielle's Hispanic background was not the reason that she was not selected; rather, Ms.Wong selected the candidate of the same ethnic background as the restaurant concept. Once again, a bona fide occupational qualification was claimed. To date, courts have been reluctant to find discrimination in these instances, but as the concept of diversity becomes mainstream, it will become very difficult to maintain race, gender, and similar characteristics as selection criteria for conceptual themes.

What Would You Do? (page 160 & 161)

Samuel needs to consult the Americans with Disabilities Act. This law clearly includes alcoholism (as long as the potential employee is not presently using alcohol and is currently in treatment for the disease as a disability). Accordingly, as long as Alex can perform the essential functions of the job (including being at work on time, consistently, and routinely), then the appropriate thing to do in these circumstances is to hire Alex. However, if Alex discontinues treatment, indulges in alcohol, or fails to perform the essential functions of the job, he is no longer a protected employee under the Americans with Disabilities Act.

8

LEGAL ASPECTS OF
EMPLOYEE MANAGEMENT

MANAGER'S BRIEF

Managers reading this chapter will gain much information helpful in legally managing employees after they are hired. Recommendations for the content of an employment offer letter and an employee manual, including general policies, compensation, benefits, and special areas, are detailed. Procedures to reduce workplace discrimination and sexual harassment are discussed, including employer liability, zero tolerance sexual harassment policies, managing complaints, third-party harassment avoidance, and the need for liability insurance. The Family and Medical Leave Act is fully explored. Legal aspects of compensation relating to minimum wage and overtime, tipped employees, tip pooling, and a wide range of taxes and tax credits are presented. Basic processes for managing employee performance (evaluation, discipline, and termination) are presented as well as a relatively new process for in-house dispute resolution.

The "do's and don'ts" of employment claims and appeals and records required by the Federal agencies are presented. Finally, the posting of employment information and the use of surveillance tactics are discussed.

THE EMPLOYMENT RELATIONSHIP

EMPLOYMENT AGREEMENT
The terms of the employment relationship between an employer and employee, specifying the rights and obligations of each party to the agreement.

After an employee is legally selected, the conditions of the **employment agreement** can be clarified.

All employers and employees have employment agreements even if nothing is in writing or work conditions are not discussed in detail. They can be as simple as an agreement on an hourly wage rate for an hour's work and at-will employment for both parties. Employment agreements may cover one employee only or a group of employees. Generally, restaurant employment agreements are established orally or by offer letter.

Offer Letter

Properly composed offer letters can help prevent legal difficulties because they detail the employer's job offer to the employee. Some employers believe such letters should be used only for managerial positions. However, to avoid difficulties, all employees should have signed offer letters in their personnel files. Components of a sound offer letter include:

- Position offered
- Compensation
- Benefits (if any)
- Evaluation period and compensation review schedule
- Start date
- Employment location
- Special conditions (i.e., at-will relationship)
- Reference to the employee manual for information about workplace policies
- Signature lines for employer and employee

Consider Antonio, who applies for a position, is selected, and is given an offer letter. In the letter a special condition of employment is stated, that Antonio must submit to and pass a mandatory drug test. Although Antonio can

sign the letter when received, his employment is not finalized until he passes the drug test.

Additional rules that Antonio will be expected to
follow or benefits he may enjoy are included in the
employee manual.

> **EMPLOYEE MANUAL** A docu-
> ment detailing an employer's
> policies, benefits, and em-
> ployment practices.

Employee Manual

An offer letter does not usually specify all policies and procedures to which the
employer and employee agree. These are typically contained in the employee
manual, which can be as short as a few pages or as extensive as several hundred
pages. Employee manuals are often reviewed by courts to help define terms of
the employment agreement if a dispute arises. Topics covered by an employee
manual vary, but common areas include:

General Policies

- Probationary periods
- Performance reviews
- Disciplinary process
- Termination
- Attendance
- Drug and alcohol testing
- Uniforms
- Lockers
- Personal telephone calls
- Appearance and grooming

Compensation

- Pay periods
- Payroll deductions
- Tip reporting requirements
- Timekeeping procedures
- Overtime pay policies

- Meal periods
- Schedule posting
- Call-in pay
- Sick pay
- Vacation pay

Benefits

- Health insurance
- Dental insurance
- Disability insurance
- Vacation accrual
- Paid holidays
- Jury duty
- Funeral leave
- Retirement programs
- Duty meals
- Leaves of absence
- Transfers
- Educational reimbursement plans

Special Areas

- Policies against harassment
- Grievance and complaint procedures
- Family medical leave information
- Dispute resolution
- Safety rules
- Security rules
- Emergency preparedness

An employee manual should be kept current, and it should be clear that the employer, not the employee, retains the right to revise it.

Many restaurants issue employee manuals with a signature page so employees can verify that they have read the manual. This helps to demonstrate that the employee acknowledges that he or she is familiar with the employer's policies and procedures. Use wording similar to the following on a signature page. (It should be in a type size larger than that surrounding it.)

The employer reserves the right to modify, alter, or eliminate any and all of the policies and procedures contained in this manual at any time.

An additional approach involves giving a written test covering manual content before the employee begins work. Test results are kept on file.

To clarify "at-will" status, the following wording should be included at the bottom center of each page: *"This is not an employment contract."* A more formal statement should be placed at the beginning of the manual, such as:

This manual is not a contract, expressed or implied, guaranteeing employment for any specific duration. Although [the restaurant] hopes your employment relationship with us will be long-term, either you or the company may terminate this relationship at any time, with or without cause or notice.

The employee manual must be very carefully drafted to avoid altering the At-Will Employment doctrine. It should be thoroughly reviewed by an employment attorney each time it is revised.

WORKPLACE DISCRIMINATION AND SEXUAL HARASSMENT

As noted in Chapter 7, various laws prohibit discrimination on the basis of an individual's race, religion, gender, national origin, disability, age (over 40), and, in some states and communities, sexual orientation.

The federal government has taken the lead in outlawing discrimination in employment practices. Many states, and even some towns and cities, also have anti-discrimination laws. Generally, state laws duplicate federal laws prohibiting practices such as discrimination based on race, color, national origin, and so forth.

Managers must know the provisions of a state's civil rights laws. Many states add categories of prohibited behavior not covered under federal law. These may include discrimination based on marital status, arrest record, or sexual orientation. Moreover, although federal civil rights laws apply to businesses engaged in interstate commerce (which includes most restaurants), many state laws extend to other businesses such as bars, taverns, and "places of public accommodation." State anti-discrimination laws are enforced by state civil rights agencies, which can impose severe penalties, including fines, on violators.

Prohibitions of employment discrimination apply in the selection of employees (see Chapter 7) as well as after hiring. With the diversity of restaurant employees, the variety of attitudes about work, family, and fellow employees is not surprising. Managers cannot create conformity in their employees' value systems; they can, however, prevent discrimination by staff, co-workers, and third parties such as guests and suppliers.

Preventing Discrimination

Workplace discrimination is enforced by the Equal Opportunity Employment Commission (EEOC). Applicants and employees can bring discrimination claims to the EEOC and/or their state's EEOC counterpart. Officials investigate charges and issue a determination of whether they believe discrimination has occurred. If a discrimination charge is filed, the EEOC can examine all policies and practices for violations—not just the circumstances surrounding a particular incident. If there is sufficient evidence of discrimination, the EEOC works first with employers to correct problems and voluntarily settle a case before it reaches the courts.

If a settlement is not reached, the EEOC may file a lawsuit on behalf of the claimant or grant the claimant the "right to sue" the employer. If the EEOC does not find sufficient evidence of unlawful discrimination, the claimant may accept that finding or privately pursue a lawsuit against the employer.

Penalties for discrimination violations can be severe. Claimants can recover back and future wages, the value of lost fringe benefits, attorneys' fees, and injunctive relief, including job and seniority reinstatement. Federal fines can be as much as $50,000 (for businesses with fewer than 100 employees) to $300,000 (for corporations with 500 employees or more).

The best way to avoid litigation is to prevent incidents before they occur. This involves ensuring that company policies and the manager's own actions do not adversely affect members of a protected class.

Common areas of potential conflict in restaurants concern appearance and language. Employers can require employees to wear uniforms or adhere to certain grooming standards (such as restrictions on wearing jewelry) if all employees are subject to these requirements and if policies are established for a necessary business reason. Although the courts have not outlawed the establishment of "English-only" rules in business, lawsuits have occurred when companies discriminate against people with pronounced accents or who do not speak English fluently—especially in positions where English fluency is not a bona fide occupational qualification.

Managing Diversity

Beyond preventing discrimination, managers have a legal obligation to establish a work environment that accepts all people. Failure to do so can be recognized by the courts as discrimination. Racial slurs, ethnic jokes, and other offensive practices should not be tolerated.

Managers who effectively work with people from diverse backgrounds will likely be more successful than their counterparts who do not, but they will need to manage people in a cultural environment vastly different from their own.

Recognition of individual differences is the first step toward effectively managing these differences. One management myth is that because all workers are equal under the law, all workers must be treated exactly the same. This is not always the case. Effective managers treat people equitably—not necessarily uniformly. If one worker enjoys showing pictures of grandchildren, the manager can show an interest in them. If another worker prefers privacy, it is equally acceptable for the manager to avoid asking that employee about grandchildren. The manager, by recognizing and acting on real differences between the two employees, is treating them equitably. They are both being treated with respect for their own cultural values.

The recognition of cultural differences is the first step toward harmony. The culturally unaware manager who does not recognize, for example, the uniqueness and importance of the Asian worker's culture, denigrates that culture just like one who is openly critical of it. Managing cultural diversity will remain an important fact of operational and legal life.

Sexual Harassment

It has become increasingly important that managers know the attitudes and conduct that fall under the two types of sexual harassment recognized by federal and state law:

QUID PRO QUO Latin term meaning "something given in return or exchange for something else."

- **Quid pro quo** sexual harassment, in which the perpetrator asks for sexual favors in exchange for workplace benefits from a subordinate or punishes the subordinate for rejecting a request for sexual favors

- Hostile environment sexual harassment, in which the perpetrator, through language or conduct, creates an intimidating or hostile working environment for individuals of one gender

The federal Civil Rights Act prohibits sexual harassment in the workplace. Penalties for violating this Act are the same as those for other civil rights violations: the employee's recovery of lost wages, benefits, attorneys' fees, and job reinstatement. Many states have also adopted sexual harassment laws that carry additional damages, fines, or penalties.

Employer Liability

Certain behavior once tolerated in the workplace is no longer acceptable. There has been an explosion of sexual harassment claims pitting employee against supervisor, employee against employee, women versus men, men versus women, and same-sex complaints.

VICARIOUS LIABILITY A party's responsibility for the acts of another that result in an injury, harm, or damage; see also *respondeat superior* in Chapter 3.

The U.S. Supreme Court has held that an employer is subject to **vicarious liability** to a victimized employee for a hostile environment created by a supervisor with authority over the employee. "Uninvited and offensive touching," "lewd remarks," or "speaking of one gender in offensive terms" can create a hostile employment environment.

The Court determined that if a superior commits harassment, the employer may avoid liability if the following requirements are met:

- The employer exercised reasonable care to prevent and promptly correct any sexually harassing behavior.

- The plaintiff employee unreasonably failed to take advantage of any preventive or corrective opportunities provided by the employer.

Courts have held that if a supervisor's harassment ultimately resulted in a tangible employment action, such as an employee's termination, demotion, or reassignment, the employer will be held strictly liable for acts of sexual harassment by supervisors.

As a result of this ruling, the main (and often only) legal defense for managers to allegations of sexual harassment by supervisors is to demonstrate a history of preventive and corrective measures.

Zero Tolerance

To guard against liability resulting from charges of discrimination or harassment and to ensure a quality workplace, managers should allow zero (no) tolerance of objectionable behavior. Here are some means by which a zero tolerance environment is created:

- Clear policies that prohibit sexual harassment
- Workshops to train supervisors and staff how to recognize potentially volatile situations and how to minimize potentially unpleasant consequences
- Provisions for seeking and receiving relief from offensive and unwanted behavior
- Written procedures for reporting incidents and for investigating and resolving grievances

Managers should not develop a zero tolerance policy of harassment simply to avoid lawsuits. Creating a clear policy statement including severe penalties for violation helps demonstrate a good-faith effort to promote a safe, fair work environment. An effective sexual harassment policy should include:

- A statement that the restaurant unequivocally advocates and supports a zero tolerance standard for sexual harassment.
- A definition of terms and behaviors discussed in the statement.
- A description of acceptable and unacceptable behaviors (no sexually suggestive photographs, jokes, or vulgar language, etc.).
- Reasons for the policy.
- A discussion of consequences for unacceptable behavior. (List sexual harassment as a punishable offense in all company handbooks and manuals.) Types of disciplinary action should be stated for consequences of sexual harassment or hostile environment offenses.

- Specific complaint procedures an employee should follow. (Provide alternatives to bringing a complaint or concern(s) to a manager's attention. If all grievances must be cleared through the harassing supervisor, no help is given.)

- The name of the person(s) to whom complaints should be reported. (This should be someone who is not in an employee's chain of command.) Employees should know of at least two individuals capable of receiving such complaints.

- An emphasis that all complaints and investigations will be treated with absolute confidence. (All investigative materials should be maintained in separate files with restricted access.)

- A statement that the restaurant prohibits all forms of harassment and that any employee complaints about other forms of harassment relating to a protected category will be addressed under the anti-harassment policy.

A policy statement will not be effective unless it is adopted by managers and communicated to all employees. Reprint the sexual harassment policy in the employee manual. Consider posting the policy in common areas, including break rooms, and/or on bulletin boards. Discuss the policy at new employee orientation and other meetings.

A training program can help promote a safe working environment and ensure legal compliance. All employees should attend a sexual harassment training program initially during orientation and then regularly. Effective training techniques include role-playing exercises, group and panel discussions, videos, behavior modeling, and sensitivity training. Employees should learn ways to seek relief if they become uncomfortable with another person's behavior. Supervisors should be trained to identify potentially harassing situations and must understand the company's policy and their role in preventing harassment and responding to complaints.

Evaluate training results. Administer tests before and after employee training. Maintain results, document the number of harassment complaints received, and note any increases or decreases. If feedback indicates that training was ineffective, change the training. If feedback shows that an employee did not learn demonstrated skills or doesn't follow company guidelines, retrain or terminate the individual. (Based on feedback, the manager should have known this employee would violate company standards or regulations. A jury may conclude that employee termination would have prevented the incident prompting the lawsuit.)

A plaintiff's attorney will want to see whether training did, in fact, occur, the type of training, and whether it was effective. To win a lawsuit alleging ineffective training, a manager must document a training trail for a jury. Keep records of training sessions; note attendees. Keep copies of supporting materials such as videos or handouts. If tests were administered or if employee evaluations were undertaken, retain them.

WHAT WOULD YOU DO?

Joseph was a 61-year-old cook and had been employed at the restaurant for 25 years. Sandra was a new manager who conducted the property's sexual harassment training program for all new employees and managers. Training sessions used current material provided by a national trade association, and she worked hard to evaluate training effectiveness.

Joseph attended several training sessions over five years. When asked by Sandra to attend another session he stated, "I don't know why I have to go again. Every time I go I get dumber!" Joseph had made similar comments each time he attended a session and once even challenged the trainers about the "political correctness" of the training. He had also been heard making similar comments before and after work while other employees were present. No staff member had ever formally accused him of sexual harassment. The restaurant states in its employee manual that it is an "at-will" employer.

What would you do if you were Sandra?

Investigating a Complaint

Even the best prevention efforts may not eliminate offensive behaviors. Managers must have procedures that are strictly followed, and employees must be assured that they can voice concerns without fear of ridicule, retaliation, or job loss.

When a complaint is lodged or when inappropriate activity is noted, a manager should act immediately. The manager should obtain the claimant's permission to start an investigation. A written consent form such as that displayed in Figure 8.1 is recommended. (Note that the form seeks permission to disclose information to third parties, if necessary, to conduct a thorough investigation.)

Often, circumstances surrounding a sexual harassment claim are personal. An employee may lodge a complaint and later reconsider or request the investigation be altered. Managers must be sensitive to an employee's emotions but should not allow staff interference with established investigation policies. Employees may withdraw a complaint, but if they do, they should sign a "Request for No Further Action Form" (see Figure 8.2), stating that they no longer wish to pursue the claim and will be comfortable if no further action is taken.

Sometimes it is necessary to continue an investigation after an employee withdraws a complaint; a manager is not relieved from the responsibility of providing a safe working environment. The facts may be so serious that there is a

---

INVESTIGATION CONSENT FORM

I. Name: _____

II. Position and Title: _____

III. Facts of Situation: (attach as many pages as necessary)

_____

_____

_____

IV. I hereby request that the company investigate the facts set forth above. I also authorize the company to disclose as much of the facts set forth above as necessary to pursue the investigation. I also understand and acknowledge that the company shall use due diligence in keeping this matter as confidential as possible. I recognize, however, that in the course of the investigation the information may need to become public to ensure a thorough investigation.

Signature _____ Date _____
    Employee

Figure 8.1 Sample Investigation Consent Form

REQUEST FOR NO FURTHER ACTION

I. Name: _____

II. Position and Title: _____

III. On the _____ day of _____ 200__, I previously completed a Consent Form that, among other things, requested that the company investigate certain facts stated by me, a copy of which is attached to this document. I have now decided that it would not be in my best interest to pursue this matter and am comfortable with my environment in the workplace as it presently exists. I have been made aware that in the event that I become uncomfortable, I can seek the assistance and support of the company at any time, and have been encouraged to do so. At this time, however, I am requesting that at least for my benefit, no further action be taken in this regard, and I fully understand that an investigation for my benefit shall not take place. I do understand, however, that the company, after having been made aware of these circumstances, may elect to pursue an investigation on its own behalf and for the benefit of other employees.

Signature _____ Date _____
     Employee

Figure 8.2 Request for No Further Action Form

need for immediate remedial action, including suspension or termination of the alleged harasser. Failure to take such action could subject the restaurant to liability for retaining the individual, who may act inappropriately again.

If a complainant states that the mere presence of the alleged harasser causes anxiety and distress, do not temporarily transfer the complainant to another job or position. (Suggest a couple of days off with pay while the complaint is investigated.) A transfer tends to undermine the victim's confidence after being told that no retaliation would result from alerting the manager.

Investigations should be thorough. If an investigation is poorly conducted or ineffective, legal liability may result, just as if no investigation occurred. Exercise discretion when selecting employees to be interviewed. Confine the investigation to the alleged victim's co-workers who witnessed the incident, who were aware of the claimant's situation, and/or who have the employee's confidence. Obtain as much information as possible to conduct a fair investigation.

The following questions may be asked of those not directly involved in an allegation:

- *Have you noticed behavior that makes people uncomfortable? If so, did it involve sexual or ethnic matters? Will you tell me who was involved?*
- *What is the general atmosphere of the work environment?*
- *Do any employees or supervisors complain a lot?*
- *Are some people treated differently from others for reasons that are not job related?*
- *Do any employees receive favoritism for reasons other than job performance?*
- *Have you noticed any personality conflicts?*
- *Will you let me know if you think of anything else?*

Adapted from Jossem Jared, "Investigating Sexual Harassment," *Litigating the Sexual Harassment Case.* Copyright © 1994 the American Bar Association.

Managers should be tactful and alert to the interviewees' attitudes toward and relationships with the victim and the alleged harasser. Remind witnesses about the sensitive nature of the investigation and the importance of maintaining confidentiality. Conduct interviews in private. Discuss results with the accused in a nonthreatening manner. Individuals who may be able to disprove the allegations should also be interviewed.

The investigation should be carefully documented. Witness interviews should be recorded in writing and, when possible, signed statements should be obtained. A record of the postinterview decision should be kept in a separate investigation file and retained for the time required by statute of limitations on sexual harassment claims. (This can be as long as two years from the date of the incident.)

Resolving a Complaint

To avoid liability, a manager must offer evidence that a sexual harassment complaint was investigated thoroughly and that the manager took prompt remedial action to end the harassing conduct. The EEOC recognizes effective remedial action to include:

- Prompt and thorough investigation of complaints

- Immediate corrective action that effectively ends the harassment

- Providing a remedy to complainants of harassment (i.e., restoring lost wages and benefits)

- Preventing future recurrences

If investigation results are inconclusive or if, after an investigation, no corrective or preventive actions are taken, the victim can file a lawsuit against the employer. Alternatively, if an employer punishes an accused harasser without conclusive evidence, the alleged harasser can file a defamation lawsuit or an invasion of privacy action against the employer. When an investigation is inconclusive, advise the alleged harasser, inform all employees about the zero tolerance policy on sexual harassment, explain consequences for failure to follow that policy, and conduct sensitivity training. If there is a resolution, ask the complainant to sign a resolution form such as the one shown in Figure 8.3.

Third-Party Harassment

Third-party sexual harassment occurs when someone outside the workforce harasses or is harassed by an employee. Examples are a supplier or customer harassing an employee or an employee harassing a customer.

In restaurants, where interaction between customers and employees is critical, the risks of third-party harassment are great. The idea that "the customer is always right" does not extend to harassment. The law clearly states that employees need not tolerate, and should not be subjected to, offensive behavior. Employers must protect employees from third-party harassment. Managers have limited control over customers and want to build their business and goodwill. From legal and practical perspectives, however, employees must know that they should speak up when they are subject to unwelcome behavior, and managers should act quickly and reasonably to resolve any such situations that occur.

Liability Insurance

Zero tolerance will not necessarily yield zero harassment claims. Managers need liability insurance with coverage for illegal acts of discrimination, including internal and third-party sexual harassment. This coverage is not provided in ordinary liability insurance policies; it must be specifically requested. The insurance

---

RESOLUTION OF COMPLAINT

I. Name: _____

II. Position and Title: _____

III. On the _____ day of _____, 200__, I previously completed a form that alleged facts regarding the environment in the workplace, a copy of which is attached to this document. I have been made aware of the results of the investigation by the company, as well as its proposed resolution of this matter, which I understand to be as follows:

i. The alleged harasser shall undergo sensitivity training;

ii. The alleged harasser shall be suspended without pay for five (5) days beginning on the ____ day of _____ and ending on the ____ day of _____ , 200__.

iii. It is agreed by both parties that the alleged harasser shall return to work at the time stated above, but only after having undergone the sensitivity training.

I am satisfied with the resolution as set forth above and understand fully that in the event the matter is not completely resolved by the foregoing actions, I have been encouraged to bring my concerns to the company for immediate attention.

Signature _____ Date _____
    Employee

Figure 8.3 Resolution of Complaint Form

should cover liability for employer and employee acts and any damages not covered by workers' compensation policies.

FAMILY AND MEDICAL LEAVE ACT

The Family and Medical Leave Act (FMLA) entitles eligible employees to take up to 12 weeks of unpaid, job-protected leave each year for specified family and medical reasons. The Act applies to all government workers and private-sector employers with 50 or more employees within a 75-mile radius. (Employees need not all work at the same location; a multiunit operation with 50 or more employees within a 75-mile radius must comply with the act.)

Employees eligible for FMLA benefits must have worked for the employer for at least 12 months and have worked at least 1,250 hours during that time. A covered employer must grant an eligible employee up to a total of 12 workweeks of unpaid leave for:

- The birth or placement of a child for adoption or foster care
- The care of an immediate family member (spouse, child, or parent) with a serious health condition or
- Medical absence when the employee cannot work because of a serious health condition

Spouses working for the same employer are jointly entitled to a combined total of 12 workweeks of family leave for the birth or placement of a child for adoption or foster care or to care for a parent (not parent-in-law) with a serious health condition.

Under some circumstances, employees may take FMLA leave intermittently (in blocks of time) or by reducing their normal weekly or daily schedule. FMLA leave may be taken intermittently whenever medically necessary to care for a seriously ill family member or because the employee is seriously ill and unable to work.

Employers whose workers are entitled to FMLA benefits must maintain group health insurance coverage for an employee on FMLA leave if such insurance was provided before the leave, and on the same terms as if the employee had continued to work. Usually, employees are required to pay their share of health insurance premiums while on leave.

Upon return from FMLA leave, an employee must be reinstated in the original or an equivalent job. (An equivalent job need not consist of the same hours but should include the same pay and level of responsibility.)

Employees seeking to use FMLA leave may be required to provide:

- Thirty-day advance notice of need for the leave when it is foreseeable
- Medical certification supporting the need for leave due to a serious health condition

- Second or third medical opinions, if requested and paid by the employer

- Periodic reports during FMLA leave about the employee's status and intent to return to work

Covered employers must post an approved notice explaining rights and responsibilities under the FMLA. A willful violation of this requirement may bring a fine of up to $100 for each separate offense. Employers must inform employees of their FMLA rights. Information can be included in an employee manual. Provisions for leaves of absence are sometimes part of a labor union's collective bargaining agreement, and managers should be aware of those provisions.

COMPENSATION

Generally, employers may establish wages and salaries as they desire. Sometimes, however, the law affects compensation rates. The Federal Equal Pay Act provides for equal pay for men and women for equal work if the jobs require "equal" skill, effort, and responsibility and if they are performed under similar working conditions. An employee's gender, personal situation, or financial status cannot serve as a basis for wage determinations. In addition to equal pay for equal work, other laws regulate compensation levels.

Minimum Wage and Overtime

MINIMUM WAGE The least amount of wages an employee covered by the FLSA or state law may receive from his or her employer.

The Fair Labor Standards Act (FLSA) established a federal **minimum wage** to be paid to covered employees and wage rates to be paid for working overtime. Like other federal laws, it establishes a minimum standard; states can set higher standards, if desired. Figure 8.4 illustrates selected variances in federal state minimum wage and other compensation programs. The FLSA applies to all businesses with employees engaged in producing, handling, selling, or working on goods that have moved in or are manufactured for interstate commerce. A very few restaurants may be too small to be covered under FLSA. (A manager should check with the local office of the Wage and Hour Division [see, in most telephone directories, U.S. Government, Department of Labor, Wage and Hour Division].)

VARIANCE IN FEDERAL AND STATE MINIMUM WAGE AND OTHER COMPENSATION PROVISIONS

	Minimum Wage	Overtime Hours	Tip Credit	Rest Breaks
Federal	$5.15/hour	1.5 times regular rate	$3.02/hour	None required
State				
Oregon	$6.50/hour	1.5 times regular rate	None allowed	10 minutes per 4 hours worked
South Carolina	No state law	No state law	No state law	No state law
Vermont	$5.25/hour	1.5 times, but hotels and restaurants are exempt	$3.02/hour	No state law

Remember that whenever a state law or regulation is different from the federal law or regulation, the law or regulation most favorable to the employee must be followed.

Figure 8.4   Variances in Federal and State Compensation Provisions as of Jan. 1, 2001

The federal minimum wage is periodically revised by Congress. Nearly all restaurant employees are covered. (The FLSA allows an employee under 20 years of age to receive a training wage below the standard minimum for the first 90 consecutive calendar days of employment. In addition, tipped employees can be paid a rate below the minimum if reported tips plus employer wages equal or exceed the minimum hourly rate.)

The FLSA does not limit the number of hours in a day or days in a week an employee over the age of 16 may work. Employers may require an employee to work more than 40 hours weekly. However, under the FLSA, covered employees must be paid at least one and one-half times their regular rates of pay for all hours worked in excess of 40 in a workweek.

Some employees are exempt from FLSA overtime provisions. These

---

WWW: Internet Assistant

Log onto the Internet and enter: http://www.dol.gov

Select: Search

Enter: "State Minimum Wages" in the search box

Select: "Minimum Wage Laws in the States" from the search results

Select: The state where you live

Learn about:

- The minimum wage rate

- Overtime provisions (referred to as Premium Pay)

- Any exemptions or exceptions relating to restaurants

---

include salaried professional, administrative, and executive employees. Restaurant managers are exempt from overtime pay requirements if:

- They are paid more than $250 per week

- Their primary duty is managing the business or a definable subdivision of it

- They customarily and regularly direct the work of two or more full-time employees or their part-time equivalent

Wage and Hour Division investigators enforce the FLSA. When they encounter violations, changes in employment practices are recommended to bring the employer into compliance, and they may require the payment of back wages due employees. Employers who willfully or repeatedly violate FLSA requirements are subject to civil penalties of up to $1,000 per violation. Employees may also bring suit, if the Department of Labor has not, for back pay and other compensatory damages, including attorney's fees and court costs.

TIP   A gratuity given in exchange for a service performed.

Tipped Employees

Restaurants may employ servers who customarily receive **tips.**

The FLSA defines a tipped employee as one whose monthly tips exceed the minimum established by the Wage and Hour Division of the Department of Labor. Tips received by these employees may be counted as wages up to 50 percent of the minimum wage. The Wage and Hour Division also determines the minimum cash wage that employers must pay to tipped employees. If an employee's hourly tip earnings (averaged weekly) added to this hourly wage do not equal the minimum wage, the employer is responsible for paying the balance.

Consider Patricia, who is employed in a state with a minimum hourly wage of $6.00. Her employer can consider Patricia's tips as part of her wages and is required to pay Patricia only $3.00 per hour. The employer can take a **tip credit** for the other 50 percent of wages needed to comply with the law.

> **TIP CREDIT The amount an employer can consider as a supplement to employer-paid wages in meeting the requirements of applicable minimum wage laws.**

Remember that tips are given to employees—not employers—so the law carefully regulates the influence that employers have over these funds. If an employer takes control of employee tips, that employer cannot utilize the tip credit provisions of the FLSA.

Calculating Overtime Pay for Tipped Employees. Tipped employees are generally subject to the overtime provisions of the FLSA. The computation of their overtime rate when the employer claims a tax credit can be confusing. Consider a state with a minimum wage of $6.00 per hour in which the overtime provision requires payment of one and one-half the normal hourly rate for hours worked in excess of 40 hours weekly. To determine the overtime rate of pay, follow three steps:

Step 1—Multiply the prevailing minimum wage rate by 1.5.

Step 2—Multiply the allowable tip credit by the standard hourly rate.

Step 3—Subtract the result in Step 2 from the result in Step 1.

Example: Minimum wage = $6.00 per hour, allowable tip credit of 50 percent.

Step 1. $6.00 × 1.5 = $9.00

Step 2. $6.00 × .50 = $3.00

Step 3. $9.00 − 3.00 = $6.00 hourly overtime rate

Tip Pooling

In some restaurants, employees routinely share tips. The FLSA does not prohibit tip pooling, but it is an area that requires caution. A tip is given to an employee—not to the employer. A tip is different from a service charge collected from the customer by the employer and distributed in a manner determined by the employer.

> **SERVICE CHARGE** An amount added to a customer's bill in exchange for services provided.

Generally, when a tip is given directly to an employee, the manager has no control over what that employee will ultimately do with the tip. An exception is a **tip pooling** arrangement.

> **TIP POOLING** An arrangement in which service providers share their tips with each other on a predetermined basis.

Tip pooling is complex, because the logistics of providing service are complex. When a server clears and resets a table, serves guests and again clears the table, the question about who should benefit from a customer's tip is easily answered. When, however, a hostess seats a guest, water and bread are provided by a busperson (who has previously set the table), a bartender provides drinks, and a server delivers drinks and food to the table, the question of who deserves a portion of the tip may be answered differently.

Managers can assist employees in developing a tip pool arrangement that is fair, based on the duties of each service position. Participation should be documented in the employee's personnel file, and a tip pooling consent form should be used. (See a sample in Figure 8.5.)

Employees cannot be required to share tips with others who do not cus-

---

TIP POOLING CONSENT FORM

1. Employee name

2. Date

3. A complete explanation of the facility's tip pooling policy.

4. The statement, "I understand the tip pooling policy and procedures stated above, and agree to participate in the tip pooling and redistribution program."

5. Employee signature line below the above statement.

Figure 8.5 Sample Tip Pooling Consent Form

tomarily receive tips, such as janitors, dishwashers, and cooks. Employers whose employees receive credit card tips can reduce such tips by an amount equal to the fees levied by the credit card company. Even a well-constructed, voluntary tip pooling arrangement can be a source of employee conflict. Because state laws vary, it is wise to check with a state hospitality association or a Wage and Hour regulator to determine the applicable laws and regulations.

WHAT WOULD YOU DO?

Stephen is a busperson at a restaurant; he clears tables, replenishes water glasses, and resets tables. His employer pays a wage rate below the minimum because of the tip credit provisions of the FLSA minimum wage law.

Stephen read the tip pooling policy and signed a document stating that he understood it and voluntarily agreed to participate in tip pooling. The policy stated, "All food and beverage tips will be combined at the end of each meal period and then distributed, with buspersons receiving 20 percent of all tips collected."

John, a customer, always enjoyed dining in Stephen's assigned section because Stephen was attentive and quick to respond to his needs. John tipped well, and the dining room staff were aware that John always requested to be seated in Stephen's section.

One day after John had finished his meal and added his generous tip to the credit card charge slip, he stopped Stephen and gave him a $20 bill, saying, "This is for you. Keep up the good work." A bartender observed the exchange.

Stephen did not place John's tip into the tip pool, stating that the gratuity was clearly meant for him alone. His supervisor demanded that Stephen contribute the tip to the pool. Stephen refused.

What would you do if you were Stephen's supervisor?

Taxes and Credits

Employers must pay taxes on the compensation they pay employees and withhold taxes from employee wages. Federal and state statutes govern the types and amounts of taxes to be paid or withheld. Sometimes tax reductions (credits) are granted to employers or employees.

Income Tax. Employers are required to withhold state and federal income taxes from the paychecks of nearly all employees. These taxes are paid by the employee but are collected by the employer and forwarded to the Internal Revenue Service and state taxation agency. The amount to be withheld is based on the employee's wage rate and the number of federal income tax dependents and deductions the employee has declared. Tips are considered wages for income tax purposes if they are paid by cash, check, or credit card and amount to more than $20.00 per calendar month.

FICA. The Federal Insurance Contribution Act (FICA) funds the Social Security program and Medicare. Employers and employees must contribute to FICA. These taxes, often called Social Security taxes, must be paid on the employee's wages, including cash wages and the cash value of all remuneration paid any way other than cash. The amount of FICA tax and the level of employee's wages subject to it are adjusted regularly by the federal government.

FUTA. The Federal Unemployment Tax Act (FUTA) requires employers (not employees) to contribute a tax based on the size of the employer's total payroll—which includes tip income and remuneration paid in forms other than cash.

EIC. The Earned Income Credit (EIC) is a refundable tax credit for workers whose incomes fall below established levels. The credit increases for families with two or more children, for families with a child under one year old, and for families that pay for health insurance for their children. Most workers entitled to the EIC choose to claim the credit when they file their federal income taxes. However, employees who elect to submit an Earned Income Credit Advance Payment Certificate can obtain the money in advance by receiving part of the credit in each paycheck.

Employers must include the EIC in the paycheck of any employee who submits the Certificate but are not required to verify the worker's eligibility for the credit. Funds for EIC payments do not come from the employer but are deducted from the income and payroll tax dollars employers would normally deposit with the IRS.

WOTC. The Work Opportunity Tax Credit (WOTC) gives employers a tax credit of up to $2,100 for hiring certain disadvantaged workers, including some disabled persons, recipients of Aid to Dependent Children, qualified veterans, qualified ex-felons, youths living in urban empowerment zones, some summer workers, and food stamp recipients.

MANAGING EMPLOYEE PERFORMANCE

Some restaurant workers are entering the workforce for the first time; others have years of experience. Regardless of ability or background, managers must have a fair, valid, and defensible system of employee evaluation, discipline, and, if necessary, termination.

Evaluation

Employee evaluation is often the basis for granting pay increases, for determining eligibility for promotion or transfer, or for modifying employee performance. The subjective nature of many evaluation methods makes them susceptible to misuse and bias. When an employee can demonstrate that the evaluation system is biased against a class of workers protected by the law, employer liability can be great.

> **EMPLOYEE EVALUATION** A review of an employee's performance, including strengths and shortcomings; typically completed by the employee's immediate supervisor.

Some large and many multiunit restaurants utilize formal procedures for employee evaluations. In smaller operations, an informal process may be used. In all cases the manager must ensure that all employees are evaluated on the basis of work performance (and nothing else), using only previously established tools and expectations such as job descriptions.

An undeserved negative employee evaluation resulting in a worker's loss of employment may subject the employer to even greater liability. **Wrongful termination** is the unlawful discharge of an employee. Although the at-will employment status exists in most states, employers should not unfairly evaluate employees and use these evaluation results as the basis for termination.

> **WRONGFUL TERMINATION** An employer's violation of the employment relationship, resulting in the unlawful firing of an employee.

Discipline

Managers can establish disciplinary rules and policies that do not violate the law. Even potentially controversial policies, such as drug testing or surveillance, have been upheld by the courts when they do not discriminate against specific employee groups.

Workplace rules should be communicated by written policies and procedures (including an employee manual), coaching, and formal training sessions.

Consistent enforcement is also important. (If a manager, in violation of stated sanitation policies, allows the cook to work without an effective hair restraint on Monday, will the employee understand why the rule is enforced on Tuesday?)

WHAT WOULD YOU DO?

Gerry was a cook whose attendance and punctuality were good. The property's employee manual (which all employees signed when hired) included the following policy:

> *To be fair to everyone, including your fellow employees and our guests, you must be at your workstation regularly and on time.*

Gerry had been working for ten months when, one day, he was 15 minutes late for work. Although Gerry was aware of the rule about punctuality, his supervisor, Pauline, rarely enforced it. Employees who were 5 to 20 minutes late may have been scolded, but usually no disciplinary action was taken unless, according to Pauline, an employee was "excessively" tardy. She preferred to, in her words, "cut them some slack" and was considered a popular supervisor.

On the day Gerry was late, several problems occurred in the kitchen. Frozen food deliveries arrived early with no cook available to put them away, the Sanitation Inspector arrived for an unannounced inspection, and the dish machine broke, so the dishes had to be manually washed. Pauline was angry, and when Gerry arrived, she terminated him, stating, "If you can't get here on time, I don't need you here at all!"

Gerry filed suit, claiming he was terminated because of his ethnic background. Pauline countered that Gerry was an "at-will" employee and that the property could terminate employees as it saw fit, especially when an employee was in violation of a communicated work rule.

What would you do if you were Gerry?

PROGRESSIVE DISCIPLINE An employee development process that provides increasingly severe consequences for continued violation of workplace rules.

Many organizations implement a policy of **progressive discipline** for minor work-rule infractions and for some major ones; employees pass through various stages, which are designed to help them to comply with stated workplace rules.

Progressive disciplinary systems usually follow five steps:

1. *Oral warning.* The employee is reminded about workplace rules and their importance, what constitutes a violation, and how to avoid violations.

2. *Documented oral warning.* The supervisor makes a written record of the oral reprimand, and the document is signed by the supervisor and the employee (who receives a copy). A copy is also retained in the employee's file.

3. *Written warning.* This is an official reprimand, generally accompanied by a plan to stop the unwanted behavior and to establish the consequences of continued infractions. A copy is placed in the employee's file, and the employee also receives a copy.

4. *Suspension.* The employee is placed on paid or unpaid leave for a time designated by the manager. A record of the suspension, its length, and conditions, is placed in the employee's file.

5. *Termination.* The employee is terminated for continued and/or willful disregard of the workplace rule(s).

Figure 8.6 shows a form useful to document actions in a progressive discipline process.

Not all incidents of workplace rule violation are subject to progressive discipline. Destruction of property, carrying weapons, falsifying records, on-the-job substance abuse, and some safety violations may be cause for immediate termination. Managers should insure that the restaurant reserves the right to immediately terminate an employee for a serious workplace violation as part of the progressive disciplinary procedure.

Termination

Although state and federal governments give employers wide latitude to hire and fire workers, the At-Will Employment doctrine does not allow an employer unrestricted freedom to terminate employees. An employer *may not* legally terminate an employee if such action is taken:

- *In violation of the regulations set forth in employee manuals or handbooks.* Failure to follow procedures outlined in employee manuals and

EMPLOYEE'S PROGRESSIVE PERFORMANCE REVIEW

Date: _____

Employee's Name: _____

Employee's Position: _____

Type of Action for this Discussion:

___ Oral Warning ___ Written Warning ___ Probation ___ Suspension

Employer's view of the violation: _____

_____

Employee's view of the violation: _____

_____

Is the employee being placed on probation? ___ No ___ Yes, until (date): __/__/__

Is the employee being suspended? ___ No ___ Yes, until (date) __/__/__

What specific action steps have been agreed upon between the employee and the supervisor to improve the situation and/or resolve the violation? (action steps and date):

_____

_____

I have reviewed and discussed this performance violation with my supervisor and understand the terms listed above to correct my performance.

_____   _____

Employee's signature   Date

_____   _____

Manager's signature   Date

Figure 8.6 Progressive Discipline Documentation Form

handbooks may result in legal action because of the expressed or implied conditions these documents may establish.

- **To deny accrued benefits.** Benefits can include bonuses, insurance premiums, wages, stock or retirement options, and time off with pay. (If an employee is fired for cause, termination may be legal and accrued benefits may be forfeited.)

- **Because of legitimate illness or justifiable absence from work.** This is especially true when an employee was injured at work and has filed a workers' compensation claim. If absences become excessive, the employer may be able to insist that the employee accept disability status.

- **For attempting to unionize co-workers.**

- **For reporting violations of law.** In some states, private business **Whistle Blowers' Protection Acts** have been passed so that employees reporting violations by their employers will not be terminated unjustly. These laws penalize employers that retaliate against workers reporting alleged violations of health, safety, financial, or other regulations and laws.

> **WHISTLE BLOWERS' PROTECTION ACT** A law that protects employees who have reported alleged illegal employer acts from employer retaliation.

- **For belonging to a protected class of workers.** Employers may not fire employees solely because they are over 40, of a particular race, color, religion, gender, or national origin or because they are disabled. Moreover, employers may not treat these workers differently from others who are not members of a protected class.

- **In some limited cases, without notice.** Under some circumstances, related to massive layoffs or property closings, employers may not fire workers without notice. In general, large employers are covered by the Worker Adjustment and Retraining Notification (WARN) Act. WARN provides protection to workers, their families, and communities by requiring employers to provide a 60-day notice of unit closings and mass layoffs. (An applicable closing occurs when an operating unit is shut down for more than six months, or when 50 or more employees lose their jobs during any 30-day period at a single employment site.)

Consider a large independent restaurant employing 150 people that is purchased by new owners on June 1. On June 2, it is announced that all employees will be terminated by the old owners and rehired by the new owners. Employees will be subject to review before rehiring. The WARN Act allows time for any employees preferring not to work for the new company to secure other employment.

- ***When the employee has orally been promised continued employment.*** The courts have sometimes ruled that an oral employment contract is in effect if an employer publicly and continually assures employees about the security of their employment.

- ***In violation of a written employment contract.*** This is true whether the contract is written for an individual worker or for a worker who is a member of a labor union with a Collective Bargaining Agreement.

Sometimes an employer must produce evidence that an employee was terminated legitimately and legally. The following guidelines help to ensure defensible terminations:

- ***Conduct and document regular employee evaluations.*** Rarely does employee performance become poor overnight. Generally, problems can be identified during regular evaluation sessions. These should be performed in a thoughtful, timely manner with opportunity for employee input. Written evaluations should be reviewed by upper management to ensure consistency among reviewers.

- ***Develop and enforce written policies and procedures.*** Managers may be accused of unfair discharge policies if they cannot show that employees were told, in writing, about the rules of employee conduct. All employees should be given a copy of employment rules, this is a good practice and can help to avoid lawsuits. Employees should be able to thoroughly review and ask questions about the rules, and they should then sign a document stating that they have done so. This document should be placed in the employee's personnel file.

- ***Prohibit "on the spot" terminations.*** Restaurants are fast-paced environments, and tensions sometimes run high. However, it is never a good idea for a manager to terminate an employee without adequate consideration. Although violent employees should be required to leave the property immediately if their presence poses a danger, other terminations made spontaneously can later be hard to defend.

- *Develop and utilize a progressive disciplinary system.* Make sure that each step is reviewed by at least one person other than the documenting manager and the employee.

- *Review all documentation before discharging an employee.* Employment termination is serious, but if sufficient evidence supports a termination, it should be done. If a progressive disciplinary process is in place, each step should be consistently followed.

- *Conduct a termination review and an exit interview.* Employees are less likely to sue if they understand why they have been terminated. Some employers refuse to tell employees, citing the "at-will" status of employment. Each approach has advantages and disadvantages. Employees shown documented evidence of consistent and excessive violation of workplace rules, and who have proceeded through a progressive discipline program, are less likely to sue because of nonrelated issues such as gender, race, ethnicity, and other protected class status. The exit interview may be witnessed by a second manager.

- *Treat termination information confidentially.* Usually, an employee's discharge is initiated by the employee's manager, but it should first be reviewed by that manager's own supervisor. Details should be shared only with those with a need to know.

In-House Dispute Resolution

The costs of a lawsuit are high, and in cases of employment litigation, the costs for a restaurant's defense against a charge of an unfair employment practice often exceed the amount of the employee's damage claim. For example, in a simple dispute in which an employee asks for $5,000 in damages, it may cost five times that amount to defend the charge.

The cost to employees to pursue unfair employment claims is high as well. Because an employee claiming an unfair practice is often no longer employed, legal expenses come when they cannot be easily paid.

Unfair employment practice cases may drag on for years, which increases legal expenses and diminishes the likelihood of an amicable settlement. Both parties may realize that a day in court is often too long in coming and too expensive to undertake.

**IN-HOUSE DISPUTE RESOLU-
TION** A process funded by
employers that encourages
the equitable settlement of
an employee's claim of unfair employment practice
prior to or without resort-
ing to litigation.

An **In-House Dispute Resolution** process to resolve disputes is becoming popular.

The In-House process may not be used for all
disputes; for example, issues involving workers' compensation clauses may be excluded. For applicable disputes, the process seeks to provide:

- *Fairness to employees.* Employees are involved
  in developing and implementing the program.

- *Cost savings to employers.* The process should result in reduced costs
  for employers.

- *Timely resolution of complaints.* The program has the ability to deal
  quickly with a problem. Sometimes this saves the employee–employer
  relationship, and the employee returns to work feeling that the employer really cares.

Features of an effective In-House Dispute Resolution program include:

- *Development with employee input.* Employees and employers generally develop a program that:
      Is easy to access
      Is fair
      Provides a rapid response
      Includes a legitimate appeal procedure

- *Training for mediators.* Individuals who will hear and help resolve
  disputes must be specially trained. Sometimes these individuals are
  called **ombudspersons.** Effectively trained mediators

OMBUDSPERSON An official
appointed to investigate and
resolve worker complaints.

can resolve many worker complaints without litigation, with resolutions ranging from a simple apology
to reinstatement and substantial monetary damages.

- *Employee legal assistance.* Employees may need legal advice; payment
  for this advice is provided. (Although it seems strange for employers to
  pay this cost, savings will occur if an amicable solution to the problem
  can be developed.)

- *Distinct chain of command for appeal.* Not all employees will be satisfied with their complaint resolution. Employees need to know that a

decision can be appealed without further complicating their relationship with the company. They need assurance that an appeal will be heard by those under no obligation to the first decision maker.

UNEMPLOYMENT CLAIMS

Unemployment insurance is costly and difficult to administer.

> **UNEMPLOYMENT INSURANCE** A program funded by employers, usually administered by the state and federal governments, that provides temporary monetary benefits for employees who have lost their jobs.

Background

The unemployment insurance program is operated by the federal and state governments. Each state imposes different costs to employers for maintaining the state's share of a pool of funds for assisting workers who have temporarily lost their jobs. (Figure 8.7 illustrates unemployment tax rate information for one state.)

States generally charge higher taxes to employers who use more of the fund pool and less to those with fewer claims. Therefore, two restaurants with identical revenues but different labor-related experiences pay widely different unemployment tax rates based on **unemployment claims.**

> **UNEMPLOYMENT CLAIM** A petition from an unemployed worker to the state unemployment agency asserting that the worker is eligible for unemployment benefits.

A worker submitting an unemployment claim does not automatically qualify for payments. The employer can challenge this claim. Each successful claim has an impact on the rate at which future contributions to the fund are determined. Managers should protest unjust claims for unemployment benefits.

Each state sets its own criteria for determining eligibility for unemployment benefits. Variances are numerous and include the following considerations:

- How soon can the unemployed worker petition for benefits?
- When will any allowable payments begin?
- What will be the size of the payments?
- How long will payments last?

1999 CONTRIBUTION RATES, STATE OF OHIO

For 1999, the range of Ohio unemployment tax rates (also known as contribution rates) is as follows:

Lowest Experience	Rate	0.0%
New Employer*	Rate	2.7%
Construction Industry	Rate	4.4%
Highest Experience	Rate	6.4%

*Except the construction industry.

Rate Notification

Tax rate notices are mailed for the coming calendar year on or before December 1. The tax rate is also printed on the employer's Contribution Report (UCO-2QR), which is mailed to you quarterly for reporting and payment of taxes due. To determine how much tax is due each quarter, multiply the rate by the total taxable wages you paid during the quarter.

Experience Rate

Once an employer's account has been chargeable with benefits for four consecutive calendar quarters ending June 30, the account becomes eligible for an experience rate. This rate is calculated annually and includes such factors as unemployment benefits claims by employees and average annual taxable payroll (as reported by the employer via quarterly wage reports). An (additional) delinquency rate is assigned if an employer fails to submit timely wage reports required for determination of the experience rate.

Standard Rate

If an employer's account is not yet eligible for an experience rate, then the account will be assigned the standard rate of 2.7% unless the employer is engaged in the construction industry, in which case the 1999 rate is 4.0%.

Request for Reconsideration

If an employer believes his or her unemployment tax rate was not calculated in accordance with the facts and the provisions of the law, the employer has 30 days from the date of mailing the rate notice in which to file a request for reconsideration.

Figure 8.7 Example of Unemployment Tax Rates

- What must the unemployed worker do to qualify for and continue receiving benefits?

- How long must the employee have worked for the former employer to qualify for assistance?

Generally, an employee quitting a job for a non-work-related reason is not eligible for benefits. Employees who are terminated, except for good cause associated with work performance, are generally eligible. (Laws are complex and vary widely; contact the branch of your state agency responsible for administering unemployment compensation benefits.)

Common examples of acts that usually *justify the denial* of unemployment benefits based on employee misconduct include:

- Insubordination or fighting on the job

- Habitual lateness or excessive absence

- Drug abuse on the job or that affects job performance

- Disobedience in regard to legitimate company work rules or policies

- Gross negligence or neglect of duty

- Dishonesty

Claims and Appeals

If the responsible state agency receives a request for unemployment assistance from an unemployed worker, the employer will be notified and given a chance to dispute the claim. Managers should respond to unemployment claims or information requests in a timely manner.

Managers should protest nonlegitimate unemployment benefit payments. They often have difficulty proving that workers should not qualify for benefits and, moreover, state unemployment officials often initially decide in favor of the employee.

Managers who do not agree with the state's decision can appeal. Then, both parties have the right:

- To speak on their own behalf

- To present documents and evidence

- To request witnesses to speak on their behalf
- To question witnesses and parties who oppose their position
- To examine and respond to opposing evidence
- To make a statement at the end of the hearing

An unemployment hearing is like a trial. Witnesses testify under oath. Documents including personnel information and performance appraisals are submitted as exhibits. A case must be organized before the hearing to maximize chances of success. Each party may have a lawyer present.

Decisions are not usually available immediately after the hearing. Managers will probably be notified by mail. Read the notice carefully; most judges and hearing examiners give specific reasons for rulings, which may help avoid future claims.

WHAT WOULD YOU DO?

Carolyn was employed for nine years as a cook. In accordance with restaurant policy, she submitted a request on May 1 for time off on Saturday, May 15. The property would be shorthanded on that date and denied her request. Visibly upset when the schedule was posted, Carolyn confronted her supervisor and stated, "I need off for my daughter's college graduation. I am not going to miss it!" Her supervisor, Martha, expressed regret, but all requests for that date had been denied and Carolyn was to report to work as scheduled.

On May 15, Carolyn called in sick four hours before her shift began. Martha recalled the earlier conversation, recorded the call-in as an "unacceptable excuse," and

---

WWW: Internet Assistant

The Florida Department of Labor and Employment Security has an excellent Web page containing questions with relatively generic responses about appealing unemployment compensation claims. Log onto the Internet and enter:
http://sun6.dms.state.fl.us/dles/uc/applfaq.htm#8

Review the Frequently Asked Questions (FAQs) and responses.

completed a form stating that Carolyn had quit voluntarily by refusing to work her as-signed shift. Martha referred to part of the employee manual that Carolyn signed when hired. It read:

> *Employees shall be considered to have voluntarily quit their employment*
> *if absent from work for one (1) or more consecutive days without an ex-*
> *cuse acceptable to the company.*

Carolyn returned to work the next day to find that she had been removed from the schedule and was informed she was no longer an employee. She filed for unem-ployment compensation. (In her state, workers who voluntarily quit their jobs are not eligible for unemployment compensation.)

What would you do if you were Martha?

EMPLOYMENT RECORDS AND RETENTION

Several federal and state agencies require employers to keep employee records on file or to post employment information. Although the number of require-ments is large and can frequently change, the following examples illustrate the responsibilities employers have for maintaining accurate employment records.

Department of Labor Records

The Department of Labor (DOL) requires that several types of employee records be maintained.

For Compensation. Every employer subject to the Fair Labor Standards Act (FLSA) must maintain the following employee records:

- Employee's full name and home address, including zip code
- Gender
- Position or job title
- Time of day and day of week when workweek begins

- Hourly rate of pay

- Hours worked each workday and total hours worked each workweek (a "workday" is any consecutive 24 hours and a "workweek" is a regularly recurring period of 168 hours)

- Total regular and overtime earnings for the workweek

- Total additions to, or deductions from, wages paid each pay period (includes items such as tip credit and charges for meals or uniforms)

- Total compensation paid to each employee for the pay period (which may include multiple workweeks)

- Date of paydays

- Period of time (workweeks) included in the pay period

For Employee Meals, Uniforms, and Lodging. Employers who make wage deductions for meals, uniforms, or lodging must keep records substantiating the cost for these items. Here is an example of how meal records can be developed:

Bill manages a cafeteria. Employees are allowed one meal per four-hour shift. Employees who participate are charged 25 cents per hour worked ($1.00 per meal). Bill must document the deductions he makes for the meal and the cost of providing the meal. Because it is impossible to determine the cost of each individual employee's meal, he uses the following formula:

Total food revenue − gross operating profit = cost of all meals;
Cost of all meals ÷ total meals served including employee meals = cost per meal

Bill documents this cost monthly using his Income (Profit and Loss) Statement as the source of financial information and a daily customer count for the total number of meals served. Generally, the DOL allows the manager great latitude in computing the employee meal costs and other costs of providing services. Costs must, however, be computed and maintained in the employer's records.

For Tipped Employees. Employers must keep the following records for tipped employees:

- A list of tipped employees or identification symbol for each employee whose wage is determined in part by tips

- The daily, weekly, or monthly amount of tips reported by the employee

■ The hourly deduction taken by the employer as a tip credit

■ The hours worked and amount paid to nontipped employees

In larger restaurants, the Accounting Department maintains the required records. However, the manager is responsible for producing these records if required to do so by the DOL. Under current DOL rules, an employer must maintain records for the following time periods:

■ For three years from the date of last entry—all payroll records

■ For three years from the last effective date—all certificates, including student certificates

■ For two years from date of last entry—all employee time cards

■ For two years—all schedules used to compute wages and all records explaining pay differences for employees of opposite gender in the same property

For Family and Medical Leave. The federal Family and Medical Leave Act (FMLA) requires employers to maintain the following records for at least three years:

■ Employee name, address, and position

■ Total compensation paid to employees

■ Dates that FMLA-eligible employees take FMLA leave

■ FMLA leave in hours (if less than full days are taken at one time)

■ Any documents describing employee benefits or employer policies about taking FMLA leave. (Figure 8.8 is an example of an announcement for the U.S. Department of Labor which explains details of the FMLA.)

Immigration Related Records

As discussed in Chapter 7, the Immigration Reform and Control Act (IRCA) requires employers to complete an employment eligibility verification form (Form I-9) for all employees hired after November 6, 1986. Employers must retain

Your Rights
Under The
Family and Medical Leave Act of 1993

FMLA requires covered employers to provide up to 12 weeks of unpaid, job-protected leave to "eligible" employees for certain family and medical reasons.

Employees are eligible if they have worked for a covered employer for at least one year, and for 1,250 hours over the previous 12 months, and if there are at least 50 employees within 75 miles.

Reasons For Taking Leave:

Unpaid leave must be granted for *any* of the following reasons:

- to care for the employee's child after birth, or placement for adoption or foster care;
- to care for the employee's spouse, son or daughter, or parent, who has a serious health condition; or
- for a serious health condition that makes the employee unable to perform the employee's job.

At the employee's or employer's option, certain kinds of *paid* leave may be substituted for unpaid leave.

Advance Notice and Medical Certification:

The employee may be required to provide advance leave notice and medical certification. Taking of leave may be denied if requirements are not met.

- The employee ordinarily must provide 30 days advance notice when the leave is "foreseeable."

- An employer may require medical certification to support a request for leave because of a serious health condition, and may require second or third opinions (at the employer's expense) and a fitness for duty report to return to work.

Job Benefits and Protection:

- For the duration of FMLA leave, the employer must maintain the employee's health coverage under any "group health plan."

- Upon return from FMLA leave, most employees must be restored to their original or equivalent positions with equivalent pay, benefits, and other employment terms.

- The use of FMLA leave cannot result in the loss of any employment benefit that accrued prior to the start of an employee's leave.

Unlawful Acts By Employers:

FMLA makes it unlawful for any employer to:

- interfere with, restrain, or deny the exercise of any right provided under FMLA:

- discharge or discriminate against any person for opposing any practice made unlawful by FMLA or for involvement in any proceeding under or relating to FMLA.

Enforcement:

- The U.S. Department of Labor is authorized to investigate and resolve complaints of violations.

- An eligible employee may bring a civil action against an employer for violations.

FMLA does not affect any Federal or State law prohibiting discrimination, or supersede any State or local law or collective bargaining agreement which provides greater family or medical leave rights.

For Additional Information:

Contact the nearest office of the Wage and Hour Division, listed in most telephone directories under U.S. Government, Department of Labor.

U.S. Department of Labor
Employment Standards Administration
Wage and Hour Division
Washington, D.C. 20210

WH Publication 1420
June 1993

U.S. GOVERNMENT PRINTING OFFICE:1996 171-169

Figure 8.8   Your Rights Under the Family Medical Leave Act of 1993

these forms for three years after the employee is hired or for one year after the employee leaves (whichever is later).

Age Discrimination in Employment Act Records

The federal Age Discrimination in Employment Act requires that employers retain employee records on an employee's name, address, date of birth (established only after the hiring decision), occupation, rate of pay, and weekly compensation. Records on personnel matters, including terminations and benefit plans, must be kept for at least one year from the date of the action taken.

EMPLOYMENT POSTERS

Regulatory agencies may require that certain employment-related information be posted in an area where all employees can see it. Examples include the following:

- DOL regulations require that all employers subject to the Fair Labor Standards Act (FLSA) post, in a conspicuous place, a notice explaining the FLSA. Employers are also required to post a notice in a prominent and conspicuous place explaining the Employee Polygraph Protection Act of 1988. Regulations also require every employer subject to the Family and Medical Leave Act to post a notice in a conspicuous place explaining the provisions of this law. (Posters may be obtained by contacting a regional DOL office.)

- EEOC regulations require every employer subject to Title VII of the Civil Rights Act of 1964 and the Americans with Disabilities Act of 1990 to post, in a conspicuous place, a notice about discrimination prohibited by such laws. (Posters may be combined and may be obtained by contacting a regional office of the EEOC.)

- Occupational Safety and Health Administration (OSHA) regulations require that every employer post a notice in a conspicuous place informing employees of the protections and afforded employees the obligations of the employer that are enforced by OSHA. (Posters may be obtained by contacting a regional office of OSHA.)

WORKPLACE SURVEILLANCE

Many restaurants electronically monitor employees. Some managers listen to phone calls, review voice mail, monitor E-mail and computer files (including sites visited on the Internet), and/or use some form of video surveillance. Managers may also conduct searches of employees' lockers, bags, and desks.

There is no national policy providing guidance about workplace privacy. Many managers believe they are protecting proprietary interests by monitoring employees. Moreover, as managers establish guidelines on work conduct, such as sexual harassment zero tolerance policies to comply with the law, monitoring helps ensure compliance.

Whether a particular monitoring technique is legal usually depends on four factors:

1. Did the employee have a legitimate expectation of privacy in regard to the item searched or the information, conversation, or area monitored? (In an employee lounge—probably not; in a rest room—absolutely!)

2. Has the employer provided advance notice to and/or obtained consent for the monitoring activity from the employee? (If so, it is difficult for employees to argue that they had an expectation of privacy.)

3. Was the monitoring performed for a work-related purpose and was it reasonable, given all of the circumstances? Generally, courts have allowed searches and monitoring that appear necessary to operate a business (i.e., for enforcing policies and procedures and ensuring quality service levels).

4. Was the monitoring done in a reasonable or appropriate manner? Was it discriminating? (In other words, was it used only with a minority subgroup of workers?)

Managers who monitor specific employee activities can adopt an Employee Privacy Policy (see the form in Figure 8.9) to help minimize misunderstandings and legal difficulties. Let employees know exactly what is expected of them, and allow them to question any part of the policy about which they are unclear. Laws in this area are complex and vary by location, so an attorney should review a monitoring/privacy policy before it is implemented.

POLICY REGARDING EMPLOYEE PRIVACY

The Company respects the individual privacy of its employees. However, an employee may not expect privacy rights to be extended to work-related conduct or the use of company-owned equipment, supplies, systems, or property. The purpose of this policy is to notify you that no reasonable expectation of privacy exists in connection with your use of such equipment, supplies, systems, or property, including computer files, computer databases, office cabinets, or lockers. It is for that reason the following policy should be read; if you do not understand it, ask for clarification before you sign it.

I, _____, *understand that all electronic communications systems and all information transmitted by, received from, or stored in these systems are the property of the Company. I also understand that these systems are to be used solely for job-related purposes and not for personal purposes, and that I do not have any personal privacy right in connection with the use of this equipment or with the transmission, receipt, or storage of information in this equipment.*

I consent to the Company's monitoring my use of company equipment at any time at its discretion. Such monitoring may include printing and reading all electronic and mail entering, leaving, or stored in these systems.

I agree to abide by this Company policy, and I understand that the policy prohibits me from using electronic communication systems to transmit lewd, offensive, or racially related messages.

_____   _____
Signature of employee   Date

Figure 8.9 Employee Privacy Policy Form

WHAT WOULD YOU DO?

Naomi is the Sous Chef at a restaurant. She has been there five years and is considered a creative culinary artist.

Thomas is the Executive Chef and Naomi's supervisor. Her annual evaluations have been very good, and she has been designated as "ready for promotion" in her past two evaluations. In January she announces she is pregnant and will have her baby in July. In March, Chef Thomas completes his annual evaluation of Naomi but does not recommend her for promotion to Executive Chef in a new restaurant being built by the owner. He cites "the extraordinary demands on the time of an Executive Chef," which, he claims, Naomi will be unable to meet. He also cites conversations he has overheard with Naomi in which she has declared, "I'm looking forward to spending as much time as possible with my baby."

Following her evaluation, Naomi claims discrimination against her because of her gender and retains a lawyer.

What would you do if you were the manager, responding to her attorney?

MANAGER'S "TO DO" LIST

Review the following recommendations proposed in this chapter. Analyze your interest in and need for implementing these recommendations by completing the columns on the right side of the form. Remember, when task assignments are made, time requirements for completion should also be stated. Follow up, as improvement activities evolve, to ensure that your property is moving closer to the goal of minimizing litigation risks.

Recommended Procedures	In Place Now?			Needed to Implement			Assigned To	Completion Date
	Yes	No	N/A*	Policy	Training	Other		
An offer letter completely and clearly identifying the manager's offer is provided to all applicants selected for employment.								
An employee manual is available and given to all new employees.								
The content of the employee manual addresses all applicable issues identified in this chapter under "Employees Manual."								
Employees are tested over the content of the Employee Manual.								
Employee manuals include a signature page so employees can verify that the manual has been read.								
Each page of the employee manual indicates the "at-will" employment status.								
All restaurant employees are required to follow all policies and standards relating to appearance and language except where bona fide occupational qualifications have been established.								
All managers treat all employees equitably.								
The manager has in place and has provided adequate communication and training for the avoidance of quid pro quo and hostile environment sexual harassment.								
Managers exercise reasonable care to prevent and promptly correct any sexually harassing behavior.								

*N/A = Not Applicable

Recommended Procedures	In Place Now?			Needed to Implement			Assigned To	Completion Date
	Yes	No	N/A*	Policy	Training	Other		
The operation has in place and has adequately communicated information about its zero tolerance sexual harassment policy and environment.								
An effective sexual harassment policy is developed, communicated, and made an integral part of the culture and environment of the restaurant.								
Ongoing training programs relating to harassment are established to help promote a safe working environment and ensure legal compliance.								
A program to objectively measure training results relating to sexual harassment is in place; corrective action, if any, is promptly taken to improve training effectiveness.								
Records of training activities relating to workplace discrimination are maintained, as are training materials used in the sessions.								
An effective process is in place to investigate complaints about inappropriate on-the-job activities.								
Managers know when they should—and should not— immediately terminate an employee accused of harassment.								
Procedures to investigate allegations of workplace discrimination are developed and include careful and documented (written) information from all applicable sources.								
Managers take immediate corrective action to end harassment and to prevent future occurrences.								

*N/A = Not Applicable

Recommended Procedures	In Place Now?			Needed to Implement			Assigned To	Completion Date
	Yes	No	N/A*	Policy	Training	Other		
Managers do not permit third-party harassment in the workplace.								
Adequate liability insurance for illegal discrimination acts, including internal and third-party sexual harassment, is purchased.								
Managers and employees are familiar with the Family Medical Leave Act, and procedures are in place to consistently comply with it.								
The provision of minimum wage and overtime compensation is consistently within the regulations specified by the U.S. Department of Labor.								
Procedures to accurately assess the amount of tip credit, if any, permitted by the state in which the restaurant is located are well known and consistently used.								
Procedures for correctly calculating overtime for tipped employees are well-known and consistently used.								
An effective tip pooling policy is in place where applicable; all employees are aware of it.								
A knowledgeable accountant or other professional assists the manager in establishing procedures to collect employee income tax, to compute the employer and employee shares of FICA taxes, to assess amounts due under the Federal Unemployment Tax Act, and to determine earned income credit, if any is due to affected employees.								

*N/A = Not Applicable

Recommended Procedures	In Place Now?			Needed to Implement			Assigned To	Completion Date
	Yes	No	N/A*	Policy	Training	Other		
An objective employee evaluation system is in place to reduce the chance of bias against a class of workers.								
Workplace rules are properly communicated by written policies and procedures.								
A systematic policy and process of progressive discipline is used by managers.								
All employee termination is done *legally* and practices to ensure that termination is done correctly are in place.								
An in-house dispute resolution process is in place.								
Managers use proper documentation to minimize the payment of unemployment claims.								
Managers are aware of and correctly develop and retain employment records required by the following: • Department of Labor • Immigration and Naturalization Service • Age Discrimination in Employment Act								
Employment-related information is posted in areas where all employees see it, according to regulations mandated by the DOL, EEOC, and OSHA.								
Managers develop and effectively communicate a restaurant policy relating to workplace surveillance.								

For more information and suggestions
log onto www.hospitalitylawyer.com.

*N/A = Not Applicable

CONSULTANT'S CORNER

What Would You Do? (page 183)

Sandra is aware of an employee who ridicules the concept of sexual harassment training. This presents a dangerous set of circumstances for any employer. Given the severe penalties for sexual harassment in the workplace, employers must be vigilant to ensure that their employees take the training very seriously and recognize the potential harm that can result from sexual harassment. A recommendation for Sandra may be that she have one final counseling session with Joseph, letting him know that if he does not modify his behavior and comments, he will be subject to termination.

In addition, if Sandra is concerned as to whether Joseph is involved, or has been involved, in harassment, she might undertake an investigation to determine whether or not he has been involved in harassing other employees. If he is found to have done so, then Sandra must take appropriate steps to ensure that the harassment ceases immediately, which may include individual counseling and training for Joseph and/or termination.

What Would You Do? (page 195)

The first thing that Stephen's supervisor needs to do is to refer to the tip pooling policy. If the issue of unique tips or out-of-the-ordinary tips is addressed, then the supervisor must follow the policy. However, if it is not addressed, the supervisor is in a difficult situation. If he allows Stephen to keep the tip, it will be very difficult to enforce the pooling policy for all of the other workers. On the other hand, if he forces Stephen to put the tip into the tip pool, he runs the risk of alienating Stephen. This is a very difficult issue that arises frequently in tip pooling situations.

What Would You Do? (page 198)

Gerry will more than likely pursue his claim for wrongful termination based on discrimination because of his ethnic status. He will argue that others of different ethnicity, in the same or similar circumstances, have been treated differently. He will probably also argue, assuming that there is a progressive discipline policy in the employee manual, that he was not provided the due process that was afforded to other employees.

In addition, Gerry will more than likely file for unemployment insurance, saying that he was unjustly terminated. The restaurant will counter that he was terminated for cause because he was late. However, it will be very difficult for the restaurant to sustain its position, because Gerry will more than likely be able to point to several situations in which other employees had been late but were not terminated.

It should be made clear that policies must be strictly followed in all cases, regardless of whether someone is an at-will employee.

What Would You Do? (page 208 & 209)

This is an example of a situation that has gotten out of hand. In today's tight labor market, companies have to be as flexible and accommodating as possible. We really need to work extremely hard to accommodate our employees, particularly for significant life events, which include children's graduations.

The unemployment situation is difficult, but it does appear that the supervisor technically complied with the policy by removing Carolyn from the schedule because of her voluntary resignation. The supervisor must be prepared to document the company policy and the series of events leading up to the voluntary resignation, and be prepared to explain any inconsistent approaches that have been taken in the past under the same or similar circumstances.

What Would You Do? (page 215 & 216)

Assuming that the attorney has contacted you in writing, you need to immediately forward the correspondence to your insurance carrier and ask it for guidance, assuming that there is coverage. In the event that there is no coverage and the insurance carrier does not provide counsel, then you must forward the correspondence to your own attorney and receive guidance. You should also immediately begin an investigation into the circumstances. If the investigation does support the facts as stated, then it does appear that Naomi was discriminated against on the basis of her gender (pregnancy). The issue here is whether she can perform the essential functions of the job, and there is no evidence that she will not be able to do so. On the face of the information presented, it appears that Chef Thomas has made some broad-based assumptions regarding pregnancy that have caused him to make a dangerous decision. Hiring, evaluation, and termination decisions must be based on work performance. When one strays from this criterion, litigation often results.

9

DUTIES AND OBLIGATIONS OF
RESTAURANT MANAGERS

MANAGER'S BRIEF

Managers reading this chapter will learn that they must operate in a reasonably safe manner or face potential liability for accidents and injuries that occur to their customers. They will be able to differentiate between the types of legal duties required of them and the consequences of failure to exercise reasonable care when fulfilling these duties. Managers will be able to use information about several liability concepts, including reasonable care, torts, negligence, gross negligence, contributory and comparative negligence, and strict liability. They will learn about implications of and the liability incurred with their own intentional acts, the intentional acts of third parties, and about negligence per se. Managers will learn the difference between compensatory and punitive damages and will understand the steps in a lawsuit, including receipt of a demand letter, filing a petition, and the resulting discovery, trial, and appeal processes. Alternatives to dispute resolution (mediation and arbitration) are also discussed. Finally, managers will learn how to effectively respond to an accident, including the do's and don'ts of such a response.

A CLOSE LOOK AT THE MANAGER'S
DUTIES AND OBLIGATIONS

Restaurant managers have numerous legal duties and obligations, which are reviewed in this chapter.

Duties of Care

Managers owe a **duty of care** to those who enter their properties. Some obligations are straightforward: A manager has a duty of care to provide safe and wholesome food. Managers are not required to be ensurers of their guests' safety and are not generally liable for events they cannot reasonably foresee. They are, however, required to act prudently and to use reasonable care to fulfill their duties of care.

> **DUTY OF CARE A legal obligation requiring a particular standard of conduct.**

Restaurant managers have a variety of duties of care, including the duty to:

- *Provide reasonably safe premises.* This includes all public and exterior spaces constituting the total physical facility.

- *Serve food and beverages fit for consumption.* This duty is shared with suppliers and also includes the techniques used to store, prepare, and serve food and beverages.

- *Serve alcoholic beverages responsibly.* This duty of care is examined closely in Chapter 11.

- *Hire qualified employees.* This duty is necessary to protect against charges of negligent hiring and other potential liabilities.

- *Properly train employees.* This duty must be satisfied to protect against charges of negligent acts by staff that could have been minimized by effective training.

- *Terminate employees posing a danger to other employees or to customers.* This duty is necessary to protect against charges of negligent employee retention.

- *Warn of unsafe conditions.* When a manager is aware (or should be aware) of anything posing a safety threat, such as a wet floor or a broken sidewalk, those conditions must be made known.

- *Safeguard customer property (especially when voluntarily accepting possession of it).* Managers take possession of customers' property, for example, when a guest's car is valet parked or a coat is checked. The restaurant manager has the duty of care necessary to protect these guests' property.

WHAT WOULD YOU DO?

Sayed was a customer at a restaurant when a severe thunderstorm occurred. It caused the ceiling of the men's rest room to leak. When Sayed entered the rest room, he slipped on wet tile resulting from the roof leak. He struck his head while falling and was severely injured.

His attorney contacted the restaurant owners with a claim for damages. The owners maintained that the fall was not their responsibility, claiming they were not the ensurers of guest safety. Although the owners knew about the roof's condition, it leaked only during extremely heavy thunderstorms and was too old to fix without great cost. Because the storm was not within their control, the owners maintained it was not reasonable to assume that they could have foreseen its severity and could not be held liable for the accident.

What would you do if you were the restaurant owners?

Standards of Care

Managers must exercise a **standard of care** appropriate to the given situation. This is determined, in part, on the level of services a customer reasonably expects to find in a restaurant. For example, a guest departing on a seven-day cruise would reasonably expect the ship's staff to include a full-time doctor. The same

> **STANDARD OF CARE** An industry-recognized, reasonably acceptable level of performance used to fulfill a duty of care.

guest visiting a quick-service restaurant would not expect to find a doctor available. In either case, the guest could suffer a heart attack, requiring medical care. The ship's standard of care would include medical treatment; the restaurant's would not.

Many disputes about liability and negligence in the restaurant industry involve the question of what an appropriate standard of care should be. However, such standards are constantly evolving. Generally, a manager is required to apply the same diligence in achieving a standard of care as any other reasonable manager in a similar situation. Because standards change and because standards of care will be assessed during litigation by jurists who are not familiar with the operation, a manager must stay abreast of changing procedures. For help, refer to the discussion of STEM (Selecting, Teaching, Educating, and Managing) in Chapter 1.

THEORIES OF LIABILITY

Restaurant accidents often occur because employees and customers are subject to many of the same risks within a property that they encounter elsewhere. It is just as likely that a trip and fall will occur in a restaurant's parking lot as it will in a grocery store's parking lot. Managers are not responsible to ensure that accidents *never* happen; that is impossible. They are legally obligated, however, to operate in a safe manner and to react responsibly when an accident occurs. If a manager neglects to do either, the legal system is designed to hold the restaurant accountable.

Reasonable Care

Managers must provide a reasonably safe and secure environment. The concept of "reasonability" is pervasive and sets the standard of care that managers must provide for employees and customers. That standard is addressed in the concept of **reasonable care.**

> **REASONABLE CARE** The degree of care that a reasonably prudent person would use in a similar situation.

Reasonable care requires managers to correct potentially harmful situations they know exist or that they could have reasonably foreseen. The level of reasonable care to be exercised can sometimes be difficult to establish. If an interior foyer is wet because of snow tracked in by customers, is a "wet floor" sign sufficient to provide warning? Must the floor also be mopped? If so, how frequently?

The doctrine of reasonable care places a significant burden on a manager who must use his or her skill and knowledge to operate their property in a manner consistent with that of another reasonable manager in a similar situation.

> **TORT** An act or failure to act which does not involve a breach of contract resulting in injury, loss, or damage to another. A tort can be intentional or unintentional.

Torts

A **tort** is a wrong against an individual in the same way that a crime is a wrong against the state. A customer who drinks too much and then drives an automobile is guilty of Driving Under the Influence (DUI)—a crime against the state. If that same driver injures another motorist, the intoxicated driver is guilty of a tort—an act resulting in injury to another. There are two types of torts: intentional (including assault, battery, defamation, and intentional infliction of emotional distress) and unintentional (including negligence and gross negligence).

Negligence

Negligence is the most common unintentional tort.

A person who has not used reasonable care is deemed **negligent.** Assume that a restaurant's sidewalk is not shoveled during a snowstorm. A customer (or someone just walking by) slips, falls, and is injured. If a lawsuit follows and the judge decides that the manager knew, or could have foreseen, that the slippery condition could cause injury, the restaurant could be found negligent. That is, it did not do what reasonable managers would do to protect customers and others including having the sidewalk shoveled and salted.

> **NEGLIGENCE (NEGLIGENT)**
> **The failure to use reasonable care.**

Negligence is said to legally exist when four conditions have been met:

1. A legal duty of care is present.
2. The defendant has failed to provide the standard of care needed to fulfill that duty.
3. The defendant's failure to meet the legal duty was the **proximate cause** of the harm.
4. The plaintiff was injured or suffered damages.

> **PROXIMATE CAUSE The event or activity directly contributing to (causing) the injury or harm.**

Managers are responsible for their own actions and, under the doctrine of *respondeat superior* (see Chapter 3), they can also be held accountable for work-related acts of their employees. Sometimes, managers are even held responsible for the acts of their customers. The degree of responsibility a manager has for the acts of others ordinarily depends on the act's foreseeability. If a dangerous act or condition was foreseeable and no action was taken to warn or prevent, then liability will usually occur.

Negligence can result from the failure to do something, or because something was done that probably should not have been done. In the preceding example about the sidewalk, the restaurant's negligence resulted from a failure to act. By contrast, improper chemical spraying to eliminate pests that yields contaminated food consumed by customers will likely be seen as negligence resulting from an inappropriate action—not inaction.

Managers can be considered negligent even when they are only partially responsible for the harm caused to another. Consider again the case of the icy sidewalk: Suppose a man slips and falls into the street, where he is hit by a car. The fall may have caused only minor injuries, but an even greater injury occurred when the man was hit by the car. It is likely the restaurant owner will face charges of negligence even if the most significant injuries were caused by the car rather than the fall. In this instance, the restaurant would probably be responsible for the injuries caused by the fall, and not the injuries caused by the car.

Gross Negligence

When individuals behave in a manner demonstrating total disregard for the welfare of others, they are deemed **grossly negligent.** The distinction between negligence and gross negligence is important. The penalty is usually greater for gross negligence than for ordinary negligence, because the grossly negligent individual— or a restaurant—can be assessed punitive damages to serve as an example and deter others from committing the same act. Often, it is difficult to determine the difference between negligence and gross negligence. The difference in the eyes of a jury, however, can be millions of dollars awarded to someone who can prove that he or she was harmed because of reckless actions or inactions.

> **GROSS NEGLIGENCE   The reckless or willful failure to use even the slightest amount of reasonable care.**

WHAT WOULD YOU DO?

Jaemin, a cook, accidentally dropped and broke two glass containers on a workstation table close to a tub of salad greens about to be transported to the help-yourself salad bar. She wiped the broken pieces from the tabletop and saw two large pieces of glass on top of the salad greens, which she promptly removed. She looked "carefully" at the rest of the top layer of salad greens and saw no more glass. While wondering what to do, she was called away by another cook who needed help.

Mary, a customer at the restaurant, consumed some salad containing several slivers of broken glass. She swallowed some small pieces (which were subsequently found to have become embedded in her esophagus) and was cut in the mouth and on the tongue in several places with larger pieces that had been in the glass-contaminated salad greens.

Her attorney filed a lawsuit against the restaurant, claiming that its employees were grossly negligent in serving potentially contaminated salad greens to customers by mixing the greens in a large bowl on the salad counter.

What would you do if you were the manager?

Contributory and Comparative Negligence

Sometimes customers, through their own carelessness, can be the cause or partial cause of their own injury or harm. This is called **contributory negligence.**

Consider a customer who attends an evening banquet and, during the event, goes outside to smoke. He wanders around an unmowed area on the side of the parking lot, which is not lighted, and trips over scrap wood discarded in the area. The customer claims the restaurant should have marked the lot perimeter

> **CONTRIBUTORY NEGLIGENCE**
> Negligent conduct by the complaining party (plaintiff) that contributes to the cause of injuries.

"Hazardous: Do Not Enter" and that it should have reasonably foreseen that customers would walk into the area. The restaurant's attorney may maintain that walking at night in the unlighted and unpaved area apart from a parking lot is dangerous and that the customer did not exercise reasonable care. Although many factors will determine the outcome, courts have held that an injured party's contributory negligence reduces a restaurant's liability for damages. Judges and juries will compare the negligence of both parties when assessing responsibility for injuries.

The doctrine of **comparative negligence** recognizes that reasonable care is a responsibility shared by both managers and those claiming to be injured by them. If the court determines that a plaintiff was 25 percent responsible (contributory negligence) for his injuries and the defendant was 75 percent responsible, the amount of damages awarded would be reduced by 25 percent. Comparative negligence laws vary widely across the country.

> **COMPARATIVE NEGLIGENCE**
> Shared responsibility for harm resulting from negligence. The comparison of the defendant's negligence with the contributory negligence of the plaintiff. (Also known as comparative fault.)

Strict Liability

Sometimes a restaurant is found liable for damages to others even when it has not acted negligently or intentionally. This is because some activities are considered so dangerous that their very existence imposes a greater degree of responsibility on the person conducting the activity. Assume a restaurant offering a jungle theme elected to exhibit a wild tiger as part of its "environment." If the tiger escaped from its cage, the restaurant would be held responsible for the tiger's actions, even if the restaurant could not be proved negligent in the tiger's handling. Its responsibility would arise because keeping dangerous animals in close proximity to people, which is hazardous, was voluntarily undertaken by the restaurant. In these circumstances, those who engage in the activity are judged not by their actions but by the nature of the activity itself. This creates absolute or **strict liability.**

> **STRICT LIABILITY**
> Responsibility arising from the nature of a dangerous activity rather than from negligence or an intentional act. (Also known as absolute liability or liability without fault.)

Intentional Acts

The law reserves the greatest sanctions for those who not only fail to exercise reasonable care but commit **intentional acts** that cause harm to others. If the manager of a restaurant intentionally misuses a customer's credit card (for example, use it to make purchases through an on-line catalog service), the manager and potentially the restaurant are subject to severe liability, including punitive damages and probable criminal prosecution. In some instances the courts have held restaurant operators liable for the intentional acts of third parties, such as guests. The issue is whether or not the act by the third party which caused the damage was foreseeable by the restaurant.

> **INTENTIONAL ACT   A willful action undertaken with or without full understanding of its consequences.**

WHAT WOULD YOU DO?

A manager's restaurant lounge is overcrowded (about 175 customers in a space with a fire-rated occupancy limit of 125). Two male customers begin fighting. The manager restrains one person; the bouncer holds the other. One of the fighters has been cut by a broken glass. The police determine the following:

- The fight started when one of the men walked to a table and asked a woman to dance; she declined, and everyone at the table, including the subsequently injured patron, began laughing.

- The man who was refused a dance took offense, picked up an empty beer mug, and smashed it in the face of a man at the woman's table.

- The two men had never seen each other before; the man at the woman's table had just met her a few minutes before the incident.

What would you do if you were the manager?

Negligence Per Se

The description of the brawl in the preceding section does not provide enough facts to learn whether the incident and resulting injury were foreseeable by the manager. But what is readily apparent from the facts is the concept of **negligence per se.**

> **NEGLIGENCE PER SE** A term applied when a rule of law is violated, and this violation is considered so far outside the scope of reasonable behavior that the violator is assumed negligent.

Recall that the lounge had more than the allowed number of customers. Is this negligence per se? Quite possibly. The injured man's attorney will certainly argue that the occupancy restrictions should have been maintained, not just for reasons of fire safety, but for physical safety as well; fights, altercations, and injuries are more likely to occur when there is not enough space between patrons. The occupancy restrictions would have helped maintain order. An expert in building safety and security would likely concur.

Managers must always follow the law. It may be tempting to "pack the house," but there can be serious consequences if an injury occurs and an ordinance has been violated. Local, state, and federal laws should always be obeyed.

LEGAL DAMAGES

If an injured party suffers a demonstrable loss as a result of a tort, the law requires that the entity responsible for the loss be held accountable. The process involves awarding damages to the injured party. There are several types of damages for personal injuries most likely to be encountered by a manager.

> **COMPENSATORY DAMAGES** Damages awarded to restore an injured party to the position he or she was in before the injury (also referred to as actual damages).

Compensatory Damages

Compensatory damages are actual, identifiable damages resulting from wrongful acts. Examples of actual damages include doctor, hospital, and other medical bills, pain and suffering, lost income resulting from injury, and the actual cost of repairing damage to real or personal property. The recovery of these damages compensates the injured party for out-of-pocket costs and for pain and suffering. If a janitor accidentally leaves some tools in an entryway and a customer falls and breaks her watch, the cost of replacing the watch can be easily identified; the restaurant may be expected to reimburse the customer. The same can be true of any medical bills the customer incurs.

Punitive (or Exemplary) Damages

Punitive damages seek to serve as a deterrent to the one who committed a tort and to others not involved in the wrongful act. The objective is for the individual who was grossly negligent, or who acted maliciously or intentionally to cause harm, to pay damages beyond those actually incurred by the injured party. In this way, society establishes that this behavior will not be tolerated and that those who commit such acts will pay for having done so.

> **PUNITIVE DAMAGES   A monetary amount used as punishment and to deter the same wrongful act in the future by the defendant and others.**

Generally, punitive damages are awarded only when a defendant's conduct was grossly negligent (the reckless disregard or indifference to a plaintiff's rights and safety) or intentional. A manager can be found to have reckless disregard for customer safety if, for example, the manager knew that dishes were not effectively sanitized because of a dish machine breakdown, but continued to use the unsanitized serviceware, and customers contracted a food-borne illness.

ANATOMY OF A PERSONAL INJURY LAWSUIT

Today, even for an excellent manager, the threat of a lawsuit is very real. Some lawsuits are frivolous; others raise serious issues. In either case, managers must know how lawsuits are filed, how they progress through the court system, and the role a manager plays in the process.

> **PERSONAL INJURY   Damage or harm inflicted upon a person's body, mind, or emotions.**

Personal Injury

Much of a manager's concern focuses on the potential for damages resulting from **personal injury.** Managers provide food and beverages to customers, and the process of doing this can place a restaurant in potential jeopardy. The old phrase, "Accidents can happen" has been replaced with "Accidents can happen, and if they do, the affected parties may sue!"

Even though effective managers try to avoid them, accidents and injuries will occur, and sometimes the responsibility for them is unclear. Consider Arjay, who leaves a restaurant after dark alone to get into his car. While in the parking lot, he is assaulted. He suffers physical harm, fear during the attack, and a lingering concern about being out after dark alone. Here are a few questions that can be raised in this case:

- Were the parking lot lights working well enough to minimize the chance of an assault?

- Was the manager vigilant in eliminating hiding places for potential assailants?

- Was the guest warned that the parking lot might not be safe?

- Had the restaurant experienced similar incidents in the past? If so, what precautions were taken to prevent future incidents?

In this example, there is no clear reason to believe that the restaurant is responsible for the incident. However, the court gives Arjay and his attorney the right to file a personal injury lawsuit to determine whether, in fact, the restaurant was totally or partially responsible for the assault. In doing so, Arjay will seek damages incurred from the assault. The lawsuit will be time-consuming for the manager and expensive to defend. The reality, however, is that such lawsuits are filed daily, and it is rare that a manager does not become involved, to some degree, in a suit sometime during his or her career. The following paragraphs examine the anatomy of a personal injury lawsuit from inception to conclusion.

Demand Letter

Typically, a manager learns that a lawsuit is impending when a **demand letter** is received. It comes from an attorney who has agreed to take the plaintiff's case. As seen in Appendix K, the typical demand letter tells the plaintiff's version of the facts surrounding an alleged personal injury, may include the monetary amount of

DEMAND LETTER Official notification, typically delivered to a defendant by registered or certified mail, that details a plaintiff's cause for impending litigation.

damages being sought, and usually indicates a deadline for the manager to respond to the charges.

Attorneys generally accept a personal injury case with one of three payment plans. The first is an hourly fee: The attorney bills the client (plaintiff) at an hourly rate for each hour the attorney works. In this case, the plaintiff should seek a conclusion quickly so as to minimize the attorney fees to be paid. In a second plan, the attorney agrees to take the case for a flat fee. (Then it is in the best interest of the attorney to seek a quick resolution.)

CONTINGENCY FEE   A method of paying for a civil attorney's services whereby the attorney receives a percentage of any money awarded as a settlement in the case. Typically, these fees range from 20 to 40 percent of the total amount awarded.

The third payment plan is the **contingency fee.** Lawyers representing defendants charged with crimes are not permitted to charge contingency fees and, in most states, contingency fee agreements must be in writing. When a contingency plan is used, the plaintiff and the attorney both have an incentive to seek the most favorable—not necessarily the fastest—settlement.

Regardless of the payment form, the demand letter is the first step in the litigation process. If the response to the demand letter does not satisfy the plaintiff, the attorney will likely file suit against the defendant.

Filing a Petition

Filing a petition (or pleading a complaint) initiates a lawsuit. The **petition** identifies the plaintiff and the defendant. It describes the

PETITION   A document that officially requests a court's assistance in resolving a dispute.

matter it wishes the court to decide. Included will be the plaintiff's request for damages. The plaintiff may, for example, ask for monetary damages. When the petition has been filed with the administrative clerk of the court, the lawsuit officially begins.

Once the petition is filed with the court, the court will notify the defendant of the plaintiff's charge and will include a copy of the complaint in the notification. Then the defendant must respond in writing within the time specified in the court's notice.

Discovery

In the discovery phase of a civil lawsuit, both parties seek to learn the facts necessary to best support their position. This can include answering questions via interrogatories or depositions, requests for records or other evidence, and sometimes visiting the scene of the incident that caused the complaint.

The discovery process can be short or lengthy. Either side may ask for information from the other and, if necessary, a judge will rule on whether the parties must comply with these requests. Sometimes, one party may obtain a subpoena, demanding that specific documents be turned over or that specific individuals be called to testify in court. A subpoena may also be used to obtain further evidence or witnesses during a trial.

The plaintiff has the burden of proving the allegations in the petition to the finder of fact (judge or jury) that a particular view of the facts is true. In a civil case, the plaintiff must convince the court "by a preponderance of the evidence" (that is, by more than 50 percent of the believable evidence). In a criminal case, the government has a higher standard and must convince the court "beyond a reasonable doubt" that a defendant is guilty.

> **INTERROGATORIES Questions** that require written answers, given under oath, asked during the discovery phase of a lawsuit.

> **DEPOSITIONS Oral answers,** given under oath, to questions asked during the discovery phase of a lawsuit. Depositions are recorded by a certified court reporter and/or on videotape.

> **SUBPOENA A court-** authorized order to appear in person at a designated time and location or to produce evidence demanded by the court.

Trial and Appeal

During a trial the plaintiff seeks to persuade the judge or jury that his or her version of the facts and points of law should prevail. Likewise, the defendant tries to persuade for his or her view. Most personal injury cases are tried by jury. After a jury is selected, the trial process, although varying somewhat by state, is as follows:

- Presentation by plaintiff
- Presentation by defendant
- Plaintiff's rebuttal
- Summation by both parties
- Judge's instructions to the jury about applicable laws and procedures
- Jury deliberation
- Verdict

- Judgment or award

- Appeal of verdict and/or award

APPEAL   To make a written request to a higher court to modify or reverse the decision of a lower-level court.

Either side can **appeal** a verdict or award. In a personal injury lawsuit, it is common for a losing defendant to appeal the size of the award if it is considered excessive.

MANAGER'S ROLE IN THE LITIGATION PROCESS

Although a restaurant's or manager's attorney will advise the manager at each step in the lawsuit, there are some management do's and don'ts that are common. For example, when a demand letter is received, provide it to the appropriate insurance company and your attorney promptly. Follow their recommendations. Be cooperative with any investigations the insurance company or attorney may instigate.

Ordinarily, a representative of the court (constable, sheriff, etc., or a private person authorized by the court) will personally hand the manager the pleading so that the court knows it has been received. A manager served with a pleading must recognize that the pleading and the restaurant's obligations to respond are time sensitive. The manager should deliver the pleading to the attorney, make certain that the insurance company obtains a copy, and retain a copy for future reference.

During the discovery process managers are often asked to turn over business records, including invoices, reports, and information stored electronically. Plaintiffs must often provide medical records and reports, doctor bills, receipts for damages, and other personal information. Frequently, a manager or staff member is asked for a personal statement during the discovery process or even to testify as a witness during the trial.

The cost of responding to discovery requests by testifying or preparing documents can be expensive, time-consuming, and disrupting. The better organized the manager is at the outset, the less burden the discovery process will be. Work closely with the attorney; be cooperative and meet all time limits imposed for responses, because a missed deadline can cause severe repercussions.

Request attorney updates frequently. Schedules for trial dates and the times persons will be unavailable, such as during vacations, for scheduled surgeries, and so forth, should be shared.

If the case is appealed, a manager's involvement in the appellate process will be minimal, if at all. This process rarely requires anything new—that is, anything that was not provided before the trial. Managers should continue to maintain records of the case and keep track of any witnesses.

ALTERNATIVE DISPUTE RESOLUTION

There are alternatives to resolving personal injury claims in court. At any time during the litigation process, the parties can agree on a settlement. Two other common methods are mediation and arbitration. Both can be highly effective alternatives to the time, cost, and stress involved in going through a trial.

In mediation, a trained and neutral individual (the mediator) facilitates negotiation to achieve a voluntary resolution of the dispute. Generally, one full day of mediation can result in a compromise acceptable to both parties. Mediation can involve sessions jointly held with both parties, their attorneys, and a mediator, or separate meetings with each party, his or her attorney, and the mediator. The costs of mediation depend on the complexity of the case but are generally far less than those involved in going to trial. If the mediation is unsuccessful, the parties may still pursue a trial. If a settlement is made, the parties sign a settlement agreement, which, if drafted properly, is an enforceable contract.

In arbitration, a neutral third party (usually chosen by mutual agreement of both parties) makes a binding decision after reviewing the evidence and hearing the arguments of all sides.

If mediation or arbitration is used, managers should make sure that they have guidelines about what can be said and when it can be said. Be patient. The negotiation process can sometimes appear tedious, but the art of compromise

---

WWW: Internet Assistant

Log onto the Internet and enter: http://www.spidr.org

Select: Ethical Standards of Professional Responsibility

Review the document developed by the Society for Professionals in Dispute Resolution (SPIDR).

usually takes time. Be flexible and willing to compromise. Many times, an apology at this point in the process will help pave the way for compromises on other significant issues, such as the amount of money to be paid.

RESPONDING TO AN INCIDENT

Despite careful planning, preparation, and prevention techniques, customers can be seriously injured. When accidents occur, a manager must act in a way that best serves the interests of the operation and the injured party.

The time immediately following an accident is critical in determining a restaurant's legal liability. Managers must know what to do and, just as important, what not to do during this critical time.

The moments following an accident can be confusing and tense. There are several steps owners and managers should follow during this crucial time period.

Step 1—Do call 911. First obtain qualified, professional help. Do not allow an untrained person to determine whether an injury requires professional medical treatment. A delay creates a greater chance of liability. Call 911!

Step 2—Do attend to the injured party. Let the injured party know that emergency assistance has been requested. Help make the person as comfortable as possible. If certified care providers are available, allow them to administer appropriate aid. Restrict the movement of the injured party as much as possible unless the injury makes immediate movement necessary.

Step 3—Do be sensitive and sincere. Do not treat the injured person as a potential liability claim. Many injured persons who later filed lawsuits do so, in part, because of the insensitive treatment exhibited by the establishment after the accident. Treat the injured party with sensitivity, sincerity, and concern.

Step 4—Do not apologize for the accident. Showing sensitivity, sincerity, and concern does not mean that you are responsible for the accident. Until the investigation is completed, a manager does not know whether an apology is appropriate.

Step 5—Do not admit fault; do not take responsibility for the accident.
Statements made immediately after an accident are often based on first impressions without knowing all of the facts. However, such a statement can have a

profound impact on the injured party and/or a judge or jury, who may perceive it as a credible admission of guilt or liability. Even when the circumstances surrounding an incident seem glaringly obvious, do not admit fault or responsibility. There is no reason to discuss liability, negligence, or responsibility. The focus must be on the customer's injuries—not the cause of the accident.

Step 6—Do not offer to pay all medical expenses of the injured party. By offering to pay medical expenses, the manager may be entering into a contractual arrangement to pay for treatment costs. This contract may be enforceable even if the accident investigation determines that the restaurant was not at fault. In minor injury situations, a manager can offer to call a doctor or treatment center, but the injured party should choose the provider. In very limited circumstances, the manager may agree to pay for the initial treatment only, but this must be specified in writing to the medical provider.

Step 7—Do not mention insurance coverage. Fortunately, most restaurants have insurance for many types of accidents and injuries. Unfortunately, this insurance will sometimes produce "dollar signs" in the eyes of the injured party. (It is easier to pursue a big, indifferent, and unfamiliar insurance company than a warm, concerned, and well-meaning manager.)

Step 8—Do not discuss the accident's cause. This is a no-win situation. If the injured party argues or implies that the restaurant is at fault and the manager agrees, fault has been admitted. If the manager disagrees, this will only create ill feelings. Remaining silent is not an admission of liability and is preferable to arguing. The best alternative is for the manager to assure the injured party that a complete investigation will be conducted and that the findings can be discussed when it is completed.

Step 9—Do not correct employees at the scene. This immediate reaction can have a very serious negative impact. Reprimanding employees is sometimes interpreted by the injured party that a mistake was made or that the restaurant caused the accident. Managers cannot change what has already occurred. They can only hope to positively influence the future decisions of the injured party. This can best be accomplished by focusing on the injured party and not on the restaurant. There will be time to assess each employee's performance and take appropriate corrective action, if warranted, after the investigation is completed.

Step 10—Do a complete and thorough investigation. Much information will be learned immediately after the accident. If other guests saw the accident, request that they write down what they saw. Ask them to sign and date their statements and to leave their addresses and phone numbers in case they have to be contacted. It may take years for a claim to be resolved, and attorneys and investigators may need to locate persons who gave statements. An incident report (see Appendix L) can summarize information. Evidence wins lawsuits; the more evidence and documentation available, the better the chances for a favorable ruling or one that minimizes the amount of damages to be paid.

Employee witnesses should also complete and sign written reports. They may end employment before an accident claim is resolved. Depending on why he or she left, an employee's perceptions of an accident, including the events leading up to it, may change over time along with their overall perception of the restaurant and its managers. An employee who first recounted a positive rendition of the events from the employer's perspective may "recall" information that makes the employer look negligent if his or her employment status is terminated at a later date.

Step 11—Do complete a claim report and submit it to the insurance company immediately.   Most insurance policies require prompt notification of all potential claims if they are to provide coverage. Insurance companies want their experts to become involved in an investigation as early as possible. Failure to report the claim may cause it to be excluded from coverage.

Step 12—Do not discuss the accident or investigation with anyone except those who absolutely need to know.   Conversations with and opinions provided to another person can cause problems. Restrict conversations to the restaurant's attorneys or authorized insurance company representatives.

Step 13—Do not discard records, statements, or other evidence until the case is finalized.   Cases can be resolved in several different ways: The claim can be settled before trial, it can be tried in court and decided, or perhaps, be appealed. Sometimes a potential injury claim may not be filed as a lawsuit immediately, but the case cannot be considered closed until the statute of limitations for filing a lawsuit runs out (ordinarily two years from the date of injury in a personal injury claim). Managers who are not absolutely certain as to whether a claim has been finalized should check with their attorney or the insurance company and request a letter of consent to destroy the evidence.

It is imperative that a manager take charge of the scene immediately after an accident occurs and is the only one talking to the injured party. Managers need to be prepared to react and think quickly under pressure and must continue to plan and implement prevention procedures. However, managers should also be prepared for reality. Accidents do happen, and the first minutes after an accident occurs can be crucial in minimizing the negative impact of a potential claim.

MANAGER'S "TO DO" LIST

Review the following recommendations proposed in this chapter. Analyze your interest in and need for implementing these recommendations by completing the columns on the right side of the form. Remember, when task assignments are made, time requirements for completion should also be stated. Follow up, as improvement activities evolve, to ensure that your property is moving closer to the goal of minimizing litigation risks.

Recommended Procedures	In Place Now?			Needed to Implement			Assigned To	Completion Date
	Yes	No	N/A*	Policy	Training	Other		
Managers identify potentially dangerous public and nonpublic areas of the premises, develop a "safety inspection checklist," and routinely confirm that these areas are maintained in safe condition.								
Managers establish proper food storing, preparing, holding, and serving temperatures, train employees in these standards, and routinely confirm that all temperature requirements are maintained.								
A system is in place to warn employees and customers about conditions on-site that are temporarily unsafe.								
Managers stay abreast of constantly changing standards that affect procedures for care of the property and its management.								
Managers correct potentially harmful situations as soon as they are discovered.								
Managers have procedures in place to consistently ensure that all applicable local, state, and federal laws are always obeyed.								
If a manager receives a demand letter in advance of a potential lawsuit, this letter is immediately shared with the restaurant's attorney and insurance company.								
In the event of a lawsuit, managers carefully follow the instructions of their attorney.								
During a trial resulting from a lawsuit, the manager carefully follows the advice of the restaurant's attorney.								

*N/A = Not Applicable

Recommended Procedures	In Place Now?			Needed to Implement			Assigned To	Completion Date
	Yes	No	N/A*	Policy	Training	Other		
During the discovery phase of a lawsuit, the manager provides all information requested by the restaurant's attorney.								
If an accident occurs, procedures are in place to ensure that the following process consistently occurs: • Call 911. • Attend to the injured party. • Be sensitive and sincere. • Do not apologize for the accident. • Do not admit fault. • Do not offer to pay for medical expenses. • Do not mention insurance coverage. • Do not discuss the accident's cause. • Do not correct employees at the scene. • Do a complete and thorough investigation. • Complete a claim report and submit it to the insurance company immediately. • Do not discuss the accident or investigation with anyone except those who need to know. • Do not discard records, statements, or other evidence until the case is finalized.								

For more information and suggestions
log onto www.hospitalitylawyer.com.

*N/A = Not Applicable

CONSULTANT'S CORNER

What Would You Do? *(page 225)*

The restaurant owners must immediately advise their insurance company of the claim. In addition, they should probably repair the roof as quickly as possible.

Even though hospitality operators are not ensurers of their guests' safety, they are responsible for warning them of dangerous situations and using reasonable diligence to maintain the safety of the premises.

It is also quite apparent from the facts that the owners knew about the leak but failed to repair it because of what they considered to be excessive cost. Experience tells us that juries do not reward business owners for putting profits ahead of the safety of their guests.

What Would You Do? *(page 228 & 229)*

This example reinforces the duty of the operator to serve food and beverages that are fit for human consumption. In this case, the restaurant obviously failed to meet that standard of care. Although it is too late for this situation, all employees must be trained to know that if there is ever a question of contamination of a food or beverage product, that product is not served and is discarded. In this case, the cost of the bowl of salad would be miniscule as compared with the probable costs of settlement to resolve the claim.

The manager must forward the complaint immediately to the restaurant's insurance carrier and seek counsel elsewhere, if it is not provided by the insurance carrier.

What Would You Do? *(page 230)*

Historically, courts have decided that a manager is not responsible for damages suffered by a customer that were caused by the intentional actions of a third party, when the third party was a customer. The courts' rationale is that the intentional or criminal act of a third party cannot be foreseen by the manager; therefore, it would be impossible for the manager to take precautions or preventive measures to keep the act from happening.

Recently, however, some courts have concluded that if violent acts have previously occurred at the property, or even if the property is in a "high-crime zone," an incident and resulting injury may be considered foreseeable. In these cases the manager may be held responsible for failure to use reasonable care in managing the restaurant.

10

A MANAGER'S LEGAL
RESPONSIBILITIES TO CUSTOMERS

MANAGER'S BRIEF

Managers reading this chapter will learn about the importance of properly accommodating customers and will discover who can (must) be admitted to a restaurant and for whom admission can be denied. The need for and the procedures to help ensure a safe environment for customers are explored, with special emphasis on the Americans with Disabilities Act (ADA). Responsibilities to noncustomers (guests of customers, invitees, and trespassers) are also explored, as are the reasons and procedures for legally removing customers from the restaurant. The legal aspects of managing guests' property are reviewed. Readers will learn about bailment relationships, including alternative types and liabilities that are established, and about handling property of unknown ownership.

ACCOMMODATING CUSTOMERS

Restaurants cannot exist without customers. However, with customers come a wide range of legal challenges to be considered.

Definition of Customers

The law views a manager's responsibility to those entering a property differently, based on the visitor's characteristics. Consider Lisette, who owns a restaurant. During a time when the restaurant is closed to the public, a robber enters, and because the person is not familiar with the property, accidentally falls down some stairs. Clearly, the law does not require that Lisette inform would-be criminals about her property's layout. Contrast that example with a **customer** who experiences a similar fall. This is why it is important to understand the distinction between who is and who is not a customer.

> **CUSTOMER** A visitor (guest) who lawfully utilizes a property's food, beverage, and/or entertainment services.

Duties of care apply to customers and, usually, to guests of customers. A customer is not limited merely to whoever pays the bill. All diners are considered to be guests of the facility.

WHAT WOULD YOU DO?

Tamir was a truck driver for a produce company. While he was making a delivery to a restaurant, the cook invited him to try some chicken salad prepared earlier following a new recipe.

The salad had been in a bowl at room temperature for several hours. Approximately four hours after eating it, Tamir became afflicted with a foodborne illness. He filed suit against the restaurant, whose attorney maintained that because Tamir was not a paying customer and had been invited to sample the salad without cost, the restaurant had no liability.

What would you do if you were the restaurant manager?

> **PUBLIC ACCOMMODATION** A facility providing entertainment, space, or seating for the use and benefit of the general public.

Admitting Customers

As facilities of **public accommodation,** restaurants historically have been required to admit everyone wanting to enter. More recently the right of a restaurant to refuse to serve a customer has expanded. However, federal, state, and local laws prohibit discrimination in public accommodations. Violations of these laws can result in civil or criminal penalties. Beyond legal expenses, discrimination can also cost a restaurant significant lost revenue resulting from negative publicity and can damage a company's reputation. Managers must know about their responsibilities to admit customers and the circumstances that would give them the right to deny admission.

It is a violation of the federal Civil Rights Act to deny any person admission to a public accommodation on the basis of race, color, religion, or national origin. It is also a violation to admit persons and to then **segregate** them to a specific section(s) of the facility or discriminate against them in the manner of service or types of products provided.

> **SEGREGATE** **To separate a group or individual on any basis, but especially by race, color, religion, or national origin.**

State and local civil rights laws are usually more inclusive. They may expand the "duty to admit" to categories not covered under federal law, such as age, marital status, and sexual orientation. They may also have strict penalties for violations.

It is legal and, in fact, sometimes mandatory for a public accommodation to separate guests based on some stated or observed characteristic. Many communities, for example, require that restaurants provide distinctly separate spaces for smoking and nonsmoking customers. In other cases, customers under a specific age may be prohibited from a restaurant's bar area. These practices are not illegal because they do not discriminate against a protected class of individuals as defined by the Civil Rights Act.

Denying Admission to Customers

Although it is illegal to unlawfully discriminate against potential customers, managers can sometimes refuse to admit or service them. Here are some situations in which admission can be denied:

- *The customer cannot show the ability to pay for the services provided.* Managers must clearly show that *all* potential customers are subjected to the same "ability to pay" test. For example, if only youths of a specific ethnic background are required to demonstrate ability to pay before ordering, the manager is discriminating on the basis of ethnicity and is in violation of the law.

- *The individual has a readily communicable disease.* An operator is not required to ignore the safety of other customers to accommodate someone who may spread a disease to others.

- *The individual wishes to enter the facility with a prohibited item.* It is permissible to refuse service to those attempting to bring animals into a restaurant (with the exception of guide animals for the visually impaired), as well as those carrying guns, knives, or other weapons.

- *The individual is intoxicated.* It is legal to deny service to customers who are visibly under the influence of drugs or alcohol, and admitting or serving them may cause great risk. (See Chapter 11.)

- *The individual presents a threat to employees or other guests.* If a customer behaves in a threatening or intimidating manner to either employees or other customers, that individual need not be served, as long as this policy is applied uniformly to all customers. If such a situation arises, document the situation using an Incident Report Form (see Appendix L.)

- *The individual does not want to become a customer.* Although restaurants are places of public accommodation, they are also businesses. A customer would not be permitted to enter a high-check-average restaurant on a busy night, order a cup of coffee rather than a full meal, and remain there for several hours. A reasonable person would assume that tables in a restaurant are reserved for those wishing to dine. Denying service to someone who does not want to eat is allowable.

- *The individual is too young.* Restaurants serving alcoholic beverages may be legally required by state or local ordinances to prohibit those under a predetermined age from entering. In some areas, young people may eat in a bar when a person of legal age accompanies them. In other communities, a young person may not even be allowed to sit in a dining area permitting them to view the bar area. Managers should make sure that they are up-to-date on regulations regarding minors.

- *The facility is full.* A restaurant that is full can deny space to a potential customer. In fact, it is a violation of fire safety laws to allow customers in excess of a specified number to occupy a public space. Moreover, if a customer arrives unreasonably late for a dinner reservation, the restaurant is not obligated to seat the customer, because the late arrival would constitute a breach of contract by the customer.

- Restaurants may also establish reasonable clothing standards for admission, but they must be evenly applied.

FACILITY MAINTENANCE

The manager has a responsibility to operate the facility properly and safely. Failure to do so places the restaurant operation at risk for a personal injury lawsuit.

Safe Environment

The restaurant must meet applicable building codes. Usually, this involves maintaining the property in compliance with local, state, and federal laws. Managers must operate in a manner that is reasonable and responsive to the safety concerns of employees and customers. A safe property requires a well-maintained physical plant and effective operating policies and procedures.

Many lawsuits filed against restaurants have resulted from accidents occurring on the grounds or inside the facilities. Consider Soeki, who arrived at a restaurant well after sundown in a freezing rain. On his way from the parking lot to the entrance, he slipped on some ice and hurt himself. If he sues, the manager must demonstrate that proper procedures were in place to maintain the parking lot safely during the winter. If this cannot be demonstrated with proper documentation, the case may be lost.

Managers can help protect the restaurant operation against slip-and-fall and other accident claims by taking the necessary steps to maintain the physical facility, to implement effective operating policies and procedures, and to document these efforts. Courts will measure a manager's negligence by the standard of care applied and on the level of reasonable care expected by customers and provided by similar properties.

Americans with Disabilities Act

Restaurants must be accessible to all. The Americans with Disabilities Act (ADA) addresses the requirements involved in removing barriers so as to enable access to public accommodations. Restaurants and bars are among the private establishments that are generally covered by this federal law.

The ADA requires public accommodations to provide goods and services to persons with disabilities on an equal basis with the general public so that everyone can benefit from the country's businesses and services and all businesses can benefit from the patronage of all Americans. The ADA mandates that any private entity owning, leasing, or operating a public accommodation must:

- Provide access into the facility. Barriers must be removed to make facilities available to and usable by people with mobility impairments to the extent that this is readily achievable. Examples include parking spaces for disabled persons, wheelchair ramps and lifts, and accessible rest room facilities.

- Provide auxiliary aids and services so that disabled people have access to effective means of communication. This involves providing aids and services to those with vision or hearing impairments. This requirement is flexible. For example, a braille menu is not required if servers are instructed to read the menu to customers with sight impairments.

- Modify policies, practices, and procedures that may be discriminatory or have a discriminatory effect.

- Ensure that there are no unnecessary eligibility factors that tend to screen out or segregate individuals with disabilities or limit their full and equal enjoyment of the place of public accommodation.

Compliance with ADA generally involves the removal of physical barriers and discriminatory policies. Requirements in regard to physical barriers are generally achievable if managers consider four recommended compliance priorities:

- Priority 1: Accessible approach and entrance
- Priority 2: Access to goods and services
- Priority 3: Access to restrooms
- Priority 4: Any other measures necessary

When a facility is not in compliance with ADA, changes in the property must be made if it is "reasonable" to do so. Because reasonableness is determined on a case-by-case basis, it is important to plan and document compliance efforts. The following steps can be helpful:

- ***Plan the evaluation***—Set an evaluation completion date, decide who will conduct the survey, and obtain floor plans.

WWW: Internet Assistant

To evaluate a facility for its compliance with the recommended priorities, managers must compare their property with ADA requirements. A thorough checklist to help do this is found on the World Wide Web at: http://www.usdoj.gov/crt/ada/racheck.pdf.

- *Conduct the survey*—Use a checklist (See the preceding WWW: Internet Assistant) to evaluate the property; use a tape measure and record results.

- *Summarize recommendations*—List identified barriers with ideas for removal. Consult with building contractors, if necessary, and estimate costs.

- *Plan for improvements*—Prioritize needs, make barrier removal decisions, and establish time tables for completion.

- *Document efforts*—Record what has been done, plan for an annual review, and monitor changes in the law.

ADA compliance laws are complex, but managers must familiarize themselves with them. Before building a new facility or renovating an existing one, select an architect or contractor who is familiar with ADA requirements. Make sure that your construction and/or renovation contract specifies who is responsible for ensuring ADA compliance.

WWW: Internet Assistant

Log onto the Internet and enter: http://www.usdoj.gov/crt/ada/adahom1.htm

Select: Technical Assistance Materials

Select: ADA Technical Assistance Materials

Scroll down and select: ADA Regulations for Title III

Browse through the standards established for accessible design

---

WHAT WOULD YOU DO?

Liana is the Area Vice President of franchising for a quick-service restaurant company whose growth has been rapid. The company is considering purchasing a small chain of 15 units consisting of older buildings in excellent locations, which would be converted to units owned and operated by her company.

What should she do (how should she respond) if the President questions the need for compliance with ADA requirements for these new units?

RESPONSIBILITIES TO NONCUSTOMERS

Customers are not the only individuals who may lawfully enter a restaurant. Owners, managers, employees, suppliers, and a customer's own invited guests all may utilize its facilities and services. Persons may also enter for a variety of reasons other than to become customers. A person may enter to visit a friend, to ask for directions, to use the rest room or a telephone, or to commit a crime. Managers have responsibility for the safety and well-being of those who are not customers (although the level of such responsibility varies by type of noncustomer).

Guests of Customers

Most restaurants allow customers great freedom in permitting invited friends and family members to accompany them in dining and meeting rooms and lounges within the property. Most customers expect, and most restaurants allow, guests of customers to enjoy the privileges enjoyed by the customer. Obviously, it is unlawful for a manager to refuse to allow guests of customers on a discriminatory basis. In addition, managers may impose the same standards of reasonable conduct on customers' guests as on the customers themselves.

From the viewpoint of personal injury liability, the guests of a customer, if they are on-site in accordance with restaurant policy, should be treated in the same manner as a customer; they should be provided a reasonably safe and secure facility. A question arises, however, about a restaurant's liability for the acts of those not associated with the restaurant. Under many state laws, a restaurant has no legal responsibility to protect others from the criminal acts of third parties. A legal responsibility may be created, however, if the danger or harm was foreseeable. For example, consider an assault in a parking lot. If dangerous incidents of a similar nature had occurred on or near the restaurant's parking lot in the past, a jury may find that a restaurant could have anticipated a recurrence and should have taken reasonable steps to prevent it. (These precautions are discussed more fully in Chapter 12.)

Invitees

A customer is an **invitee** of a restaurant. Other individuals who are not customers can also be considered invitees. Invitees enter a property because they have been expressly invited by the owner or because their intent is to utilize the property in a manner permitted

> **INVITEE   An individual who is on a property with the expressed or implied consent of the owner.**

by law and the property's owner(s). In either case, the restaurant is required to use reasonable care in maintaining the facility and to notify or warn the invitee of potential danger.

Invitees include employees, managers, contractors, vendors, and individuals such as those entering to ask directions, use a telephone, or make a purchase. Because restaurants are open to the public, the number of situations in which an invitee enters the premises can be great.

Consider Ara, the manager of a restaurant attached to a large shopping mall. Because of its location, many shoppers enter the restaurant's lobby. If an individual were hurt in the lobby, Ara would likely be responsible to show that he and his staff had demonstrated reasonable care in maintaining the area. This would be true even if the invitee had no intention of utilizing any of the restaurant's services. The fact that the restaurant decided to locate within the mall would demonstrate to most juries and personal injury attorneys that the restaurant could have reasonably foreseen a large number of shoppers in the area and that it should take reasonable care to protect their safety.

Trespassers

Legally, managers do not owe the same duty of care to someone who is unauthorized to be on a property as they do to one who is authorized. For example, a restaurant that mops its floors nightly has a duty to place Wet Floor signs around any wet area that is likely to have foot traffic passing through it.

However, the manager does not have a duty of care to illuminate those signs when the restaurant is closed and the lights are turned off. Assuming that access is restricted, a burglar who enters the restaurant after hours has no legal right to expect that the manager will warn about slippery floor conditions.

Some cases of trespass can be complex, and managers should be careful to distinguish between a trespasser and a wandering guest. Consider Deitra, a customer of a dimly lighted restaurant lounge. While seeking the ladies' room, she accidentally opened a storage room door, walked into a storage rack, and was injured. The restaurant's attorney argued that Deitra was a trespasser inasmuch as customers are not allowed in storage areas. Her attorney argued that she was a customer and that the restaurant was negligent because it should have had signage and the storeroom door should have been locked. A manager can expect that customers, if allowed, may wander into restricted areas. When they do, they will still generally be considered customers.

WHAT WOULD YOU DO?

Chia-Ning had been visiting an employee in a restaurant that had been open only three days. She was assaulted in the parking lot when she left. Her attorney threatened to sue the restaurant for injuries. Lashondra, the restaurant's attorney, indicated that the restaurant was not responsible for the acts of third parties, and because it had no history of criminal activity on its grounds, it could not have foreseen any potential problem. In addition, Chia-Ning had not been a customer of the restaurant.

Chia-Ning's attorney replied that many restaurants experience problems in their parking lots, so the manager should have anticipated potential problems. He also stated that Chia-Ning was an invitee of the property, and therefore the restaurant was required to guard her interest in the same manner as it would guard the interest of a customer.

What would you do if you were Lashondra's client?

REMOVAL OF CUSTOMERS

A manager must remove customers from a restaurant in a way that is legally sound. Generally, customers can be removed for lack of payment, for inappropriate conduct, or because of certain conditions of health.

Lack of Payment

When customers order food, it is reasonable to assume they will pay their bills. Sometimes, for a variety of reasons, they will not pay. In a restaurant, the manager has few options for collecting. Clearly, the manager can refuse to serve anything additional to the guest during that visit and can rightfully refuse service in the future as long as the bill remains outstanding. However, if the customer leaves the restaurant, there is often little that can be done to recover losses.

Often, the arrival of a law enforcement official at a restaurant is sufficient to encourage the customer to pay the bill. However, the police will rarely, if ever, arrest a customer for failure to pay a bill. Efforts to collect on money owed the restaurant should be pursued according to applicable state and local laws. This usually involves filing a suit in **small-claims court** or another appropriate court to obtain a judgment against the debtor (nonpaying customer). The cost of doing so is high, in both time and money, so it is best to avoid the situation whenever possible. Measures to protect a restaurant from customers who have no intention of paying their bills are discussed in Chapter 12.

> **SMALL-CLAIMS COURT A court designed especially to hear lawsuits involving relatively small sums of money. Such courts provide a speedy method of making a claim without the need to hire a lawyer and engage in a formal trial.**

Inappropriate Conduct

Customers who pose a threat to the safety and comfort of other customers or employees may be removed from a restaurant. In fact, a manager has a duty of care to provide a facility that is reasonably safe for everyone. A customer who is extraordinarily loud, abusive, or threatening to others should be removed. Many disruptive situations are best handled jointly by the manager and local law enforcement officials.

The question of whether a guest should be refunded any prepaid money or charged for any damages is determined according to the situation. In general, however, a guest who has received products and/or services and who is removed for inappropriate behavior must still pay for those products/services. Whether the manager levies the charge is subject to principles of sound business judgment.

Accident, Illness, or Death

The severe illness or death of a customer creates a traumatic experience for any restaurant. People can have accidents, get sick, die, attempt suicide, or overdose on drugs in restaurants just as they can elsewhere. In such circumstances, it is important for everyone to know exactly how to respond. The priority should be to maintain the dignity of the customer while providing appropriate medical attention.

When an emergency requires the removal of a customer, extreme care is necessary. The following procedures can be helpful:

- Train employees as to their roles in responding to a medical emergency.

- Instruct employees to contact the manager immediately if it appears that a customer is seriously ill, unconscious, or nonresponsive.

- Call 911 or another emergency care provider. (If the circumstances seem suspicious, notify the police.)

- Determine whether other customers are at risk and whether the area needs to be secured against entry by others.

- Designate someone to keep unauthorized persons away from the area until the emergency medical team arrives.

- Document the incident, using an Incident Report (see Appendix L).

- Only comfort the customer unless you are medically trained to provide aid.

- When the emergency medical team arrives, provide any information available to establish the customer's identity.

- If the customer is removed from the property, secure and hold any personal property. (The length of time personal property must be retained and the method of disposing of it at the expiration of that time period varies from state to state.)

- Report the incident to local law enforcement authorities if required to do so by law.

LIABILITY FOR GUEST PROPERTY

A restaurant manager's responsibility extends to the security of customers' property.

Common-Law Liability

Under common law, innkeepers and those providing food and beverages were held responsible for the safety of a traveler's property. If common law had not mandated a protected environment, robbers and thieves would have made inns unsafe and travel would have been greatly restricted.

In today's world, restaurant customers still face the threat of robbery. Credit cards, cash, and personal property such as cameras and furs are "fair game" for those who are dishonest. Unfortunately, even restaurant employees can be a threat to customers' property. Managers must remain vigilant for all kinds of wrongdoers, from sophisticated con artists to "grab and go" thieves, because today's law may hold a restaurant liable for the safety of its customers' property.

Property liability, however, extends beyond the threat of theft. Consider Miguel, who allowed a restaurant's valet parking staff to park his new (and expensive) convertible. While retrieving the car, a valet driver hit a concrete pillar, damaging the car extensively. As may be expected, Miguel was upset and would, in all likelihood, hold the restaurant responsible for the damage. In this case, the property, although not stolen, was clearly damaged while in the possession of the restaurant.

BAILMENTS

Restaurants are not generally covered under state laws that limit the liability of innkeepers for guest property. However, restaurants have responsibilities for the safety of their customers' property, especially in situations when the restaurant takes temporary possession of that property.

> **BAILMENT** The delivery of a property item for some purpose with the expressed or implied understanding that the person receiving it will return it in the same or similar condition in which it was received when the purpose has been completed.

These responsibilities have been established by the courts through use of a legal concept called **bailment.** Coat checks and valet parking are two examples of bailments. Restaurant managers must understand their responsibility for a customer's property when a bailment is established.

Bailment Relationship

In a bailment relationship, a person gives property to someone else for safekeeping. For example, a restaurant customer may check a coat in a coatroom.

The diner assumes that the restaurateur will safely hold the coat until it is reclaimed. Although there may or may not be a charge for the service, the manager assumes responsibility for the safety of the coat when it is received. In this situation, a bailment has been created.

BAILOR   A person who gives property to another in a bailment arrangement.

In a bailment relationship, the person who gives property to another is the **bailor.** The person who takes responsibility for the property after receiving it is the **bailee.**

BAILEE   A person who receives and holds property in a bailment arrangement.

To create a bailment, the property must be delivered to the bailee, who has a duty to return the property to the bailor when the bailment relationship ends. If a customer gives a coat to a coatroom attendant, the bailment relationship begins when the attendant accepts the coat and ends when the coat is returned to the customer.

GRATUITOUS BAILMENT   A bailment in which there is no payment (consideration) in exchange for the promise to hold the property.

A bailment may be for hire (the bailor may have to pay the bailee to hold the property, such as when paying for valet parking), or the relationship may be a **gratuitous bailment.**

Types of Bailments

There are three types of bailments:

1. Bailments that benefit the bailor—This arrangement exists, for example, when a refrigeration repairman asks whether his tools can be left in a restaurant's storeroom for the night so they can be used the next day to finish a repair job. The restaurant that accepts the tools for safekeeping also accepts the responsibility of a bailment relationship and must exercise a high degree of care for the safety of the property (tools). If the manager is unwilling to do so, possession of the property should be refused.

2. Bailments for the benefit of the bailee—When a manager borrows chafing dishes from another restaurant to service a large wedding, the bailment benefits only the bailee. This bailment can be gratuitous, or the dishes can be rented. In either case, the bailee benefiting from the relationship is responsible for the safety of the property while it is in his or her possession.

3. Bailments for the benefit of both parties—When a restaurant agrees to park its guests' cars while they dine, this is a bailment that benefits both parties. The guests (bailors) gain the convenience of having their cars parked, and the restaurant (bailee) gains from the increase in business arising from the parking service.

Although the laws vary somewhat among these three arrangements, managers should realize that customer property in their possession subjects them to the duty of reasonably caring for that property. Managers should exercise as much care for customers' property as they would for their own property. If this cannot be done, it is best not to enter into a bailment relationship.

WHAT WOULD YOU DO?

The Fox Mountain Country Club was a popular location for weddings in a midsized town. In winter, the country club offered a free coat check service operated by a staff member.

At a banquet function, Rosa gave her full-length sable coat to the uniformed coat check attendant. She was given a small plastic tag with a number that corresponded to the number on the coat hanger where her coat was hung. Rosa remarked to the attendant that the coat was "very valuable" and she hoped the attendant would protect it carefully.

When Rosa returned to retrieve the coat, it was missing. The coat check attendant apologized profusely. He stated he had left the coatroom unattended only twice that evening: one time was for a 15-minute dinner break and the other for a 5-minute cigarette break. The coatroom door was left open and unlocked so that customers leaving early could retrieve their coats.

The manager was called, and he pointed to a sign prominently displayed near the coatroom, stating, "The restaurant is not responsible for lost or stolen property." He recommended that Rosa refer the matter to her insurance company.

What would you do if you were Rosa?

Liability Under a Bailment Relationship

A restaurant is liable for a customer's property if a bailment relationship is established. Many restaurants provide coat racks or unattended coatrooms.

Generally, a restaurant is not responsible for theft or damage to a customer's property on an unattended coat rack, because the restaurant did not legally take possession of the property; a bailment was never created.

This concept also applies to items inside bailed property. A restaurant that offers valet parking would be liable for damage to a customer's automobile. When the car keys are given to the valet, possession of the car transfers to the restaurant; a bailment is established. However, the restaurant would probably not be liable for the loss of an expensive camera left inside the car; it knowingly accepted ownership of only the automobile. No bailment relationship was established for the camera inside the car.

In cases where a bailment relationship does not exist and a restaurant does not assume liability, managers should still exercise a degree of care over their guests' property to avoid the risk of alienating a customer and a potential negligence lawsuit.

When a bailment relationship has been established, a restaurant will be liable for loss or damage to a guest's property. Often, a restaurant's liability for damage will be limited if it (the bailee) proves that the standard of care required under the law was exercised.

WHAT WOULD YOU DO?

Suppose you manage a restaurant in a downtown area of a city. No parking is available directly adjacent to your facility. For five years, your customers have had valet parking service provided by A-1 Parking, whose valet drivers gave customers a claim check for their cars and drove them to the A-1 garage. When customers finished dining, the valet radioed the parking lot with the claim check number, an A-1 driver delivered the car, and the customers paid a parking fee.

The arrangement has been a good one; no trouble has ever been reported. Today the owner of A-1 announced his retirement and asked whether the restaurant owner wanted to buy the business.

What would you do if you were the restaurant owner?

A bailee can also reduce liability by establishing a set liability limit with the bailor if the limitation does not violate the law or public policy. A restaurant may post a sign saying that it will reimburse customers for lost property up to a stated amount. Some states recognize this sign as a reasonable agreement between bailor and bailee to limit liability; other states do not. A manager should know state law or consult an attorney before posting such a sign.

In all cases, if loss or damage to a customer's property results from the restaurant's own negligence or fraud, it will be liable for the full value of that property. In contrast, if a customer's negligence contributes to the loss, the restaurant's liability may be reduced or eliminated.

Perhaps the most difficult application of bailment and liability concerns the safekeeping of customers' automobiles. When a restaurant offers valet parking, the situation is clear. The guest gives the key to the valet, which creates a bailment relationship and places liability for the automobile with the restaurant. When the restaurant has an agreement with an independent parking garage, it may still be liable for a customer's automobile because the garage could be considered an agent of the restaurant.

Many restaurants have free parking lots on-site but accept no liability for their customers' automobiles. Customers may park on the lot if they desire but must keep their car keys with them. No bailment relationship is established between the customer and the restaurant that would cover any loss or damage to a car. However, some states consider the availability of a parking lot to be a gratuitous bailment that would hold the restaurant liable for any damage. In cases when customers keep their car keys, but a fee is charged to use the parking lot, the courts may decide that this charge creates a bailment relationship and may hold the parking lot owner liable.

The laws covering liability for automobiles vary widely between states. Managers should have a thorough knowledge of the liability provisions of their state's laws.

Detained Property

Bailees and bailors have significant responsibilities when a bailment is created. The bailee can charge a fee to cover costs, such as a parking fee, associated with holding or protecting property. The bailor may have to pay reasonable charges for property that has been held. If the bailor is unwilling or unable to pay the agreed-upon charges, the bailee may detain the goods of the bailment as a lien until full payment is made.

Consider a restaurant that charges a parking fee. A customer claims dissatisfaction with the meal and refuses to pay for the meal and the parking fees. If the manager withholds the automobile until payment is made, it would be considered **detained property.** During the time the property is detained the restaurant, as bailee, will be obligated to protect the detained property from harm with the same measure of care normally exercised.

> **DETAINED PROPERTY**
> Personal property held by a bailee until the bailor makes lawful payment.

This situation illustrates why a manager must use legal knowledge and good judgment. The manager may be within legal rights to detain the automobile and demand payment. However, that action may not be in the restaurant's best interest. To maintain good customer relations and to avoid a lawsuit, the manager may decide that the best approach is to release the automobile. Detaining property can subject one to a possible lawsuit if not done properly and is a procedure that should be pursued only after careful consideration of legal consequences.

PROPERTY OF UNKNOWN OWNERSHIP

Managers or their staff members may find personal property whose ownership is uncertain. Under common law, there are three classifications of property whose ownership is in doubt. Each carries unique responsibilities for the manager.

Mislaid Property

Mislaid property is property whose owner has forgotten where it has been placed. A customer may enter a restaurant with an umbrella and forgoet to retrieve it when leaving. The umbrella is considered mislaid property, and the manager is responsible to keep it safe until the owner returns. If the manager gives the umbrella to someone claiming to be the owner but who, in fact, is not, common law would find the manager liable to the real owner for the umbrella's value.

> **MISLAID PROPERTY** Personal property put aside on purpose but then forgotten by the rightful owner.

Managers are required to use reasonable care to protect mislaid property until the rightful owner claims it. If the rightful owner does not return in a reasonable amount of time, ownership transfers to the property's finder. Most restaurants require employees to turn in any mislaid property found in the normal course of their work. Ownership of the mislaid property then transfers to the employer, not the employee.

Lost Property

Lost property is property whose location has been accidentally or inadvertently forgotten by the owner. Under common law, individuals finding lost property in a public place may keep it unless the rightful owner returns to claim it. In many states, the finder has a legal obligation to make a reasonable effort to locate the rightful owner of lost and mislaid property.

> **LOST PROPERTY** Personal property inadvertently put aside and then forgotten by the rightful owner.

As in the case of mislaid property, employees finding lost property must turn it over to their employer even if the property was found in a public place. A restaurant janitor who finds a portable computer in the restaurant's waiting area is required to turn the property over to the restaurant, because the manager may be responsible for the computer's value if the rightful owner returns to claim it.

How long must a finder of lost property retain it? It may be expected that the length of time would increase with the value of the property. A pair of diamond earrings found in a rest room would likely require a greater holding time than an umbrella at a restaurant table. Many managers require all property to be held a minimum time before it is given to the employee who found it (as a reward for honesty) or to charity. Appendix M shows a sample form a restaurant can use to properly track "lost and found" items.

Abandoned Property

An owner who abandons property has no intention of reclaiming it. It can be difficult for a manager to know when property has been abandoned.

> **ABANDONED PROPERTY** Personal property deliberately put aside by the rightful owner with no intention of returning for it.

Under common law, a finder has no obligation to care for or protect abandoned property, nor is the finder required to seek the owner. Broken umbrellas and sunglasses, old coats and books are examples of abandoned property found in restaurants. It is a good idea to be very sure that any property found in a restaurant is, in fact, abandoned before it is considered as such. When in doubt, treat the property as mislaid or lost.

Disposing of Unclaimed Property

When an item of value is found, a manager should attempt to return the property to its rightful owner. If this is not possible, the manager should try to safely protect the property until the rightful owner returns for it. Only after it is clear that the original owner will not be returning should the property be disposed of.

The following guidelines can help when devising a policy to protect the rights of original property owners and reward employee honesty:

- Review your state's lost and found laws to determine any unique requirements.

- Require all employees and managers to turn in all personal property found in public places (foyers, coatrooms, rest rooms, etc.).

- Keep a Lost and Found Tracking Form to record applicable information. (See Appendix M.)

- If the value of the item is significant, take all reasonable efforts to locate the rightful owner; document these efforts.

- Hold found property for a period of time recommended by your company or a local attorney. (Sixty days should be a minimum.)

- Permit only the manager or a designee to return found property to alleged owners; take extra care to return an item only to its rightful owner.

- If the original owner does not come forward, dispose of the property according to written procedures shared with all employees after review by your attorney. Many managers give found property to the employee who turned it in, as a reward for employee honesty. Other facilities donate valuable lost property to a local charity.

MANAGER'S "TO DO" LIST

Review the following recommendations proposed in this chapter. Analyze your interest in and need for implementing these recommendations by completing the columns on the right side of the form. Remember, when task assignments are made, time requirements for completion should also be stated. Follow up, as improvement activities evolve, to ensure that your property is moving closer to the goal of minimizing litigation risks.

Recommended Procedures	In Place Now?			Needed to Implement			Assigned To	Completion Date
	Yes	No	N/A*	Policy	Training	Other		
Managers are aware, inform their employees about, and consistently follow provisions of the federal Civil Rights Act relating to denying persons admission to a public accommodation and/or to segregating them to specific sections of the facility or discriminating in any manner of service.								
Managers know, train staff to adhere to, and consistently follow all provisions of state and local civil rights laws relating to public accommodations.								
Managers are aware of those times when admission to customers can be denied: • They cannot show ability to pay for services. • They have a communicable disease. • They wish to enter with a prohibited item. • They are intoxicated. • They pose a threat to employees or customers. • They don't seek to become customers. • They are too young. • The facility is full. • They are not dressed appropriately.								
Managers take necessary steps to maintain the physical facility, including: • Implementing appropriate policies and procedures • Training employees • Developing and using an effective safety inspection checklist • Promptly correcting any observed problems								

*N/A = Not Applicable

Recommended Procedures	In Place Now?			Needed to Implement			Assigned To	Completion Date
	Yes	No	N/A*	Policy	Training	Other		
Managers check applicable laws, contact local community fire inspection and other departments, and contact their insurance offices to help ensure that they are in compliance with all reasonable aspects of the Americans with Disabilities Act (ADA).								
Before a new facility is built or an existing one is renovated, an architect or contractor is selected who is familiar with ADA; the construction/renovation contract specifies responsibility for ensuring ADA compliance.								
Managers have a firm idea about and consistently provide a reasonable standard of care relating to the safety of customers, their guests, and invitees.								
Managers develop and consistently use reasonable policies and procedures to remove customers in cases of: • Lack of payment • Inappropriate conduct • Accident, illness, or death								
Managers have in place, train employees to use, and consistently follow a plan to effectively respond to customers' health emergencies.								
Managers and staff are knowledgeable about laws in their state related to common-law liability for customers' property.								

*N/A = Not Applicable

Recommended Procedures	In Place Now?			Needed to Implement			Assigned To	Completion Date
	Yes	No	N/A*	Policy	Training	Other		
Managers have policies and procedures in place and train employees to consistently use reasonable care in protecting customers' property.								
The manager carefully considers and discusses with an attorney bailment liability and aspects of responsibility for valet parking for customers if offered.								
The manager has in place and consistently uses a policy relating to lost and found property, including that which is abandoned.								
The manager is aware of any applicable laws relating to the disposition of found property.								

For more information and suggestions
log onto www.hospitalitylawyer.com.

*N/A = Not Applicable

CONSULTANT'S CORNER

What Would You Do? *(page 246)*

First, the argument that the restaurant could not be liable because Tamir was not a paying customer is without merit. Second, the manager needs to retrain the entire kitchen staff on appropriate sanitation and food safety procedures.

What Would You Do? *(page 252)*

Unless these properties fall within very narrow exceptions (e.g., historical landmarks)— and it is unlikely that they all would—the company would have to bring each property into compliance with the Americans with Disabilities Act. It is a wise business that considers the cost of compliance with the ADA prior to purchasing a property, because renovations in some instances can be extensive. The types of renovations that may be required include ramps to the entryway, expanded bathroom areas, and a reduction in the number of parking spaces available, inasmuch as two of the presently existing parking spaces may be required to create one parking space for disabled persons. In that instance, the operator must consider whether it will still have the requisite number of parking spaces to comply with the zoning requirements in the location for each outlet.

What Would You Do? *(page 254)*

It may be important initially to establish Chia-Ning's status. She really does not fall into the trespasser category, which might lessen the duty of care owed by the operator. The facts do not tell us whether or not she purchased any products or services while she was on the property.

It would probably be helpful for the restaurant to adopt a policy that precludes friends from coming to the property merely to visit the employees.

The manager is certainly going to argue that the restaurant was not in a high-crime area and that it had not had any incidents in the prior three days. Accordingly, it was not foreseeable that a person would be assaulted in the parking lot. Assuming that position is correct and there have been no incidents in the area or in the parking lot within the last three days, then the restaurant will probably prevail in this case of "intentional act (assault and battery) by a third party" against an invitee.

What Would You Do? *(page 259)*

Rosa will more than likely pursue the claim through her insurance company. The scenario will go something like this: The insurance company will pay Rosa. Through what is known as subrogation, the insurance company, after paying Rosa for the coat, will now own the claim against the restaurant. It will then look to the restaurant to recover the money that it had to pay out on the claim. In this "bailment" situation, it must be made clear to managers that in a bailment situation like this, when they accept property for safekeeping, they have an obligation to return it in the same or similar condition in which it was received. If the operator of a coat check needs a break, then another employee must relieve that operator at the coat check service. The restaurant's reliance on the exculpatory clause will probably be in vain because of its negligence in leaving the coat check unattended.

What Would You Do? (page 260)

The issue to be determined by the restaurant is whether or not it wants to go into the "bailment" business. As the situation exists today, the valet company possibly pays a small fee to the restaurant for being allowed to be the valet provider and assumes all of the risk associated with the bailment of the vehicles.

There is probably a reason that most restaurant companies contract with third parties to provide valet parking for their customers. It may be that a company's expertise in serving food and beverages may not translate into expertise in valet parking and caring for guests' automobiles.

The manager should do a significant risk assessment and cost–benefit analysis to determine whether the parking service would be a good investment. The manager also needs to check the agreement with the valet operator to see whether, if the restaurant chooses not to purchase the business, it has any influence over the type of operator that ultimately does purchase the business and whether it has the ability to terminate the agreement with the old operator and negotiate a new agreement with the purchaser.

What Would You Do? (page 264)

The manager in this instance should probably allow her to have the jacket. You want to create and enforce a policy that encourages your employees to turn items in. In this instance Esmeralda probably had an obligation to turn the coat in. She did so in good faith. However, if the manager does not allow her to keep the jacket it is doubtful that she or other employees will follow the same course in the future.

11

LEGAL CONCERNS IN SERVING FOOD AND BEVERAGES

MANAGER'S BRIEF

Managers reading this chapter will learn about their responsibilities to serve safe and wholesome food and to comply with truth-in-menu regulations. They also will learn about their responsibilities when serving alcoholic beverages and will obtain information about the content of effective training programs for those serving alcoholic beverages.

SERVING FOOD

WHOLESOME FOOD Food that is safe for humans to consume.

Managers have a legal obligation to sell only **wholesome food.**

Uniform Commercial Code Warranty

WARRANTY An assurance that a statement made or facts expressed in a contract are correct as stated or expressed.

The manager's responsibility to serve food safe for human consumption is covered by the Uniform Commercial Code (UCC) and other state and local laws. UCC regulations state, *"A warranty that the goods shall be merchantable is implied in a contract for their sale if the seller is a merchant . . . the serving for value of food or drink to be consumed either on the premises or elsewhere is a sale."* (UCC§ 2-314)

MERCHANTABLE Suitable for buying and selling.

Restaurants sell food, and there is an implied **warranty** that the food is **merchantable.**

FOODBORNE ILLNESS Sickness caused by consuming unsafe foods or beverages.

A manager must operate the facility to protect guests from **foodborne illnesses** or other injury caused by unwholesome food and beverages.

Guest Safety

Local health departments perform routine inspections of restaurants and may conduct training or certification classes for those who handle food. Managers must know local health department requirements and work hard to ensure that only safe food is served. Otherwise, the results can be catastrophic.

Consider Elida, who built her restaurant's reputation by serving quality food at fair prices. A careless cook forgot to refrigerate chicken stock and used it the next day to flavor an uncooked sauce. Several individuals became very ill, and the local media reported that an elderly lady was hospitalized after eating at the restaurant. Customer counts dropped, and Elida lost her business (and that was even before the elderly diner filed a lawsuit).

The law is clear. Managers will be held responsible for the illnesses suffered by their guests that are the result of consuming unwholesome food. Managers must make every effort to comply with local ordinances, train their staff in effective food handling techniques, and **document** their efforts.

DOCUMENT To maintain a written record what one has done.

WWW: Internet Assistant

For ServeSafe information, visit the National Restaurant Association's Web site at www.restaurant.org

---

The National Restaurant Association's ServeSafe program can help a manager to ensure the safety of the food being served.

WHAT WOULD YOU DO?

Olga and her friends had lunch at the Regal House. She selected a bowl of the "Chef's Special Vegetable Soup." Three hours later she suffered seizures and had difficulty breathing because the soup had contained monosodium glutamate (MSG), a food item to which she always suffered severe reactions. Olga recovered, but her attorney contacted the property, seeking money damages for her suffering.

What would you do if you were the manager of the Regal House?

Managers should take all reasonable measures to ensure that food is safe to serve. It is always best to **disclose** ingredients and warn customers about potential concerns.

DISCLOSE To reveal fully.

If a food safety–related incident does occur, the following steps should be taken to prevent further harm and limit potential liability:

- Document the name, address, and telephone number of the customer; note what was consumed and when.

- Obtain the name and address of the physician treating the customer. If the customer has not contacted a physician, encourage him or her to do so.

- Contact the physician to determine whether a case of foodborne illness has been diagnosed.

- Notify local health department officials immediately if a foodborne illness outbreak is confirmed; they can determine the source of outbreak and try to identify affected guests and employees.

- Evaluate and, if necessary, modify the property's training and certification efforts relating to the areas involved in the incident.

- Document your efforts and notify your attorney.

What a restaurant serves is important, but *how* that restaurant serves its food can be just as important. Managers must be experts with skill and judgment to ensure proper delivery of prepared food and beverages. The UCC addresses the responsibility for proper food service:

> *Where the seller . . . has reason to know . . . that the buyer is relying on the seller's skill or judgment to select or furnish suitable goods, there is . . . an implied warranty that the goods shall be fit for such purpose. (UCC§ 2-315)*

Managers cannot serve unwholesome food, nor can they serve safe and wholesome food in an unsafe or negligent manner. Consider Armando, who ordered Cherries Jubilee for dessert. When the server prepared the dish, a small amount of alcohol splashed out of the flambé pan and landed on Armando's arm. As he jumped back to try and avoid the burning liquid, he fell and severely injured his back. In this case the restaurant would face severe penalties for its server's carelessness even though the quality of the food served was acceptable.

Managers should frequently review all food temperatures and production/delivery techniques. If an incident involves *how* food was served rather than *what* food was served, complete an incident report as soon as possible. (A sample copy of an Incident Report is found in Appendix L.)

WHAT WOULD YOU DO?

Enriqueta, a secretary, treats her children to breakfast at a fast-food restaurant. She orders hot chocolate, and the children select orange juice. Her youngest child, who is six years old, asks whether she may try the hot chocolate. (The beverage has been served in a Styrofoam cup with a plastic lid.)

Enriqueta replies that the chocolate is "probably too hot for her to try." (This comment is overheard by several guests sitting nearby.) The child reaches for the drink anyway, and her mother, in an effort to pull it away, spills the beverage on her own hands, causing severe burns. Her lawyer states that Enriqueta has suffered second-

and third-degree burns and will be forced to miss work for three weeks. Upon returning to work, her typing speed is severely reduced because of scarring on her left hand. The attorney threatens to sue for damages, including medical expenses, lost wages, and a large amount for punitive damages.

What would you do if you were the manager?

TRUTH-IN-MENU CONCERNS

Managers should advertise food and beverage products most advantageously. If hamburgers contain eight ounces of ground beef (before cooking), a manager can tell customers in an advertising program, the menu, and servers' oral descriptions. A manager cannot, however, misrepresent products in violation of the **Truth-in-Menu** laws. These laws (perhaps better described as "accuracy in menus") protect consumers from **fraud** by food and beverage sellers.

> **TRUTH-IN-MENU** The collective name given to laws and regulations implemented to ensure accuracy in menu wording.

> **FRAUD** A deliberate misrepresentation.

Many managers believe that Truth-in-Menu laws are of recent origin; they are not. The federal government, as well as many local communities have a long history of regulating food advertisement and sale, beginning in 1906 when the Food and Drug Act and the Federal Meat Inspection Act authorized the federal government to regulate the safety and quality of food. In 1990, the Nutrition Labeling and Education Act (NLEA) made the disclosure of nutrition information by food purveyors mandatory for most foods. Among the few foods initially exempted were restaurant items. Regulations are now in place which require restaurants to provide to customers, upon request, back up data evidencing a nutrition or health claim (cookbooks, analyzes, etc are useful tools).

Managers must comply with all current Truth-in-Menu laws. The key is honesty in menu claims about what is charged and what is to be served. If one dozen oysters are offered at a given price, one dozen oysters should be served and the bill should match the menu price. Likewise, the customer should know if the menu price includes a mandatory service or cover charge.

WHAT WOULD YOU DO?

Ignach hosts ten guests at a restaurant. Unfortunately, the service, in his opinion, is terrible.

When the check arrives, he notices that a 15 percent charge has been added to the total price of the food and drinks the group consumed. When he inquires about the charge, his server informs him it is policy to assess a 15 percent "tip" to the bill of all parties larger than eight persons. The policy, says the server, is not printed on the menu, but is to be orally explained to customers making a reservation for more than eight people. Ignach's reservation was made by his secretary, and she mentioned no such policy to him.

Ignach refuses to pay the extra charge, claiming he, not the restaurant, should determine the amount, if any, of gratuity. The manager explains that the server has misspoken: The extra charge is a "service charge," not a tip, but Ignach still refuses to pay the added charge.

What would you do if you were the manager?

Accuracy in menu involves more than honestly and precisely telling customers about prices. It also involves care in describing preparation style, ingredients, origin, size, and health benefits. The National Restaurant Association (NRA) and many state associations have material to assist managers in the preparation of menu copy.

Following are some concerns to address in developing menu copy.

Preparation Style

How an item is prepared is important. "Grilled" items must be grilled (not just manufactured food with "grill marks" that is steamed before service). "Homemade" must designate a product prepared on-site, not commercially

---

WWW: Internet Assistant

For information on accuracy in menu and nutrition labeling, visit the National Restaurant Association's Web site at www.restaurant.org.

baked, and "fresh" means a product has never been frozen, canned, dried, or processed. Note the specificity of preparation style for the following items. Federal guidelines have been developed for these and numerous other foods:

- Breaded shrimp—Includes only the species *Pineaus.* The tail portion of the commercial species must constitute 50 percent of the total weight of a finished product labeled "Breaded Shrimp." "Lightly Breaded Shrimp" must have shrimp content of 65 percent by weight of the finished product.

- Kosher-style—A flavored or seasoned product that has no religious significance.

- Kosher—Products prepared or processed to meet specific Jewish dietary and handling requirements.

- Baked ham—A ham heated in an oven for a specified period of time. (Many brands of smoked ham are not oven-baked.)

Ingredients

Menus should accurately state the ingredients in a food item. Managers need not divulge recipes (ingredient lists), but there are situations in which listed ingredients must accurately match those used to make the item. If Kahlua and Cream is on a bar menu, the liqueur and the dairy product used should be those stated. Kahlua is a Mexican coffee liqueur, and cream is defined as a product made from milk with a minimum fat content of 18 percent. Managers can offer less expensive coffee liqueur and half-and-half (12 percent milk fat) can be served, but to call such a drink Kahlua and Cream is unethical at best and illegal in many areas.

Whenever a specific ingredient is listed on a menu, that item should be served. If the menu says "Maple Syrup," colored table syrup or maple-flavored

---

WWW: Internet Assistant

For a review of how the NLEA applies to restaurants and to see other definitions, visit the following Web site: www.fda.gov/opacom/backgrounders/foodlabel/newlabel.html

syrup should not be served. If substitutions must be made, customers should be informed of the substitutions before they place their orders.

Origin

The origin of a product or its ingredients can be important. Many consumers prefer Colorado trout to generic trout, Washington apples to others, and blue-point (Long Island) oysters to those from other areas. It can be tempting to use these terms to describe menu items that contain lesser-costing products. To do so is fraudulent and sends the wrong message to employees (who know about the substitutions).

Size

Product size can be an important factor in determining how much a customer will pay for a menu item. Consider Medardo's menu consisting of prime steak sold in a variety of sizes. His 8-ounce steak sells for $17.95, the 12-ounce for $23.95, and the 16-ounce for $25.95. The portion size of the steak will be important to his customers' concept of value.

Whether it is the size of eggs sold at breakfast or the use of the term "Jumbo" in referring to shrimp, specifying size on a menu is important. The law expects a manager to deliver what is promised. This is not always easy to do, because this area is complex. For example, "large" East Coast oysters must legally contain no more than 160 to 210 oysters per gallon; "large" Pacific Coast oysters legally may contain not more than 64 oysters per gallon. Food suppliers can help managers to learn food industry purchasing standards so that they can know what they are buying.

To avoid difficulties, a simple rule of thumb is, "If you say it, serve it."

Health Claims

For years, the only menu item most restaurants offered for a healthful choice was a "diet" plate of cottage cheese, fruit, and, perhaps, grilled meat. Today's health-conscious consumer demands more. Restaurants provide details about the nutrition of their menu items. The federal government, however, issues strict guidelines about what can and cannot be stated about menu offerings. Therefore, Truth-in-Menu concerns not just what is charged and what is served, but also nutritional claims.

Some menus identify nutritionally modified dishes with symbols, such as a red heart to signify that the dish fits within a diet pattern meeting general dietary recommendations. Other managers make claims about "low fat," "light," or "heart healthy." The Food and Drug Administration (FDA) has regulations ensuring that health claims can be substantiated. The Nutrition Labeling and Education Act (NLEA) applies to restaurant menu items making a claim about a food's nutritional content or health benefits. These regulations affect all eating establishments, regardless of size. The FDA estimates that more than half of all menus make some claims for nutrition or health benefits and are, therefore, covered by the regulations.

Nutrient claims relate to an item's nutrient content (for example, an item may be claimed to be low in fiber.) Health benefit claims relate to the relationship between a nutrient or food and a disease or health condition (a dish low in fat, saturated fat, and cholesterol may be claimed to help reduce the risk of heart disease). These claims may initially appear on the menu in simple terms such as "heart healthy." However, further information about the claim should be available elsewhere on the menu or provided upon request.

Currently, the law does not require managers to provide nutrition information about foods for which no nutritional or health claims are made. However, they must be careful that general guidance on the menu doesn't become a claim ("Fruits and vegetables can help reduce cancer risk"), because it would require the item to meet FDA's nutrition information and claims requirements.

Food manufacturers may do chemical analyses to determine the nutritional value of their products. Because this is not practical for restaurants, managers may back up their claims with any "reasonable" reference, such as databases, cookbooks, or other secondhand sources providing nutrition information.

The FDA grants restaurants more flexibility, because many restaurants don't produce foods according to the exacting standards that apply to food manufacturers. Enforcement of the regulations governing menu claims is provided by the state and local public health departments that have direct jurisdiction over the particular restaurants.

The following are examples of nutrient and health benefit–type claims and their meanings under FDA regulations:

Nutrient Claims

- Low sodium, low fat, low cholesterol—means the item contains low amounts of these nutrients.

- Light or Lite—means the item has fewer calories and less fat than the food to which it is being compared (Light Italian Dressing). Managers may use the term "lighter fare" to mean the dishes contain smaller portions, but its meaning must be clarified on the menu.

Health Benefit Claims

- Heart healthy—includes items low in saturated fat, cholesterol, and fat that provide, without fortification, significant amounts of one or more of six key nutrients. (This claim indicates that a diet low in saturated fat and cholesterol may reduce the risk of heart disease.) "Heart healthy" can also include an item low in saturated fat, cholesterol, and fat that provides, without fortification, significant amounts of one or more of six key nutrients and a significant source of soluble fiber (found in fruits, vegetables, and grain products). This claim indicates that a diet low in saturated fat and cholesterol and rich in fruits, vegetables, and grain products containing some types of fiber (particularly soluble fiber) may reduce the risk of heart disease.

It may be necessary to have menu items with nutritional health claims reviewed by both your attorney and a dietitian. Menus must be accurately developed to avoid violation of the law. This includes the careful monitoring of what servers *say* about menu items, and how items are promoted through menu copy, photographs, flyers, and promotions.

ALCOHOLIC BEVERAGE SERVICE

A wide variety of alcohol-related laws exist throughout the United States. Managers have a responsibility to know and carefully follow all applicable laws.

WWW: Internet Assistant

For an example of one restaurant group's approach to providing consumer information about menu items, visit the Burger King site at www.burgerking.com

Background

Alcohol is a drug that has historically been used to treat disease. It is also a substance that has, for many people, an addictive characteristic and is classified as a **depressant.**

> **DEPRESSANT   A substance that lowers the rates of vital body activities.**

Society tightly regulates the dispensing of many depressants. Pharmacists, for example, must go to school for many years in order to be permitted to legally dispense tranquilizers, Valium, and other depressants with prescriptions from medical doctors who are licensed to so prescribe. Alcohol, in contrast, can, in many states, be provided by an 18-year-old bartender or server with little, if any, training.

The alcohol content in the standard servings (drinks) of beer (12 ounces), table wine (5 ounces), and distilled spirits ($1\frac{1}{2}$ ounces in a mixed drink) is equal. The service of all alcoholic beverages must be treated in the same serious manner. Employees must realize that it is not what they serve, but how much they serve, that is most important.

> **BLOOD ALCOHOL LEVEL (BAL) A percent measurement of the concentration level of alcohol in the bloodstream. (Also known as blood alcohol content or concentration [BAC].) For example, in some states a BAC of .08 is considered the legal limit for a person to operate a motor vehicle.**

The amount of alcohol consumed by an individual in a specific time period is measured by the individual's **blood alcohol level (BAL).**

Many factors, in addition to the number of drinks consumed, influence an individual's BAL. The liver digests alcohol at a constant rate of about one drink per hour; a 150-pound man typically reaches a BAL of .10 by drinking two to four drinks in one hour. The effects of increasing BALs are shown in the following chart:

BAL LEVEL	EFFECT
.06 – .10	Significant decrease in reaction time and visual abilities
.11 – .15	Slurred speech and volatile emotions
.22 – .25	Staggering, difficulty in talking, and blurred vision
.40	Induced coma
.50	Cessation of breathing and heart failure

Alcohol affects individuals differently. It has the chemical and physical properties of a drug, and, as with many sedatives, its basic effect is sleepiness. It causes euphoria at a low dosage but can result in reduced memory, judgment, and intellectual functioning. Increasing dosages produce a hypnotic state, numbness, coma, and, in some cases of overdose, even death.

Specific BALs are used to define legal **intoxication,** but managers cannot easily test guests for BAL. Serving alcohol to an intoxicated guest is illegal. For this reason, a manager must rely on legal knowledge, operational procedures, and staff training programs to avoid doing so. Serving alcohol is a privilege with great responsibility attached to it. It is regulated by law and cannot be taken lightly.

INTOXICATION (LEGAL)   The point at which an individual's BAL equals or exceeds the standard established by the state.

Each state regulates the sale of alcohol as it sees fit, but in all cases a **liquor licensee** must apply for and obtain a **liquor license** or permit to sell alcohol.

LIQUOR LICENSEE   An individual or entity that has been issued a liquor license by the proper state authority.

In addition to licensing, special rules may apply to specific situations in which alcohol is sold. In each case, however, its service is tightly regulated.

LIQUOR LICENSE   A state permit for the sale and/or service of alcoholic beverages.

Alcohol Service Liability

Who should be responsible for the sometimes negative effects of alcohol consumption? When intoxicated individuals have caused damage or injury to themselves or others, laws impose some portion of responsibility on those who sell or serve alcohol. Consider Robert. If Robert is 25 years old, drives to the grocery store, buys a case of beer, goes home and overindulges in alcohol, most would say it is his right to do so even if excessive drinking is unwise. If, however, Robert was 17, enters a bar, overindulges in alcohol served to him by a bartender, and while driving home kills an innocent pedestrian, most would agree that Robert, the bartender, and/or the bartender's employer all share some responsibility for the tragic result of his intoxication. Laws have been enacted in all states to prevent the sale of alcohol to minors and to those who are intoxicated. These laws typically provide punishment for situations such as the following:

- Minor in possession
- Minor driving while intoxicated (DWI)
- Possession of fake identification
- Adult purchase of alcohol for a minor
- Restaurant or bar that sells alcohol to a minor

Third-Party Liability. To understand the complex laws that regulate liability for illegally serving alcohol, managers must understand that there can be at least three parties involved in an incident resulting from the illegal sale of alcohol:

- **First Party:** The individual buying and/or consuming the alcohol
- **Second Party:** The establishment selling or dispensing the alcohol
- **Third Party:** An individual not directly involved in a specific situation relating to the sale or consumption of alcohol

In the preceding example of the underage drinker, Robert is the first party, the bar serving the alcohol to Robert is the second party, and the innocent pedestrian is the third party.

There is a misconception that the law has only recently established potential responsibility for an entity that serves alcohol to an intoxicated person. That is really not the case. Historically, a property that negligently served alcohol to an obviously intoxicated guest could be sued for negligence if harm came to the guest (and a jury could consider the contributory negligence of the guest). What is relatively new in many areas is that **third-party liability** can also be imposed on those who serve alcohol.

> **THIRD-PARTY LIABILITY** A legal concept stating that the second party in an alcohol transaction is liable for the acts of the first party and also for any harm suffered by a third party as a result of the first party's actions.

Managers must understand their responsibility and resulting liability when serving alcohol. There is a difference between a host who holds a party where alcohol is served and an establishment licensed to sell alcohol.

Social Host Liability. Historically, courts have not found those who host social parties where alcohol is served to be liable for the actions of their intoxicated guests. Although this position may change, the current thinking of most courts is that a **social host** has no common-law duty to stop service of alcohol to an intoxicated adult guest.

> **SOCIAL HOST** A nonlicensed provider of alcohol, typically at a party or similar gathering.

There are several reasons that a social host is not held to the same standard of care as a licensed provider of alcohol. Consider Ruma, who hosts a party in his home. In analyzing the situation, it may be noted that:

- Ruma's guests will likely make their own decisions about how much to drink.

- It is unlikely that Ruma has acquired the knowledge and training to identify those who have become intoxicated.

- He has no effective means of controlling the number of drinks consumed by his guests.

- If many guests attend his party, it will be difficult to know who, if anyone, is becoming intoxicated.

Despite the court's position on social host liability, the slogan "Friends don't let friends drive drunk" is a good rule. Ruma should be responsible and cautious about allowing guests unlimited alcohol consumption.

Managers should understand that the courts will not view their operations like that of a social host. As a license holder, the manager and the operation will be held responsible for alcohol service in a very different way.

Dram Shop Liability. Before the 1990s, most courts did not hold those licensed to serve liquor responsible for damages sustained by a third party resulting from the intoxication of a liquor licensee's customer. Today, nearly every state has established dram shop laws that impose third-party liability on those who sell or serve alcohol.

> **DRAM SHOP A name given to a variety of state laws establishing a liquor licensee's third-party liability.**

Under the dram shop legislation of most states, liquor licensees are responsible for harm and damages to both first and third parties, subject to any **contributory negligence** offsets, if the following circumstances exist:

> **CONTRIBUTORY NEGLIGENCE Negligent conduct by the complaining party (plaintiff) that contributes to the cause of the injuries.**

- The individual served was intoxicated.

- The individual was a clear danger to him- or herself and others.

- Intoxication was the cause of the subsequent harm.

WHAT WOULD YOU DO?

Mark entered a restaurant's bar, sat down, and, according to eyewitnesses, uttered just a single word to the bartender: "Draft."

Because the bartender had only one brand of beer on draft, she pulled the beer, handed it to Mark, and accepted the five-dollar bill offered in payment. Mark left the bar 15 minutes later without having said a word to anyone and left the change from his five-dollar bill on the bar.

Subsequently, Mark was involved in an auto accident in which a ten-year-old boy was injured. The boy's parents are suing the restaurant and a bar where Mark had consumed ten beers in three hours before driving to the restaurant. The bartender wants to know whether she will be held liable and asks you, the restaurant manager.

What would you do (say) to the bartender?

Common law held an innkeeper or tavern operator responsible for harm to drinkers if they injured themselves after consuming too much alcohol. Now, as can be seen in the following excerpt from one state's dram shop law, the server of alcohol can be held responsible for injuries to third parties.

If any person, by himself or his agent, sells any alcoholic liquor to an intoxicated person, and such purchaser, in consequence of such intoxication, thereafter injures the person or property of another, such seller shall pay just damages to the person injured, up to the amount of twenty thousand dollars, or to persons injured in consequence of such intoxication up to an aggregate amount of fifty thousand dollars . . . provided the aggrieved person(s) give written notice to such seller within sixty days of the occurrence of such injury to person or property of his or their intention to bring an action under this section. . . . Such notice shall specify the time, the date and the person to whom such sale was made, the name and address of the person injured or whose property was damaged, and the time, date and place where the injury to person or property occurred.

Training for Responsible Service

Many state legislatures limit the liability of those who serve alcohol by enacting regulations that reduce, to some degree, the liability of properties that thoroughly train employees involved in the sale of alcohol.

A manager's greatest area of alcoholic beverage liability is related to serving those who are underage and/or intoxicated. To help limit this liability,

WWW: Internet Assistant

To learn more about TIPS, visit the following Web site: www. gettips.com.

servers of alcoholic beverages must be well trained, and training should be documented and ongoing. Usually, responsible alcohol server training is mandated or strongly encouraged. The absence of this training would be harmful in the event of a lawsuit alleging the irresponsible service of alcohol. The National Restaurant Association, the American Hotel and Motel Association, and many private organizations provide excellent training materials that can help make training easier. Training for Intervention Procedures (TIPS) is an excellent responsible server program. TIPS incorporates a commonsense approach to serving alcohol responsibly in a variety of settings.

Approved Course. The training program used will likely need approval by the agency monitoring alcohol service in the area. If an in-house training program is developed, it too must be submitted for approval. The best nationally available training programs will likely be preapproved for use in your area, but it is the manager's responsibility to make certain of this. Never purchase or use a nonapproved program. (A jury may perceive the use of such training as an indication that the manager was not serious about responsible alcohol server training.)

Whether a manager creates a responsible server program or purchases and implements one of the many for sale, it is important to ensure that the program addresses several issues.

Alcohol Absorption into the Bloodstream. An understanding of how alcohol works in the body is crucial to understanding the server's role in responsible alcohol service. Servers need to know the basics of alcohol absorption and the factors affecting blood alcohol level (BAL), including:

- *Body weight:* The larger the body, the more the alcohol is diluted. Given the same amount of alcohol, a large person will be less affected by the alcohol than a smaller person.

- *Food consumption:* The consumption of food slows the rate at which alcohol is absorbed into the system. In addition, different foods affect absorption rates differently.

- *Amount of sleep:* Tired people feel the effects of alcohol more than those who are well rested.

- *Age:* Younger people feel the effects of alcohol more quickly than older people.

- *Health:* The liver plays an important part in removing alcohol from the system; those with liver problems may be more likely to become intoxicated.

- *Medication:* Many medications do not mix well with alcohol; sometimes they can be dangerous.

- *General metabolism:* Some people absorb alcohol faster than others.

Legal and False Identification. Many minors wishing to drink obtain false identification (ID) cards or papers in an effort to gain access to places where they can buy alcoholic beverages. Managers are not expected to know whether a minor is presenting a false ID to purchase alcohol, but they must use reasonable care in spotting those who do possess and attempt to use those documents. A major component of any responsible alcohol server program is instruction on the identification of false IDs. Provide instruction in the following topic areas:

- Alteration of type style, including font and point size, in an ID document

- Cut-and-paste techniques used to create an ID document

- Physical identification/picture match

- Relamination detection

- Random information verification (address, Social Security number, etc.)

- List of qualifying ID documents

WHAT WOULD YOU DO?

Michele entered a restaurant's lounge. She was stopped briefly by a security guard, who inspected her photo ID as he had been trained to do during a one-hour orientation class he attended on the first day of work.

The photo ID she presented showed her age to be 21 years and 3 months. The photo on the picture ID was clearly her own. She was not asked to remove the ID from her wallet. Michele entered the bar and, over three hours, consumed five drinks, each containing approximately 1.5 ounces of 80-proof alcohol.

After leaving the lounge, Michele was involved in a traffic accident that seriously injured a man. His family sued Michele and the owner of the restaurant/lounge when it was revealed that Michele was only 20 years old and not of legal age to drink alcohol.

What would you do if you were the owner?

Early Intervention. It is against the law to serve an intoxicated person, but it is often a challenge to identify a person who is intoxicated. The number of drinks served over a given time yields an indication of possible BAL, but many other factors affect it. (See the preceding discussion of BAL.)

An effective server training program teaches servers to note observable behavioral changes that occur with advancing stages of intoxication. When noted, there are specific techniques to help limit the quantity of alcohol served and, if necessary, to refuse service completely.

Documentation of Training Effectiveness. It is not enough for employees to attend training sessions; they must also demonstrate mastery of the training content. The best off-the-shelf materials have examination components to test trainee competence. The tests should be both reliable and valid. Examinations should be scored by an independent source, and results should be reported to managers promptly. If a manager must defend the use of a particular server training program in court, the defense almost always will need to address the program's actual effectiveness. An inability to demonstrate server training results may damage the manager's ability to prove that the training was conducted in a responsible manner.

WHAT WOULD YOU DO?

Bill attended a reception at a restaurant with an open bar. Over $2\frac{1}{2}$ hours, it was determined that he consumed approximately nine drinks. There were three bartender stations available; no bartender personally served him more than three drinks. One of the bartenders finally did detect a significant change in Bill's behavior, and when Bill requested another drink, that bartender refused to serve him and called a manager.

The manager talked with Bill, determined that he was likely intoxicated, asked for and received his car keys, and instructed a worker to drive Bill home and give the car keys to his wife. This was done; however, an hour after being taken home Bill was involved in a fatal one-car accident. His wife brought suit under dram shop legislation. She stated that her husband was upset at his treatment by the manager and that she "couldn't stop him" when he took the car keys from her. She held the operation responsible because "They got him drunk." As additional evidence of irresponsibility, she pointed to the tipping policy in place during open bars. (Bartenders are paid a percentage of the revenue from the alcoholic beverages served. This leads, claimed her attorney, to overpouring, as bartenders seek to build revenue and, in so doing, their own income.)

What would you do?

MANAGER'S "TO DO" LIST

Review the following recommendations proposed in this chapter. Analyze your interest in and need for implementing these recommendations by completing the columns on the right side of the form. Remember, when task assignments are made, time requirements for completion should also be stated. Follow up, as improvement activities evolve, to ensure that your property is moving closer to the goal of minimizing litigation risks.

Recommended Procedures	In Place Now?			Needed to Implement			Assigned To	Completion Date
	Yes	No	N/A*	Policy	Training	Other		
Review your last health inspection score with your inspector. Make sure you understand all deficiencies and seek the inspector's advice for improvement.								
Meet with key members of your team to detail procedures for foodborne illness claims if you are off-site when a claim is made.								
Review food and beverage holding temperatures/standards. Make sure they are documented and well communicated to staff.								
Analyze standard recipes to determine whether there are any ingredients known to cause allergic reactions. If there are, eliminate the ingredient(s) or the menu item or ensure that customers are clearly informed about the use of the ingredient(s).								
Examine your menu carefully for terms relating to Truth-in-Menu or an item's health benefits. Make sure statements are accurate.								
Review tipping/service charge policies and ensure that these are stated on the menu or that customers are clearly informed about them before they order.								
Examine the third-party liability portion of insurance policies with your insurance carrier.								

*N/A = Not Applicable

Recommended Procedures	In Place Now?			Needed to Implement			Assigned To	Completion Date
	Yes	No	N/A*	Policy	Training	Other		
Contact your local alcoholic beverage regulatory agency to determine whether the alcohol server program you use meets standards; document the response.								
Check employee files of all who serve alcohol; make sure you have documented their completion of a qualified alcohol server training program. Offer the training frequently.								
Prepare and deliver a training segment for your staff explaining third-party liability.								

For more information and suggestions
log onto www.hospitalitylawyer.com.

*N/A = Not Applicable

CONSULTANT'S CORNER

What Would You Do? (page 273)

Not a good situation; the property is in a tough spot. The interaction with Olga's lawyer will likely include you and your attorney. There is not much you can do other than answer questions honestly and completely.

The presence of MSG probably *should* have been revealed, or the recipe modified to eliminate its use. From now on, if any ingredient used is unusual or known to cause allergic reactions, reveal this to your customers *before* they order. Better yet, avoid using ingredients that can cause allergic reactions.

What Would You Do? (page 274)

Contact your attorney and insurance company. This one is not likely to go away. The question here will be fairly straightforward. Was the chocolate served at a temperature too hot to be safe? The fact that Enriqueta knew it was hot is not very important, nor are the specifics about how the chocolate was spilled. You, as manager, must demonstrate that the drink was served at an appropriate temperature. Ask your beverage equipment manufacturer for guidelines about proper temperature setting. Your trade association may also publish serving temperature recommendations. Be careful if you cannot really be sure what the serving temperature was (which would be the case, for example, if the server microwaved water and then added a chocolate powder to make the hot chocolate). Be sure to establish standards and ensure that all food and beverages are served at their proper temperatures. Frequent checks of temperature-holding equipment are critical.

What Would You Do? (page 276)

You can't ask the police to help you collect your money; they won't. You may also have difficulty calming the customer, because the service was not good. Although a tip is voluntary, a service charge is not. You must decide between the poor "goodwill" you will incur and the money you are owed. It may be best to waive the charge this time. In the future, make sure that every customer knows, ahead of time, what the charges will be. (Consider stating the charge on the menu.) If you do, your ability to enforce the service charge, even if the customer alleges poor service, is enhanced.

What Would You Do? (page 284–285)

Food and beverage operators have an obligation to serve alcohol responsibly. A legal standard that has been established in almost every state is to not serve a person who is obviously intoxicated. In this particular set of circumstances, it would be very difficult for the restaurant to be held responsible, given the fact that Mark failed to display any outward signs of intoxication and/or that his consumption was not unusual. Obviously, there will be a different situation for the prior place of service.

The bartender in this case may be sued but will probably be dismissed from the case prior to its going to trial.

What Would You Do? (page 287 & 288)

Most jurors will not be impressed with only one hour of training for those who check IDs. When an owner is diligent in checking IDs, this helps limit liability. (The same is true for server training.) The best approach here is to demonstrate how well trained your staff is. Serving minors is illegal, as is serving intoxicated persons. Liability is reduced when a manager can show that great care has been used to prevent violations. Train, Train, Train!

What Would You Do? (page 288)

Even if the manager and servers perform well, as in this case, it is important that policies and procedures do not make it appear that the operation is irresponsible. The lawyer will cite the tipping policy as evidence that the restaurant was encouraging the overconsumption of alcoholic beverages by its guests. This will be an issue any time drinks are discounted.

In this situation it does not appear that the restaurant served the guest while he was intoxicated. In addition, it appears to have used due diligence and reasonable care in delivering the guest safely to his home and entrusting the car keys to his wife.

The outcome might be different in this situation if, in fact, the restaurant had continued to serve the guest while he was intoxicated.

12

LEGAL ASPECTS OF SAFETY AND SECURITY MANAGEMENT

MANAGER'S BRIEF

Managers reading this chapter will learn that the safety of customers and employees is critically important, as is protecting a restaurant's assets. They will learn basics important in the design of safety programs to help protect people and security programs to help protect property. Procedures to protect a restaurant from consumer theft, fraudulent payments, and internal theft are presented. Finally, managers will learn how to devise, implement, and assess emergency plans to safeguard individuals and assets and to respond to crises threatening people, property, or the business itself.

CREATING A PROTECTED ENVIRONMENT

Managers have no task more important than taking reasonable care to protect the safety of employees and customers. They must also protect business assets. These responsibilities require an examination of routine safety and security processes and emergency procedures.

Safety and Security Management

Managers are responsible for numerous activities designed to protect people and property, which are part of a **safety program** and a **security program.**

SAFETY PROGRAM
Procedures and activities to ensure the physical protection and good health of customers and employees.

SECURITY PROGRAM
Procedures and activities designed to protect the property and assets of customers, employees, and the business.

Policies, procedures, and training programs constituting safety and security programs must be planned, implemented, and continually assessed. Large restaurant companies employ Directors of Safety and Security, who design and encourage on-site safety and security efforts. In smaller restaurants, the manager is responsible to meet the expectations of the general public, customers, employees, and others who will be protected from harm. Failure to do so can result in tremendous liability if lawsuits occur.

Courts will not expect managers to guarantee, against all possible calamities, the safety of everyone coming in contact with a restaurant. They will expect managers to use good judgment when managing procedures that show concern for the well-being of people and the security of their property.

WHAT WOULD YOU DO?

Angelo frequently dined at a particular restaurant. One day he sat down, and the wooden chair collapsed; his neck was injured as he fell. He sued, charging negligence, based on the belief that the normal wear and tear of chairs is something the manager should have known would occur, and that an inspection program should have been in place to identify weakened chairs.

What would you do if you were the manager?

Crisis Management

Managers sometimes face challenges that are anything but minor. Consider Samir, who manages a restaurant near a community that has been destroyed by a tornado. He knows that storms often occur with little warning and wonders what he and his staff would do if a storm threatened his restaurant. He also wonders what he can do now to prepare in case a tornado strikes his property.

CRISIS   An occurrence with potential to jeopardize the health and well-being of individuals and/or the business.

Examples of **crisis** situations having potential for devastating damage to restaurants include:

- Power outages
- Vandalism
- Arson/ fire
- Bomb threats
- Robbery
- Looting
- Severe storms, including
    Hurricanes
    Tornadoes
- Earthquakes
- Floods
- Snow and ice
- Civil disturbances
- Accidents/injuries
- Drug overdoses
- Medical emergencies, including cardiopulmonary resuscitation (CPR)
- Death/suicide of customer or employee
- Intense media scrutiny
- Adversarial governmental agency investigation

Although managers do not have control over some crises, such as storms, it is reasonable to assume that a manager could preplan for them. Crisis management involves preplanning, responding properly during a crisis, and assessing performance afterward to determine whether improvement is possible.

The legal implications of safety, security, and crisis management are important, as are the financial, marketing, public relations, and morale issues associated with creating a protected environment. Managers must keep current on changing trends and products related to customer, employee, and asset safety to ensure the physical safety of those entering their property and to reduce legal liability.

SAFETY AND SECURITY PROGRAMS

It is difficult to provide a step-by-step list of activities which, if implemented, will minimize the chances of accident, injury, or loss. Managers must assess their safety and security program needs, develop and implement programs to address them, and effectively monitor results with the goal of constant improvement.

Advantages of Preplanning

The advantages of a safe and secure environment go beyond protecting customers, employees, and business assets and include:

- *Increased employee morale.* When employees see safety and security programs being implemented, they know this benefits them.

- *Improved management image.* Often, managers are accused of placing the needs of the business ahead of the needs of people. Implementation of safety and security programs demonstrates management's concern for staff and customers and confirms that management cares for people as well as profits.

- *Improved effectiveness in recruiting employees.* Effective safety and security programs can affect recruiting. Consider the parents of a teenage worker counseling their child about a job offer. Uniformed security guards, closed-circuit cameras, and a management dedicated to safety will be important in the decision-making process.

- *Reduced insurance rates.* Insurance companies often reward businesses for safety and security efforts by reducing insurance premiums.

- *Reduced employee costs.* Employees who avoid injury are more productive and reliable than those who do not. Worker's compensation claims are lower in a safe work environment, and lost productivity from injury-related absence is reduced.

- *Improved operating ratios.* A safe and secure facility has lower costs. When theft by customers and employees is reduced, profitability increases. Well-conceived programs to reduce theft and raise awareness about security measures yield lower operating costs and higher gross operating profits.

- *Support if accidents occur.* When accidents do happen, attorneys and managers will want documented evidence that programs were in place to reduce the chance of a mishap. Juries will be interested in whether managers exercised reasonable care in the operation of their property. Attorneys can best do their job when managers have done their job professionally.

- *Increased customer satisfaction.* The restaurant that does not protect its inventory affects the customer. Inventory stockouts and/or the need to increase prices to cover higher costs promote customer dissatisfaction.

- *Marketing advantages.* When a restaurant takes a genuine and documentable proactive stance in safety and security, it becomes easier to market the property to the general public.

- *Reduced likelihood of negative press.* Today's media typically sensationalize misfortunes. Managers can often avoid accidents and thereby escape the negative press that would otherwise result. It is always easier to avoid accidents than to defend oneself in the press.

Four-Step Safety and Security Management Process

Legally, a manager's basic obligation is to act responsibly in the face of threats to people and property. One way to manage those responsibilities is to use a four-step safety and security management process, as described in the following paragraphs.

Recognize the Threat. Safety and security programs start by recognizing that a threat to people or property exists. Consider Tunc, who manages a pizza parlor. Over the past six months, four customers and two employees have complained about vandalism to their cars. Prior to these incidents, he never had a problem. Now he realizes the need to act responsibly to serve the interests of his customers, employees, and their property.

It is common to assess the need for safety and security programs as they relate to:

- Customers and employees and their property
- Other affected persons and their property
- Business assets

A number of safety and security concerns follow. The list is not exhaustive but does indicate areas within a restaurant to be considered in developing a safety and security program.

Areas of Safety and Security Concern

Customers	Employees
- Parking lots	- Work site safety
- Public areas	- Workplace violence
- Dining rooms	- Worker accidents
- Bars and lounges	- Employee locker rooms
- Rest rooms	
- Meeting (function) rooms	

Customers' Property In

- Coatrooms

- Parking lots

Business Assets

- Cash

- Operating supplies

- Food and beverage inventories

- Equipment and serviceware

- Telephone access

All People and Property

- Medical emergency

- Criminal activity

- Natural disaster

- Utility outages

Respond to Threat. After a threat to safety or security is identified, a response can be developed. Responses can include:

- *Training for threat prevention.* If, for example, employee safety is threatened by back injuries caused by improper lifting, training employees in proper lifting techniques may reduce or eliminate that threat.

- *Increased surveillance or patrol.* Sometimes the best response to a threat is to increase necessary scrutiny. In the parking lot problem described earlier, Tunc could increase parking lot monitoring. Routine patrols by management, employees, and an outside security firm or the police may help to deter vandals.

Some safety and security threats can be addressed by using video cameras in stairwells, halls, and storerooms. Often the presence of the camera itself deters crime. (Camera systems can either record activity in an area or show such activity without recording it).

WHAT WOULD YOU DO?

Assume that your restaurant has had two customer assaults in the parking lot in the last three months. You consider installing a closed-circuit video camera (CCVC) system and/or increasing the lighting levels for the lot. You decide to install six cameras that do not record but permit security personnel to "see" all areas of the lot from a central viewing area.

One night after dark, Authella is assaulted in the parking lot while leaving the restaurant. She sues, claiming that the failure to monitor the cameras was a direct cause of her assault. She also states that the cameras' use was deceptive; they gave her a false sense of security because, she says, "The cameras showed that the restaurant cared about my security." According to time sheets provided under subpoena, an employee was assigned to view the cameras in their central location for an average of two hours per night between the hours of 8:00 P.M. and 10:00 P.M. The assault occurred when there was no employee monitoring the cameras.

> **SUBPOENA** A court-authorized order to appear in person at a designated time and location or to produce evidence demanded by the court.

> **DEEP POCKETS** A term used to describe a defendant perceived to be wealthy.

Your attorney states that the property did what could be reasonably expected, and the restaurant should not be held responsible for Authella's injuries.

What would you do?

An owner's right to unlimited monitoring and surveillance, even in that owner's property, is not absolute. Illegally monitoring the behavior of customers and employees can dramatically increase an owner's own legal liability.

Some observers estimate that more than forty percent of U.S. businesses monitor their employees electronically (by listening in on phone calls, by reviewing voice mails, computer files, and e-mail, or by video surveillance). That percentage grows as one considers companies that monitor employees in other ways, such as by conducting searches of lockers, bags, and desks.

There is no single national policy that addresses workplace privacy. Many managers believe they are protecting proprietary business interests by monitoring employees and their work products. In addition, as companies establish work conduct guidelines, such as sexual harassment zero tolerance policies, monitoring helps to ensure compliance. The legality of a particular monitoring technique usually depends on four factors:

1. Did the employee have a legitimate expectation of privacy regarding the item searched or the information, conversation, or area monitored? (In an employee lounge, probably not; in a rest room, absolutely.)

2. Did the employer provide advance notice and/or obtain the employee's

consent for the monitoring activity? (If so, it is difficult for an employee to allege an expectation of privacy.)

3. Was the monitoring done for a work-related purpose, and was it reasonable, given all circumstances? (Generally, courts have allowed searches and monitoring necessary for operating a business—protecting trade secrets, enforcing policies and procedures, etc.)

4. Was the search or monitoring done in a reasonable or appropriate manner? Was it discriminating (in other words, used only on a minority work subgroup)?

Managers who elect to monitor employee activities can implement an employee privacy policy. (See Appendix N.) It can help lessen misunderstandings and legal difficulties to let employees know what is expected of them and allow them to question unclear parts of the policy. Laws are complex and vary by location. An employee privacy policy should be reviewed by your attorney before it is implemented.

Managers can implement other procedures to reduce safety and security problems including:

- *Systematic inspections.* Systematic inspections of facilities can often identify possible safety and security threats. Managers should carefully monitor their property's compliance against accepted standards of a safe and secure operation, and such efforts should be documented. Appendix O shows a Property Safety and Security Checklist used to monitor compliance and document the effort.

- *Modification of facilities.* When the facility itself contributes to a problem, it will require modification. Examples include replacing worn carpets that may cause falls, painting curbs to make them more visible, and adding security lighting. Kitchen equipment must be properly maintained, with repairs made as soon as reasonably possible. Facility defects that are recognized but not acted upon can be damaging in the event of a lawsuit.

- *Establishment of standard procedures.* Routine policies and procedures can be an effective response to safety and security threats. For example, when a restaurant collects cash, the money must be counted and deposited according to specific procedures. Periodic product inventories, plate counts for buffet meals, and signing in and out for management keys are examples of standard operating procedures that affect safety and security.

Implement Program(s). After a safety or security threat is identified and a response is developed, proper implementation becomes important. Large restaurants may have individuals specifically designated for these tasks; in smaller properties every employee may have responsibility for implementation. Large and small properties may be helped with temporary or longer-term assistance by a security guard company. Local law enforcement officials should always be a component of any safety and security efforts.

Safety and Security Departments. Large properties may have a Safety and Security Department, whose manager reports to the General Manager. Staff would be responsible for routine duties such as patrolling the facility, performing inspections, assisting with crime reports, and serving as liaison with insurance carriers. The department would also advise the General Manager on safety and security topics. The Educational Institute of the American Hotel and Motel Association (AH&MA) offers an excellent certification program for some members of a Safety and Security Department.

Security Guards. Managers of smaller properties may contract with a security guard company to help with program implementation. Generally, a guard's role is to:

- Observe the property
- Report observations to management (or police, if needed)
- Intervene only if it can be done safely or to protect the life of a customer or employee
- Record activities and findings

WWW: Internet Assistant

For more information on certification programs from AH&MA's Educational Institute, visit its Web site at www. ei-ahma.org

Engaging security guards is an excellent option when additional help is needed (for example, in the event of large parties or when managers believe additional safety or security protection is warranted). They are not a substitute for a complete and ongoing safety and security program. If guards are to be used, insist that the security guard company do the following:

- Provide an acceptable indemnification/hold harmless agreement
- Supply proof of liability insurance that names the restaurant as an additional insured
- Demonstrate proof that it carries worker's compensation insurance
- Supply a copy of its hiring standards and procedures
- Provide a written agreement as to the specific services it will provide

Safety Committees. A safety committee can help identify and correct safety and security problems. Ideally, it should consist of members from each department, including preproduction, production, and cleanup areas in the kitchen, and bartenders, servers, and hosts in public areas.

Meetings should be scheduled regularly. They need not be long (one hour or less). An agenda for a committee meeting may include the following:

- *Safety and security instruction.* Training videos, new policies and procedures, and related instruction can be presented. Each committee member should see his or her role as "teacher," because a worker's peers can reinforce dissemination of safety and security information.

- *Review of safety concerns.* Members should be informed about actions taken in response to concerns raised in prior meetings. Members must believe that managers will listen to their concerns and take action.

  Any new group concerns should be discussed. Suggestions, corrections, and improvements to safety and security programs should be encouraged.

- *Effectiveness report by manager.* The committee will want to know how they are doing. If accidents have decreased, say so. If they have not, this should also be stated. Let members know that you consider their contributions important to the property's success.

Staff commitment is the most significant resource available to reduce safety and security liability. Establishing a safety committee demonstrates your own commitment and is an excellent way to utilize your staff to improve the operation.

Relationship with Law Enforcement. Establishing and maintaining a good working relationship with local law enforcement officials is important. They can help in several ways:

- **Regularly scheduled meetings.** Meet on a regular basis with law enforcement officials to share mutual concerns and ideas for support. If their help is needed, a personal working relationship will help resolve difficulties quickly and efficiently.

- **Neighborhood business watch programs.** These programs involve business owners reporting any suspicious individuals or activities they encounter.

- **Property safety and security reviews.** Law enforcement officials may conduct a courtesy walk-through of the restaurant to detect possible problems and provide suggestions. They are in a unique position to "see" problems that have not been recognized.

- **Interdiction programs.** Drug enforcement officers or other officials may create an **interdiction program** so that managers and employees can inform interdiction team members in the event that they observe specific behaviors previously identified by the team.

> **INTERDICTION PROGRAM** An arrangement whereby citizens contact police to report suspected criminal activity before a crime is committed.

No law requires people to call the police if they suspect criminal activity is occurring. When you call an interdiction program, you are calling as a concerned citizen. By working together, managers and police can help prevent crimes.

- **Training programs.** Some police departments offer training in crime detection and deterrence. Classes are often free or of low cost and can be attended by managers and subordinates. Personal safety, preventing employee theft, credit card fraud, identifying counterfeit money, and detecting drug trafficking are among the possible programs.

Monitor Results. After safety and security programs are implemented, managers must be concerned about their effectiveness. If a program is not reducing or eliminating the threat to people or property, it should be reviewed and modified. Consider Burak, a delicatessen manager. In reviewing his store's sanitation performance, he noticed an average of three critical violations per inspector's visit. Burak purchased a food safety video and required each employee to view it. Now, 12 months later, the number of violations per visit is unchanged. He knows he must do more to ensure food safety. Continued monitoring indicates when program modification is required. Managers are in a much stronger legal position if they can document that a safety and security program exists and that it is effective.

Here are some indicators that can be used to measure safety and security programs:

- Number of inspections performed
- Inspection or quality scores
- Number of incidents reported
- Dollar amount of losses sustained
- Number of insurance claims filed
- Number of lawsuits filed
- Number of serious or minor accidents
- Number of lost workdays
- Amount of insurance premium increase (decrease)
- Number of drills or training exercises correctly performed

Less tangible measures include customer satisfaction scores, improved employee morale, and enhanced product marketability. Unless managers know that a program has reduced problems, they may be lured into a false sense of security that their program "works."

WHAT WOULD YOU DO?

Eun-Young was a catering supervisor who usually worked out of her home office. She communicated with her manager's office by telephone, fax, and modem, all of which were installed in her home by Advance Technology, a company that her manager selected to supply equipment and services.

When Eun-Young's modem stopped working one day, she contacted her manager's office which, in turn, called Advance Technology, requesting that a service technician be dispatched. The technician arrived, but in the course of his visit, assaulted Eun-Young. The technician was apprehended by the police and convicted of felony assault (his third such conviction in three years).

Eun-Young sued Advance Technology, claiming negligent hiring. In addition, her attorney advised her manager that she was injured on the job and would be making a workers' compensation claim.

What would you do if you were Eun-Young's manager?

CRIMES AGAINST RESTAURANT BUSINESSES

Managers must be aware of and know how to counter threats and criminal activities aimed at their businesses. Although safety and security plans may protect against some types of property theft, measures for preventing the theft of services, fraudulent payments, and internal theft—the topic of this section—require different procedures and extra vigilance.

Customer Theft of Services

Sometimes customers are legitimately unhappy about the products and/or levels of service received during a meal. They may be angry and protest all or a portion of their bills. Managers must help calm these customers and develop a solution that is fair to the customer and to the business.

In other cases individuals consume services with no intention of paying for them. In the restaurant industry, these customers are said to have "skipped," meaning they have skipped paying the cashier. The loss of revenue can be substantial if managers do not take preventive measures.

Every state has passed laws prohibiting individuals from consuming hospitality services without paying for them. These laws are strict and often carry large fines or prison terms for those found guilty. The provisions of state statutes vary widely, so managers should check with an attorney to learn the specific provisions of applicable laws.

In a busy restaurant it is sometimes easy for a customer or an entire party to leave without settling their bill unless all staff members are vigilant. The following are procedures to help reduce food and beverage skips:

■ If customers are to pay after consuming food and/or beverages, servers should present the bill promptly when diners are finished.

■ If there is a cashier in a central location in the dining area, make sure that the cashier is available and visible at all times.

■ If servers collect for their own customers' charges, instruct the servers to return to the table promptly after presenting the bill to obtain payment.

■ Be observant of exit doors near rest rooms or other areas that provide opportunities for customers to exit without easily being seen.

■ In a hotel that allows customers to charge food and beverage purchases to a room or a master bill, verify the customer's identity with both a printed and a signed name.

■ If an employee sees a customer leave without paying, the manager should be notified immediately.

■ When approaching customers who have left without paying, the manager should ask whether they have "forgotten" to pay (usually the customer will then pay the bill).

■ Should a guest refuse to pay or if he or she flees, the manager should note the following on an incident report:

    Number of customers involved

    Amount of bill

    Physical description of customer(s)

    Vehicle description, if a car is seen, and license plate number, if possible

    Time and date of the incident

    Name of the server(s) who actually served the customer(s) and who notified the manager

If a guest does leave without paying, the police should be notified. In no case should staff members or managers attempt to physically detain the customer. First, the risk of injury to the employee is great and the liability that can be involved should an employee be hurt is far greater than the value of a skipped food and beverage bill.

Fraudulent Payment

Credit cards, cash, and personal checks are the most common forms of payment for restaurant services. Unfortunately, all three can be used fraudulently.

Credit Cards. There is a federal law prohibiting the fraudulent use of credit cards. Individuals who fraudulently use credit cards in interstate commerce to obtain goods or services of $1,000 or more in any year are subject to fines of up to $10,000 and prison terms of up to ten years.

Today credit cards are issued with three-dimensional designs, magnetic strips, encoded numbers, and other features to reduce consumer fraud. Moreover, electronic credit card verification systems are fast, accurate, and designed to reduce loss.

Restaurants should always use a credit card verification service even if the number of or amount of charges is relatively small. These services charge a fee but guarantee that the restaurant will receive payment for legitimate card charges even if the cardholder does not pay the bank issuing the monthly statement. Sometimes managers face a challenge with a credit card holder who pays the full bill with his or her card but later protests all or part of that bill. Unless the customer can be satisfied, the restaurant may have to defend its procedures.

Each major credit card issuer has its own procedures, and managers should be familiar with those required by the cards they accept. Credit card companies have a responsibility to the restaurant and to the cardholder. To be fair to both, the card issuer requires the restaurant to follow its procedures for accepting cards and billing for services. Then, if customers have a legitimate complaint, they will be treated fairly. At the same time, restaurants are protected from fraud.

The following are general procedures that should be followed in accepting any type of credit card:

- Confirm that the name on the card is the same as that of the individual presenting the card for payment. (A driver's license or other acceptable forms of identification can be used.)
- Examine the card for obvious signs of alteration.
- Confirm that the card is valid; that is, that the date of usage is within the time period permitted.
- Compare the signature on the card with that written by the customer paying with the card.
- The employee processing the charge should initial the credit card receipt.

- Carbon paper, if used, should be destroyed.

- Credit card charge slips not yet processed should be kept secure to limit the possibility of theft.

- Do not issue cash in exchange for credit card charges.

- Do not write in tip amounts. These should be supplied by the customer only (unless the tip is mandatory and the customer has been told of that fact in advance).

- Tally credit card charges on a daily basis. Make sure that the aforementioned procedures have been followed. (If not, corrective action should be taken immediately.)

Cash. There are two usual ways in which guests who use cash can defraud a restaurant. The "quick change" artist intentionally tries to confuse or distract the cashier when paying a bill. The best defense is to instruct cashiers to take their time and make change carefully. Handling cash is confusing only when cashiers do so too quickly or carelessly.

Some individuals may present counterfeit money. The federal government has done much to make counterfeiting more difficult. Redesigned bills that began circulation in the late 1990s are one example of this effort. Even so, managers and applicable staff should participate in a counterfeit money detection training program if offered by local law enforcement officials.

Personal Checks. The acceptance of personal checks presents a variety of risks. Customers may write NSF (nonsufficient funds) checks or checks on closed accounts, on accounts from nonexistent banks, or on accounts owned by other people.

There are services that preauthorize the validity of personal checks, similar to credit card services. However, these services may not reimburse the restaurant for the amount of checks returned as unpayable by a bank. To minimize the acceptance of checks that cannot be collected on, use the following procedures:

- Confirm that the name on the check is the same as that of the individual presenting the check for payment. Note the source of the identification on the check used to verify the identity of the check payer (for example, driver's license number, student identification number, etc.).

- Establish a maximum amount for which a check can be written without preauthorization directly from the bank shown on the check.

- Ensure that the check has:
    The correct name of your restaurant
    The correct date
    The correct dollar amount
    The same numerical amount and written dollar amount
    A clearly identifiable address of the issuing bank
    A signature that matches the name on the check

- Examine the check carefully for any signs of alteration.

- Deposit all checks received promptly with your own bank.

- Keep a list of individuals who have passed uncollectable checks, and have cashiers refer to this list each time they are asked to accept a check.

- Insist that all checks include a telephone number and address.

- Accept out-of-town checks carefully or not at all, as these checks may be more difficult to collect on.

- Employees accepting checks should initial and date them under their initials.

If a check is returned because the account is closed or has insufficient funds to cover the amount, contact local law enforcement officials for collection assistance. Accepting partial payment of the check's original amount in exchange for not prosecuting the check writer is usually not a good idea. (This suggests that you are treating the check amount as a "loan" to be paid back rather than a debt to be paid immediately.) Local laws vary; managers should be familiar with them.

Internal Theft

The internal theft of assets by employees generally takes one of two forms: the theft of financial assets (embezzlement) or the theft of company property.

Embezzlement. Guarding your restaurant against embezzlement involves implementing and maintaining financial controls to verify:

- Product sales receipts
- Service sales receipts

- Deposits
- Accounts receivable
- Accounts payable

One procedure many managers use is to **bond** employees whose work includes handling financial assets.

Restaurant employees can also defraud customers. Common techniques include:

> **BOND(ING) An insurance agreement in which the insurer guarantees payment to an employer in the event of financial loss caused by the actions of a specific employee.**

- Charging for items not purchased and keeping the overcharge.

- Changing totals on credit card charges after the customer has left or imprinting additional credit card charges and pocketing the cash difference.

- Mis-adding legitimate charges to create a higher total and keeping the overcharge.

- Purposely shortchanging customers when making change and keeping the extra change.

- Charging a higher-than-authorized price, recording the proper price, and keeping the overcharge.

Theft of Restaurant Property. There is always potential for the theft of property (assets) because employees can personally use many restaurant items, ranging from food and beverage products to trash bags. Although it may not be possible to prevent all employee theft, a number of measures can be helpful:

- Screen employees.
  Use preemployment reference and criminal background checks.
  Consider the use of psychological prescreening tests.
- Create an antitheft atmosphere.
  Enforce all theft-related policies fairly and consistently.
  Tell employees the real cost of theft and how it affects them.
  Reward employees for efforts to reduce theft.

- Eliminate opportunities to steal

   Do not allow "off the clock" employees to remain on the property.

   Only managers should be allowed to purchase food and beverage products for their personal off-site use (and many restaurants do not permit sales to any staff member in efforts to reduce "favoritism."

   Eliminate opportunities for employees to enter or leave with unexamined packages, bags, knapsacks, etc.

   Implement effective inventory controls.

Security Safeguards

Theft by customers or employees greatly affects a manager's ability to operate profitably. Laws may help protect the operation and, perhaps, even recover damages. However, a restaurant's being the plaintiff in a lawsuit initiated by the manager can be just as costly and disruptive as defending the business against someone else's lawsuit. The best way to protect the restaurant is by establishing safeguards and procedures to prevent the various kinds of theft. Some police departments have training sessions addressing forgeries, bad checks, counterfeit money, stolen credit cards, and threats to internal security. This training, the manager's own vigilance, and effective antitheft procedures are all important. Train employees to consistently use procedures helpful in preventing crimes against the restaurant.

CRISIS MANAGEMENT PROGRAMS

The crisis management needs of restaurants vary, based on numerous factors. For example, physical location may affect the type of crisis (earthquake or tornado) and the potential frequency of a crisis (such as robbery in a high-crime area) a restaurant is likely to experience. Regardless of location, power outages, fires, workplace violence, and a variety of other circumstances can create a crisis. Managers must be ready.

Precrisis Planning

Waiting to prepare for a crisis until it occurs does not make sense. Consider Maximillian, who was dining at a steakhouse. A piece of steak lodged in his throat. No staff member had been trained for this emergency, and had it not been for a fellow diner's administering the Heimlich maneuver, Maximillian may have died. If this had happened, it is possible that the restaurant would have faced the liability costs and poor publicity arising from a lawsuit. Everyone would question: "Why wasn't the restaurant prepared for such an occurrence?"

A manager should develop and practice an **emergency plan** that identifies likely situations of crisis and details the property's response to them. Once created, the plan should be implemented.

> **EMERGENCY PLAN   The procedure(s) implemented in response to a crisis.**

Emergency Plan Development. Managers should be ready for every crisis they can foresee. Many situations will require similar responses. Training staff in the proper response to general medical emergencies prepares them for responding to slips and falls, employee accidents, customer injuries, and other safety threats. Preparing an evacuation plan will be helpful in a fire- or weather-related disaster or power outage.

All crises have some common characteristics:

- Extreme urgency
- Stopping of normal operations
- Human suffering and/or financial loss
- Potential media scrutiny
- Threat to the restaurant's reputation

Because a crisis is so potentially damaging, the emergency plan should be clearly written. It need not be unduly complicated. A planned response should be clear and simple, regardless of the number of procedures required. In its simplest form, a written emergency plan should address:

- The nature of the crisis
- Who is to be informed if a crisis may or does occur
- What is to be done in response
- When it is to be done
- Who is to do it
- Who communicates with whom about the crisis

Here are situations for which emergency plans may be developed:

- Fire
- Storms
    Hurricane
    Tornado
    Earthquake
    Winter
- Power failure
- Injury/accident
- Illness or death of customer or employee
- Evacuation of nonworking elevator
- Robbery
- Bomb threat
- Interactions with media personnel

When an emergency plan is completed, it should be copied so that each manager and affected employee can have immediate access to it. It is important to review and revise the emergency plan on a regular basis. Appendix P shows the information required in an emergency telephone list—one component of an emergency plan.

Emergency Plan Practice. After the emergency plan is developed, the required procedures should be practiced. Implementing an emergency plan may involve activities ranging from plan review to an actual run-through. Appendix Q shows an emergency plan related to a fire. The emergency plan itself becomes a blueprint for practice sessions.

Managers must determine which section(s) of the emergency plan should be practiced and with what frequency. The objective of practicing is to emphasize the most likely and most serious threats and to allow all employees with crisis responsibilities to fully understand and be able to perform their roles.

Crisis Response

If and when a crisis occurs, there will be a response from the manager, the staff, customers, and, perhaps, the media. This section examines the likely response from each party.

Management Response. During a crisis, events unfold rapidly. Managers who have prepared and practiced an emergency plan are more likely to respond professionally than those who have not.

A manager's response to a crisis depends on its nature. Consider Scot, who manages a pizza shop employing delivery drivers. One night he is notified at home that a driver has been assaulted and robbed at gunpoint. This event has far-reaching effects. Certainly it affects the assaulted employee. The other drivers may also be affected, as they may now fear an assault. This result can have an effect on recruiting new employees and retaining existing workers. The customer base and the image of Scot's business may be affected if the robbery is widely reported in the media. Insurance coverage and premiums may be affected, as may Scot's training programs related to robbery. Although it is not possible to "undo" the assault, Scot must act professionally with regard to both his employees and the business.

Appendix R identifies a manager's major responsibilities during a crisis. They can be modified to become part of each manager's and supervisor's orientation program. The fact that these guidelines exist and that managers have been thoroughly trained in them can help reduce legal liability in the event of a crisis.

Staff Response. Staff members' responses to a crisis are just as important as the manager's response. Their function is to help protect people and property without risking danger to themselves. In a fire, staff can notify customers, help to evacuate a building, secure assets (if time permits), and help calm anxious customers. These roles take on extra significance as one realizes that a manager cannot be everywhere during a crisis. In the case of a robbery or suicide attempt, the manager may not even be aware of the crisis until it has substantially passed.

It is vital that employees do nothing in a crisis to further endanger themselves, customers, or the business. Consider the supervisor who refuses to immediately summon medical help for an injured customer because he fears the restaurant may incur cost or liability if it appears that the operation is demonstrating responsibility for the injury. If the guest dies and it can be shown the supervisor's actions contributed directly to the death, the restaurant will face greater exposure to liability and costs than if the supervisor had called an ambulance. Courts will hold the manager and employees to the standard of reasonable care. Reasonable people do not value money above life. No property or amount of money is worth risking personal harm to anyone on the property. Remember to "protect people before property."

Workers themselves can become crisis victims. The threat of harm from robbery, vandalism, and even the actions of co-workers is real. Good employees will not remain with an organization that does not actively demonstrate concern for their safety. Effective managers take the security steps needed to protect employees.

If a crisis occurs, a manager must keep employees informed about it. In a serious situation, daily briefings may be required. Employees will want to know how it will affect them. (If the business will close for a time, will paychecks continue? If not, what alternative assistance may be available? Will additional hours be required of staff? If so, which ones?)

A crisis can affect employees in the short and the long run. Experiencing a crisis, especially if it causes injury or loss of life, can be stressful. Negative effects on employees can include anxiety, depression, nightmares, flashbacks, and physical effects like insomnia, loss of appetite, and headaches. Collectively, these and related symptoms are known as **posttraumatic stress disorder.** Managers have been called upon to recognize and respond to this condition in employees following a crisis.

POSTTRAUMATIC STRESS DIS-ORDER A severe reaction to an event that threatens an individual's physical and/or emotional health.

Customer Response. When a crisis occurs, customers can be involved. They can, for example, be witnesses to crimes or accidents. They themselves can be crisis victims or innocent bystanders. Although a manager cannot control a customer's response to a crisis, a manager can control his or her own response to the customer, which can have a major impact on that customer's reaction.

The manager's objective should be to show genuine concern, treat the customer fairly, and avoid any needless legal difficulty. Strategies to accomplish these ends include the following:

- Realize that the customer may be agitated, confused, scared, or angry. Accept these feelings as legitimate; consider them when speaking to the customer.

- If practical, introduce yourself and state your title. Ask for the customer's name and repeat it to make sure you say it correctly. Use the customer's name during your conversation.

- Give the customer your undivided attention, maintain eye contact, and avoid interrupting. Listen more than you talk.

- Stay calm; do not lose your temper, regardless of the customer's comments.

- Apologize for the customer's inconvenience. Be genuine. Put yourself in the customer's position and treat the customer as you would want to be treated.

- Tell the customer what is currently being done or will be done.

- Arrange for medical treatment if needed. (Don't accept blame for the cause of the crisis.) Be clear, however, as to your real concern for the customer's safety.

- Offer alternative solutions to the problem if possible; seek a solution that satisfies the customer's needs.

- Let the customer know that you will follow up to ensure that what you have promised will be done.

- Thank the customer for talking with you; make notes of the conversation if necessary.

Plaintiffs in lawsuits often state that they would not have sued if they had been treated sensitively during their inconvenience. Even in a situation such as severe weather, which is completely beyond the manager's control, customers may become upset and blame management for crisis-related difficulties. Let these customers know that you are genuinely concerned and are doing everything possible to ease their difficulties.

Media Response. When a crisis occurs, it and your restaurant may become the day's news story. Consider the restaurant robbed at gunpoint. Media reporters may call or visit the property. Although most reporters are fair and evenhanded, some are not. A poorly prepared management statement or **press release** can magnify the crisis rather than help diffuse it.

> **PRESS RELEASE An official statement from an individual or organization distributed to the media and other parties judged to be interested in its information.**

Even the best preparation cannot turn bad news into good. During a crisis a manager can help to ensure that the restaurant's side of the story is told and help to preserve its image as a professional, caring, and concerned organization. Otherwise, not only may your liability expand, but you may face litigation for failure to express an appropriate amount of concern for the crisis victims. The following guidelines can help managers who are spokespersons during a crisis:

- Be professional. Your picture may be taken or you may appear on television; dress appropriately.

- Update the press regularly. Be proactive. If you prepare a press release, distribute copies to all interested reporters.

- Clearly identify yourself and your position before talking with the media.

- Speak calmly and clearly. Project a professional image conveying that you are properly dealing with the situation.

- Avoid speculating about causes or outcomes. Speak only about those things of which you have factual knowledge.

- Express genuine concern for the victims' suffering.

- Avoid graphic descriptions of events or injuries.

- Do not release names of victims or suspects. (Refer these questions to the appropriate party.)

- Never reply, "No comment." If you truly cannot comment, give the honest reason. Legitimate reasons *not* to respond include:
  Pending legal investigation
  Incomplete information
  Responsibility falling to another (give that person's name)

- Remember that your primary responsibility in speaking with the media is to provide factual information and to express genuine concern for crisis victims. In addition, emphasize the positives of your restaurant (for example, safety and security efforts in place, training programs (relating to the crisis) implemented, and your commitment to cooperate fully with all authorities).

  - Expect tough questions; practice your answers to such queries. Do not become belligerent or hostile.

  - Never demand to review a reporter's story before it is printed. Never agree to speak **off-the-record**.

OFF-THE-RECORD   Given or made in confidence and not for publication. An oral agreement can be made between a reporter and an interviewee in which the reporter promises not to quote the interviewee's comments for publication. (These agreements are usually unenforceable.)

- If you think that you or your restaurant has been unfairly treated in a news report, contact the reporter to calmly retell the facts.

- Temporarily suspend advertising for a time appropriate for the crisis.

- Consider creating a publicity campaign to counteract any negative impact.

Some managers believe that they and their restaurant may be treated unfairly by reporters during a crisis. It is natural not to want to see the operation cast in a negative light. However, do not do anything to make a difficult situation worse. Although you cannot control reporters' actions, you can conduct yourself professionally while expressing genuine concern for crisis victims.

Postcrisis Assessment

Although evaluation of emergency plans should be ongoing, the end of a crisis is a particularly good time to do such an evaluation. Managers should review their performance, along with that of the staff, to assess their effectiveness.

A variety of approaches can be used to do a postcrisis analysis of performance, and the **STEM model** (discussed at length in Chapter 1) presented here can be useful.

> **STEM MODEL** An approach used by managers that relies on Selecting, Teaching, Educating, and Managing to reduce potential liabilities.

Consider Ji-Young, who manages a restaurant featuring fresh seafood. One of her employees drives to the airport daily to pick up incoming shipments from the East Coast. One day, as her van driver was returning from the airport, a serious accident occurred that severely injured four pedestrians. The cause of the accident was not clear when the accident occurred. Negative publicity surrounding the crash threatened the reputation of the restaurant. Regardless of the accident's cause or how the manager and her staff handled themselves, a postcrisis assessment should be performed. Using the STEM approach, she would review several elements.

Selecting. Were procedures in place to ensure that the driver was qualified? Had a background check on licenses been performed? Were vision tests mandatory or corrective glasses mandated if needed? (If an opposing attorney sues for negligence, the answers to these questions and more will be required.) Although it may be too late to correct any deficiencies related to this crisis, it is not too late to prepare for and attempt to prevent another occurrence. Ji-Young can begin reducing the potential for litigation by selecting the right employee for a specific job.

Teaching. Ji-Young must develop proper teaching methods, including feedback, such as competency testing, to ensure that training was effective. Her drivers must be trained in administering first aid. When employees know what to expect and have been properly trained, the chances of their making a mistake that would further deepen the crisis are greatly reduced.

Educating. Managers, including Ji-Young, must continuously educate themselves. If a lawsuit results from a crisis, a plaintiff's attorney will want to know a manager's competency level. Employee selection and training are ultimately management's responsibilities. An effective postcrisis assessment thus includes examining management's competencies as well. Demonstration of continuing education, certification, and expertise in specific safety and security areas can be crucial in reducing potential legal liability.

Ji-Young's performance with the press should be reviewed. Were employees instructed about who would serve as the media spokesperson? Was the spokesperson (manager) well studied and prepared? Was anything said that could actually increase the restaurant's potential liability?

Managing. The management process includes the manager's actions and the procedures they establish and require. A postcrisis assessment involves reviewing those procedures for improvement. In Ji-Young's case, a review will involve examining all hiring and training practices for van drivers, the training of employees affected by the crisis, and the procedures related to management's emergency response.

An analysis of diverse areas, including the ready availability of first aid supplies, insurance coverage, and the restaurant's relationships with law enforcement agencies, would be undertaken. Managers should use what is learned in one crisis to help prevent or minimize the negative effect of future crises. They should utilize their legal knowledge to respond in a more effective manner should a similar crisis arise in the future.

WHAT WOULD YOU DO?

Suppose you manage a 24-hour restaurant. Last week Mr. Ketchar, a customer, arrived at approximately 2:00 A.M., and after getting out of his car, he tripped over a curb and broke his hip. Because Mr. Ketchar is a very visible city councilman, the incident was reported in the local paper.

You were interviewed about the accident's cause when it was discovered that the curb had not been painted bright yellow (required by city ordinance), nor were lighting levels adequate in the area where Mr. Ketchar fell. Your two assistant managers suggest the restaurant paint the curb, install additional lighting, and inform the media of both actions. You want to veto this idea, maintaining that these actions could imply previous negligence and increase the restaurant's potential legal liability.

What would you do?

MANAGER'S "TO DO" LIST

Review the following recommendations proposed in this chapter. Analyze your interest in and need for implementing these recommendations by completing the columns on the right side of the form. Remember, when task assignments are made, time requirements for completion should also be stated. Follow up, as improvement activities evolve, to ensure that your property is moving closer to the goal of minimizing litigation risks.

Recommended Procedures	In Place Now?			Needed to Implement			Assigned To	Completion Date
	Yes	No	N/A*	Policy	Training	Other		
List several crises you could face simply because of your restaurant's location. Review your emergency plan(s) to ensure that these situations are addressed.								
Review your emergency telephone numbers list to ensure that it is both accurate and accessible to those who may need it.								
Call the chief law enforcement officer in your area and invite him or her for coffee or lunch; discuss crisis issues.								
Identify at least three measures you use to evaluate your safety and/or security efforts. Communicate your most recent assessments to your staff and set goals for your next measurement period.								
Contact your local law enforcement officials to determine whether training programs are offered to assist in your safety and security training efforts. Attend if possible.								
Evaluate and update your emergency plans. If you do not have a written emergency plan, select a committee and set a date for your first meeting to develop a plan.								
If you do not have a safety committee, select staff members. Determine the time for the first meeting and establish a list of goals and objectives for the group.								

*N/A = Not Applicable

Recommended Procedures	In Place Now?			Needed to Implement			Assigned To	Completion Date
	Yes	No	N/A*	Policy	Training	Other		
Contact the business editor of a local newspaper. Invite him or her for a property tour and an informal discussion of how your business works. Stay in touch with that individual.								
Contact the fire chief to schedule at least one annual fire drill for your property. Seek the fire department's ideas on how a drill should be implemented.								
Distribute a memo outlining factors your supervisors should use to determine which employee accidents will result in mandatory medical treatment.								
Develop (or review) procedures to be used when a customer "skips"; provide training for all staff, as applicable, to implement these procedures.								
Develop (or review) procedures to be used for processing credit card charges; provide training for all staff, as applicable, to implement these procedures.								
Develop (or review) procedures to be used for processing personal checks; provide training for all staff, as applicable, to implement these procedures.								
Ask yourself the following question: "If I were a dishonest employee, how could I steal money, food/beverage products, or other assets?" Develop and implement corrective action procedures to address any situations this self-analysis exercise identifies.								

For more information and suggestions log onto www.hospitalitylawyer.com.

*N/A = Not Applicable

CONSULTANT'S CORNER

What Would You Do? *(page 296)*

Dining room chairs should be strong enough to hold the average person eating at your restaurant. The real issue here (and the one that will be of interest to your insurance carrier and attorney) is "Was there on-going, documented chair inspection?" If you can prove there was, it will be of great help. If not, there could be significant liability here. Develop and implement the inspection program immediately.

What Would You Do? *(page 298)*

Tragic events happen; this one is as bad as it gets. Your immediate role is to professionally represent your company and business to the community. Look to your own supervisor for instruction about required actions. Don't avoid the press; they will not go away. Be prepared and demonstrate your genuine concern for those involved in this crisis. Don't forget the support your unit's employees will need during this difficult time.

It is also a good idea to review the policies that were in place so that appropriate training can occur. For instance, it is difficult to know in this situation whether or not the manager would have survived had he given them the money. Most experts agree that being able to respond to a robber's demand for money is the best policy.

What Would You Do? *(page 301–302)*

This scenario raises all of the dilemmas involved in CCVC systems. It has been agreed that they give guests a sense of security, so they let their guard down. Even if they are monitored, is it reasonable to think that a security guard who witnesses an assault taking place will be able to intervene in time to stop the attack? Accordingly, most operators have chosen not to utilize a CCVC system as a tool for guest safety, but as a tool for internal security enforcement.

What Would You Do? *(page 307–308)*

As more hospitality professionals work from their homes, the issue presented here will grow in frequency and in complexity. Your attorney can advise you about the current situation. The lesson is that vendors who have access to employee homes, and the employers themselves, will likely be held responsible for damage suffered by at-home workers. Workers can be injured at home as well as at more traditional work sites. Worker's compensation laws may protect you in some cases, depending on the situation.

Select your telecommunications and other vendors with care. Be especially careful if they will enter your employee's home.

What Would You Do? (page 322 & 323)

Your assistants are correct. Most state courts take the position that managers should not be considered negligent because they corrected a problem related to an accident. Your concern is most likely unfounded. Moreover, a second accident under the same circumstances could be extremely costly if it were proven that you knew about an existing problem but did nothing to correct it. (This is the kind of information a plaintiff's attorney loves, and your insurance company hates!) You are responsible for correcting foreseeable problem areas. In the event of a second accident, it will be hard for your attorney to convince a jury that you could not have foreseen the second accident when you had already experienced the first.

Keep in mind that you have an obligation to at least meet the requirements of the law, and in this case it appears that the law was clear that the curb should be painted—another incentive to follow your managers' advice.

APPENDICES

BANQUET CONTRACT

GROUP CONTACT: _____   EVENT DATE: _____

EVENT NAME: _____   ROOM(S): _____

CONTRACT RETURN DATE: The space listed above is on a first option basis through _____ (DATE) _____ In the event another client requests space being held on your behalf, we will request a decision within 48 hours or the space may be released.

GUARANTEE POLICY: A minimum guarantee of attendance must be received by 12:00 noon two business days prior to the event. (Thursday noon for Monday and Tuesday functions; Wednesday noon for Saturday and Sunday functions.) This is the minimum number of guests for whom you will be charged. The property will provide seating and food for 5% above the guaranteed count not to exceed ten in number. An increase in the guarantee will be accepted up to a maximum of 24 hours before the event subject to product availability. The estimated number of guests listed in this Banquet Contract will apply if the guarantee is not received two full business days prior to the event. **POSITIVELY NO REDUCTIONS IN GUARANTEE WILL BE ACCEPTED LESS THAN TWO FULL BUSINESS DAYS PRIOR TO THE EVENT.**

LONG-TERM (CONTRACT DATE MORE THAN 180 DAYS FROM EVENT) CANCELLATION POLICY: Notice of cancellation must be received in writing and confirmed by the property at least 180 days in advance of the event. By signing this contract, you agree to pay a cancellation fee for the loss of business if the event is canceled less than 180 days in advance. The cancellation fee shall equal 50% of the anticipated billing for events canceled 120–180 days in advance. If cancellation occurs 61–119 days prior to the event, a cancellation fee of 75% of the anticipated billing will apply. A cancellation that occurs 60 days or less from the date of the scheduled event will result in a cancellation fee of 100% of the anticipated billing. Any cancellation fees will be due and payable upon invoice. If another group utilizes the space, the cancellation fee may be prorated or waived. This determination will be made solely by the property after the day of the event. **Any nonrefundable deposit that must be paid under this contract is not affected by this Cancellation Policy.**

SHORT-TERM (CONTRACT DATE LESS THAN 45 DAYS FROM EVENT) CANCELLATION POLICY: Notice of cancellation must be received in writing and confirmed by the property at least 45 days in advance of the event. By signing this contract, you agree to pay a cancellation fee for the loss of business if the event is canceled less than 45 days in advance. The cancellation fee shall equal 50% of the anticipated billing for events canceled 45–30 days in advance. If cancellation occurs 29–11 days prior to the event, a cancellation fee of 75% of the anticipated billing will apply. A cancellation that occurs 10 days or less from the date of the scheduled event will result in a cancellation fee of 100% of the anticipated billing. Any cancellation fees will be due and payable upon invoice. If another group utilizes the space, the cancellation fee may be prorated or waived. This determination will be made solely by the

Appendix A   Sample Banquet Contract

property after the day of the event. **Any nonrefundable deposit which must be paid under this contract is not affected by this Cancellation Policy.**

REDUCTION POLICY: If the final guaranteed attendance is less than 50% of the original estimated attendance, a Reduction Fee will be applied. The Fee will be equal to the full meeting room rental. Reduction in estimated attendance will be accepted up to 60 days prior to the function.

BILLING: Completed credit applications will be necessary for all clients requesting direct billing. Direct billing privileges will be granted upon receipt and approval of a completed credit application. Payment is due upon receipt of the invoice. Individual account billings are due upon checkout and will be added to the Master Account if not paid.

ALCOHOL SERVICE POLICY: In keeping with our commitment to responsible service of alcohol, the property will: A) card all guests who appear to be under the age of 25; B) not serve alcoholic beverages to guests without proper ID; and C) not serve doubles, shots, shooters, or multiple liquor drinks containing more than three liquors (i.e., Long Island Iced Tea). Single drinks will be dispensed to patrons. The Banquet Manager reserves the right to refuse alcoholic beverage service to an individual or group.

REDUCTION POLICY:

Your event coordinator will contact you a minimum of **three weeks** prior to your event to plan details and menu. The property has booked space according to our understanding of your group's needs. Both parties have reviewed space to ensure accuracy.

A Banquet Event Order will follow upon completion of the details of the event for your approval. The property reserves the right to modify room assignments to maximize use of the facilities.

These Catering Policies have been reviewed and understood. I agree with the arrangements stated above and contract the facilities as given.

Please sign and return the entire approved contract to: (PROPERTY ADDRESS)

SIGNATURE: _____   DATE:_____

BANQUET MANAGER: _____   DATE:_____

Appendix A *(Continued)*

CLIENT NAME/ADDRESS:

ESTIMATED NO. OF GUESTS: _____

_____

CLIENT PHONE: _____

_____

_____

CLIENT FAX:

_____

_____

NOTE: ALL FOOD AND BEVERAGE CHARGES ARE SUBJECT TO APPLICABLE SERVICE CHARGE PLUS TAX.

Date	Time	Room	Function
Menu		Room Setup	
		Audiovisual Needs	
Beverages		Miscellaneous & Billing	

The final guarantee (number of guests) must be received by 12:00 noon two full business days prior to the event. Should the final guarantee not be received by this time, the above estimated number of guests will be the basis for billing charges. No reductions in guarantee will be accepted less than two full business days prior to the event. Please carefully review all information above and sign below. We reserve the right to relocate your function(s) to another room. Every effort will be made to contact you in advance should this be the case.

_____   _____

Guest's Signature   Date

_____   _____

Property Representative's Signature   Date

Appendix A   *(Continued)*

MEETING CONFIRMATION

DATE:

ORGANIZATION:

CONFERENCE:

GROUP CONTACT:

TITLE:

PHONE: FAX:

ADDRESS:

KEY DUE DATES: For your convenience, we have listed key dates mentioned within this Meeting Confirmation for your reference. Please review the corresponding sections for further information.

Acceptance/Signed Meeting Confirmation
Credit Arrangements/Completed Credit Application
Reservation Cutoff
Program Details/Menu Selections
Three Days Prior to Scheduled Events
Food and Beverage Guarantees

PROGRAM SPECIFICS:

Appendix B   Sample Meeting Space Contract

Dates:

DAY:

DATE:

DAY MEETING PACKAGE RATES (for all meeting attendees):

Subject to 8.25% sales tax and 20% service charge

This DAY GUEST PACKAGE RATE includes:

Lunch (Gala Dining Room): Lunch is available for seating at 11:30 A.M. or 12:30 P.M.

Meeting Room Supplies: Room setup, pads, pencils, ice water pitchers, and hard candies.

Continuous Beverage Service (7:30 A.M.–5:00 P.M.): Coffee, decaf, tea, assorted sodas, and bottled water.

Community Refreshment Breaks

Morning Break (7:30 A.M.–10:30 A.M.): Assorted baked goods (varies daily), sliced fresh fruit, assorted mini-yogurts, and orange juice.

Afternoon Break (2:00 P.M.–4:00 P.M.): Assorted afternoon snacks, fresh baked cookies or brownies of the day, candy, whole fresh fruit, and lemonade.

Standard Audiovisual

10–25 people: 2 flipcharts (including markers and masking tape), overhead projector, screen, podium, and easel.

26–50 people: 2 flipcharts (including markers and masking tape), 2 overhead projectors, 2 screens, standard microphone, VCR, easel, and message board.

51–75 people: 3 flipcharts, 2 overhead projectors, 2 screens, standard microphone, VCR, easel, and message board.

76+ people: 4 flipcharts, 2 overhead projectors, 2 screens, standard microphone, lavaliere microphone, VCR, easel, and message board.

FUNCTION ARRANGEMENTS

We have reserved meeting space as outlined below. Meeting rooms are not held on a 24-hour basis unless otherwise noted. A conference services manager personally assigned to your account will be contacting you to discuss and finalize your exact room setup requirements, menu selections, and audiovisual equipment needs.

Appendix B *(Continued)*

Please advise us of all changes to your agenda so that we may best serve your specific program requirements. Should there be a significant reduction in attendees, we reserve the right to adjust function space accordingly.

Day	Date	Time	Function	Setup	Attendance

MEETING ROOM RENTAL

The charge for meeting space will be _____ per breakout per day.

FUNCTION GUARANTEES

A final guarantee of the number of meeting attendees and/or catered food functions is due no later than three (3) business days prior to each scheduled event. This guarantee represents the minimum guest count for billing purposes and may not be reduced after this time.

CREDIT ARRANGEMENTS

Upon our accounting department's approval of your credit application, your master account will be direct-billed. Our credit terms are "Net due upon receipt of invoice" with interest charged at 1.5% on all balances over 30 days of billing date.

CREDIT APPLICATION

Credit application due: _____

CANCELLATION

Acknowledgement of a definite commitment by the restaurant will, in good faith, continue to protect the facilities and dates agreed upon, to the exclusion of other business opportunities. Therefore, the commitment of space and dates is of specified value to the restaurant. Due to the great difficulty in reselling conference space on short notice, cancellation of the entire program will be subject to an assessment according to the following schedule:

0 to 30 days prior to arrival. Full payment for all estimated banquet revenues as booked for the duration of the dates agreed upon.

31 to 60 days prior to arrival	75% of the above
61 to 90 days prior to arrival	50% of the above
91 to 180 days prior to arrival	30% of the above
181 days to 1 year prior to arrival	15% of the above
Signing date to one year prior to arrival	10% of the above

Appendix B *(Continued)*

PROGRAM ALTERATION CONTINGENCY

This agreement has been based on the sequence of days and function requirements specified. If these requirements are significantly changed, we reserve the right to alter the terms and conditions of this contract, including assessment of cancellation fees.

ACCEPTANCE

If the above details meet with your approval, please sign this letter of agreement and return to us by_____. If an approved agreement is not received by the above option date, the restaurant will release the tentative space reserved.

    We sincerely appreciate the opportunity to serve _____. You can be assured of the effort of our entire staff and my personalized attention to help make your meeting most enjoyable and successful.

ACCEPTANCE BY CLIENT	ACCEPTANCE BY RESTAURANT
Name: _____	Name: _____
Title: _____	Title: _____
Date: _____	Date: _____

Appendix B *(Continued)*

CONTRACT FOR SALE OF GOODS

Agreement made and entered into this [date] _____, by and between _____ [name of seller], of [address] _____ [city] _____, [state] _____ , herein referred to as "Seller," and [name of buyer] _____, of [address] _____ [city] _____ , [state] _____, herein referred to as "Buyer."

    Seller hereby agrees to transfer and deliver to Buyer, on or before [date] _____, the following goods:

DESCRIPTION OF GOODS

CONSIDERATION TERMS

Buyer agrees to accept the goods and pay for them in accordance with the terms of this contract. Buyer agrees to pay for the goods at the time they are delivered and at the place where he or she receives the goods. Goods shall be deemed received by Buyer when delivered to address of Buyer as described in this contract. Until such time as goods have been received by Buyer, all risk of loss from any casualty to said goods shall be on Seller.

    Seller warrants that the goods are now free from any security interest or other lien or encumbrance, that they shall be free from same at the time of delivery, and that he [or she] neither knows nor has reason to know of any outstanding title or claim of title hostile to his [or her] rights in the goods.

    Buyer has the right to examine the goods on arrival and has [number] of days to notify Seller of any claim for damages on account of the condition, grade, or quality of the goods. The notice must specifically set forth the basis of his [or her] claim, and that his [or her] failure to either notify Seller within the stipulated period of time or to set forth specifically the basis of his [or her] claim will constitute irrevocable acceptance of the goods.

    This agreement has been executed in duplicate, whereby both Buyer and Seller have retained one copy each, on [date] _____.

_____   _____
Buyer   Seller

[Signatures]

Appendix C Sample Contract for Sale of Goods

HospitalityLawyer.com
http://www.HospitalityLawyer.com
P.O. Box 22888
Houston, TX 77227
Phone: (713) 963-8800
Fax: (713) 627-9934
editor@hospitalitylawyer.com (E-mail)

Restaurant Business
P.O. Box 1252
Skokie, IL 60076-9819
http://www.restaurantbiz.com/
Phone: (212) 592-6500

Hospitality Litigation News
Tuttle & Taylor, A Law Corporation
355 South Grand Avenue, 40th Floor
Los Angeles, CA 90071-3102
http://www.tuttletaylor.com
Phone: (213) 683-0600

Nation's Restaurant News
P.O. Box 31197
Tampa, FL 33633-0692
http://www.nrn.com/
Phone: (212) 756-5199

Restaurants USA
National Restaurant Association
1200 Seventeenth Street, NW
Washington, DC 20036
http://www.restaurant.org
Phone: (202) 331-5900
        (800) 424-5156
Fax: (202) 331-2429
info@dineout.org (E-mail)

Appendix D   Publications on Government Regulations

Position Title: Executive Chef

Reports to: Food and Beverage Director

Position Summary: The department head responsible for any and all kitchens in a food service establishment. Ensures that all kitchens provide nutritious, safe, eye-appealing, properly flavored food. Maintains a safe and sanitary preparation environment.

Tasks:

1. Interviews, hires, evaluates, rewards, and disciplines kitchen personnel as appropriate.
2. Orients and trains kitchen personnel in property and department rules, policies, and procedures.
3. Trains kitchen personnel in food production principles and practices. Establishes quality standards for all menu items and for food production practices.
4. Plans and prices menus. Establishes portion sizes and standards of service for all menu items.
5. Schedules kitchen employees in conjunction with business forecasts and predetermined budget. Maintains payroll records for submission to payroll department.
6. Controls food costs by establishing purchasing specifications, storeroom requisition systems, product storage requirements, standardization recipes, and waste control procedures.
7. Trains kitchen personnel in safe operating procedures of all equipment, utensils, and machinery. Establishes maintenance schedules in conjunction with manufacturer instructions for all equipment. Provides safety training in lifting, carrying, hazardous material control, chemical control, first aid, and CPR.
8. Trains kitchen personnel in sanitation practices and establishes cleaning schedules, stock rotation schedules, refrigeration temperature control points, and other sanitary controls.
9. Trains kitchen personnel to prepare all food while retaining the maximum amount of desirable nutrients. Trains kitchen personnel to meet special dietary requests, including low-fat, low-sodium, low-calorie, and vegetarian meals.

Source: Anonymous

Appendix E Sample Job Description

Subject	Inappropriate Questions (May Not Ask or Require)	Appropriate Questions (May Ask or Require)
Gender or marital status	Number and ages of children Pregnancy, actual or intended Maiden name, former name	In checking your work record, do we need another name for identification?
Race	Race Color of skin, eyes, hair, etc. Request for photograph	(A photograph may be required after hiring for identification)
National origin	Questions about place of birth, ancestry, mother tongue, national origin of parents or spouse What is your native language? How did you learn to speak Spanish (or other language) fluently?	If job-related, what foreign languages do you speak fluently?
Citizenship, immigration status	Of what country are you a citizen? Are you a native-born U.S. citizen? Questions about naturalization of applicant, spouse, or parents	Are you a U.S. citizen? If hired, can you show proof that you are eligible to work in U.S.?
Religion	Religious affiliation or preference Religious holidays observed Membership in religious clubs	Can you observe regularly the required days and hours of work?
Age	How old are you? Date of birth	Are you 18 or older? (to comply with labor laws) Are you 21 or older? (for positions serving alcohol)
Disability	Do you have any disabilities? Have you ever been treated for (certain) diseases? Are you healthy?	
Questions that may discriminate against minorities because of economic status, etc.	Have you ever been arrested? List all clubs, societies, and lodges to which you belong. Do you own a car? (Unless required to do the job.) Type of military discharge Questions regarding credit ratings, financial status, wage garnishment, home ownership	Have you ever been convicted of a crime? If yes, give details. (If crime is job-related, as embezzlement is to handling money, you may refuse to hire.) List membership in professional organizations relevant to job performance. Do you have a reliable means of getting to work? Military service: dates, branch of service, education and experience (if job-related).
Assumptions related to sex, age, race, disability, etc.	Work is too heavy for women or disabled persons Stereotypes: buspersons should be men, room cleaners and typists should be women, bartenders should be under 40, etc.	Can you do the job?

Jack E. Miller, Mary Porter, and Karen Eich Drummond, *Supervision in the Hospitality Industry*, 3rd ed. (New York: John Wiley & Sons, Inc., 1998), 169. © 1998, John Wiley & Sons, Inc. Reprinted with permission.

Appendix F   Guidelines for Appropriate Interview Questions

Employee Consent Form for Drug Testing

I agree, fully and voluntarily, to submit to a urinalysis or blood test conducted by _____ for a drug screen as a condition of my consideration for employment. I understand that failing to meet the standards established for this test may result in the disqualification of further consideration of my application. Finally, I understand that these results will be used only as the basis for an employment decision and will not be shared with any individual or organization outside the company.

The undersigned represents that he or she has read this information in its entirety and understands it.

Employee Signature _____   Date _____

Employer Witness Signature_____   Date _____

Appendix G   Sample Employee Consent Form for Drug Testing

Employee Consent Form for Background Checks and Application Verification

I agree, fully and voluntarily, to checks related to:

1. (e.g., Criminal History)

2. (e.g., School Attendance Record)

as well as checks on information I have supplied in my employment application.

I understand that failing to meet the standards established for these checks as well as falsification of information on my application may result in the disqualification of further consideration of my application. Finally, I understand that the results of these background checks and the accuracy of my application will be used only as the basis for an employment decision and will not be shared with any individual or organization outside the company.

The undersigned represents that he or she has read this information in its entirety and understands it.

Employee Signature _____   Date _____

Employer Witness Signature_____   Date _____

Appendix H   Sample Consent Form Authorizing Background Check

U.S. Department of Justice
Immigration and Naturalization Service

OMB No. 1115-0136

Employment Eligibility Verification

INSTRUCTIONS
PLEASE READ ALL INSTRUCTIONS CAREFULLY BEFORE COMPLETING THIS FORM.

Anti-Discrimination Notice. It is illegal to discriminate against any individual (other than an alien not authorized to work in the U.S.) in hiring, discharging, or recruiting or referring for a fee because of that individual's national origin or citizenship status. It is illegal to discriminate against work eligible individuals. Employers CANNOT specify which document(s) they will accept from an employee. The refusal to hire an individual because of a future expiration date may also constitute illegal discrimination.

Section 1 - Employee. All employees, citizens and noncitizens, hired after November 6, 1986, must complete Section 1 of this form at the time of hire, which is the actual beginning of employment.The employer is responsible for ensuring that Section 1 is timely and properly completed.

Preparer/Translator Certification. The Preparer/Translator Certification must be completed if Section 1 is prepared by a person other than the employee. A preparer/translator may be used only when the employee is unable to complete Section 1 on his/her own. However, the employee must still sign Section 1.

Section 2 - Employer. For the purpose of completing this form, the term "employer" includes those recruiters and referrers for a fee who are agricultural associations, agricultural employers or farm labor contractors.

Employers must complete Section 2 by examining evidence of identity and employment eligibility within three (3) business days of the date employment begins. If employees are authorized to work, but are unable to present the required document(s) within three business days, they must present a receipt for the application of the document(s) within three business days and the actual document(s) within ninety (90) days. However, if employers hire individuals for a duration of less than three business days, Section 2 must be completed at the time employment begins.Employers must record: 1) document title; 2) issuing authority; 3) document number, 4) expiration date, if any; and 5) the date employment begins. Employers must sign and date the certification. Employees must present original documents. Employers may, but are not required to, photocopy the document(s) presented. These photocopies may only be used for the verification process and must be retained with the I-9. However, employers are still responsible for completing the I-9.

Section 3 - Updating and Reverification. Employers must complete Section 3 when updating and/or reverifying the I-9. Employers must reverify employment eligibility of their employees on or before the expiration date recorded in Section 1. Employers CANNOT specify which document(s) they will accept from an employee.

- If an employee's name has changed at the time this form is being updated/ reverified, complete Block A.

- If an employee is rehired within three (3) years of the date this form was originally completed and the employee is still eligible to be employed on the same basis as previously indicated on this form (updating), complete Block B and the signature block.

- If an employee is rehired within three (3) years of the date this form was originally completed and the employee's work authorization has expired or if a current employee's work authorization is about to expire (reverification), complete Block B and:
  - examine any document that reflects that the employee is authorized to work in the U.S. (see List A or C),
  - record the document title, document number and expiration date (if any) in Block C, and complete the signature block.

Photocopying and Retaining Form I-9.A blank I-9 may be reproduced, provided both sides are copied. The Instructions must be available to all employees completing this form. Employers must retain completed I-9s for three (3) years after the date of hire or one (1) year after the date employment ends, whichever is later.

For more detailed information, you may refer to the INS Handbook for Employers, (Form M-274). You may obtain the handbook at your local INS office.

Privacy Act Notice. The authority for collecting this information is the Immigration Reform and Control Act of 1986, Pub. L. 99-603 (8 USC 1324a).

This information is for employers to verify the eligibility of individuals for employment to preclude the unlawful hiring, or recruiting or referring for a fee, of aliens who are not authorized to work in the United States.

This information will be used by employers as a record of their basis for determining eligibility of an employee to work in the United States. The form will be kept by the employer and made available for inspection by officials of the U.S. Immigration and Naturalization Service, the Department of Labor and the Office of Special Counsel for Immigration Related Unfair Employment Practices.

Submission of the information required in this form is voluntary. However, an individual may not begin employment unless this form is completed, since employers are subject to civil or criminal penalties if they do not comply with the Immigration Reform and Control Act of 1986.

Reporting Burden. We try to create forms and instructions that are accurate, can be easily understood and which impose the least possible burden on you to provide us with information. Often this is difficult because some immigration laws are very complex. Accordingly, the reporting burden for this collection of information is computed as follows:1) learning about this form, 5 minutes; 2) completing the form, 5 minutes; and 3) assembling and filing (recordkeeping) the form, 5 minutes, for an average of 15 minutes per response. If you have comments regarding the accuracy of this burden estimate, or suggestions for making this form simpler, you can write to the Immigration and Naturalization Service, HQPDI, 425 I Street, N.W., Room 4307r, Washington, DC 20536. OMB No. 1115-0136.

EMPLOYERS MUST RETAIN COMPLETED FORM I-9
PLEASE DO NOT MAIL COMPLETED FORM I-9 TO INS

Form I-9 (Rev. 11-21-91)N

Appendix I   Sample Form I-9

U.S. Department of Justice
Immigration and Naturalization Service

OMB No. 1115-0136

Employment Eligibility Verification

Please read instructions carefully before completing this form. The instructions must be available during completion of this form. ANTI-DISCRIMINATION NOTICE: It is illegal to discriminate against work eligible individuals. Employers CANNOT specify which document(s) they will accept from an employee. The refusal to hire an individual because of a future expiration date may also constitute illegal discrimination.

Section 1. Employee Information and Verification To be completed and signed by employee at the time employment begins.

| Print Name: Last | First | Middle Initial | Maiden Name |

| Address (Street Name and Number) | Apt. # | Date of Birth (month/day/year) |

| City | State | Zip Code | Social Security # |

I am aware that federal law provides for imprisonment and/or fines for false statements or use of false documents in connection with the completion of this form.

I attest, under penalty of perjury, that I am (check one of the following):
☐ A citizen or national of the United States
☐ A Lawful Permanent Resident (Alien # A_____)
☐ An alien authorized to work until ___/___/___
(Alien # or Admission #)_____

| Employee's Signature | Date (month/day/year) |

Preparer and/or Translator Certification. (To be completed and signed if Section 1 is prepared by a person other than the employee.) I attest, under penalty of perjury, that I have assisted in the completion of this form and that to the best of my knowledge the information is true and correct.

| Preparer's/Translator's Signature | Print Name |

| Address (Street Name and Number, City, State, Zip Code) | Date (month/day/year) |

Section 2. Employer Review and Verification. To be completed and signed by employer. Examine one document from List A OR examine one document from List B and one from List C, as listed on the reverse of this form, and record the title, number and expiration date, if any, of the document(s)

| List A | OR | List B | AND | List C |

Document title:_____
Issuing authority:_____
Document #:_____
Expiration Date (if any): ___/___/___
Document #:_____
Expiration Date (if any): ___/___/___

CERTIFICATION - I attest, under penalty of perjury, that I have examined the document(s) presented by the above-named employee, that the above-listed document(s) appear to be genuine and to relate to the employee named, that the employee began employment on (month/day/year) ___/___/___ and that to the best of my knowledge the employee is eligible to work in the United States. (State employment agencies may omit the date the employee began employment.)

| Signature of Employer or Authorized Representative | Print Name | Title |

| Business or Organization Name | Address (Street Name and Number, City, State, Zip Code) | Date (month/day/year) |

Section 3. Updating and Reverification To be completed and signed by employer.

| A. New Name (if applicable) | B. Date of rehire (month/day/year) (if applicable) |

C. If employee's previous grant of work authorization has expired, provide the information below for the document that establishes current employment eligibility.

Document Title:_____ Document #:_____ Expiration Date (if any):___/___/___

I attest, under penalty of perjury, that to the best of my knowledge, this employee is eligible to work in the United States, and if the employee presented document(s), the document(s) I have examined appear to be genuine and to relate to the individual.

| Signature of Employer or Authorized Representative | Date (month/day/year) |

Form I-9 (Rev. 11-21-91)N Page 2

Appendix I (Continued)

LISTS OF ACCEPTABLE DOCUMENTS

LIST A		LIST B		LIST C
Documents that Establish Both Identity and Employment Eligibility	**OR**	Documents that Establish Identity	**AND**	Documents that Establish Employment Eligibility

LIST A — Documents that Establish Both Identity and Employment Eligibility

1. U.S. Passport (unexpired or expired)

2. Certificate of U.S. Citizenship (INS Form N-560 or N-561)

3. Certificate of Naturalization (INS Form N-550 or N-570)

4. Unexpired foreign passport, with I-551 stamp or attached INS Form I-94 indicating unexpired employment authorization

5. Alien Registration Receipt Card with photograph (INS Form I-151 or I-551)

6. Unexpired Temporary Card (INS Form I-688)

7. Unexpired Employment Authorization Card (INS Form I-688A)

8. Unexpired Reentry Permit (INS Form I-327)

9. Unexpired Refugee Travel Document (INS Form I-571)

10. Unexpired Employment Authorization Document issued by the INS which contains a photograph (INS Form I-688B)

LIST B — Documents that Establish Identity

1. Driver's license or ID card issued by a state or outlying possession of the United States provided it contains a photograph or information such as name, date of birth, sex, height, eye color and address

2. ID card issued by federal, state or local government agencies or entities, provided it contains a photograph or information such as name, date of birth, sex, height, eye color and address

3. School ID card with a photograph

4. Voter's registration card

5. U.S. Military card or draft record

6. Military dependent's ID card

7. U.S. Coast Guard Merchant Mariner Card

8. Native American tribal document

9. Driver's license issued by a Canadian government authority

For persons under age 18 who are unable to present a document listed above:

10. School record or report card

11. Clinic, doctor or hospital record

12. Day-care or nursery school record

LIST C — Documents that Establish Employment Eligibility

1. U.S. social security card issued by the Social Security Administration (other than a card stating it is not valid for employment)

2. Certification of Birth Abroad issued by the Department of State (Form FS-545 or Form DS-1350)

3. Original or certified copy of a birth certificate issued by a state, county, municipal authority or outlying possession of the United States bearing an official seal

4. Native American tribal document

5. U.S. Citizen ID Card (INS Form I-197)

6. ID Card for use of Resident Citizen in the United States (INS Form I-179)

7. Unexpired employment authorization document issued by the INS (other then those listed under List A)

Illustrations of many of these documents appear in Part 8 of the Handbook for Employers (M-274)

Form I-9 (Rev. 11-21-91)N Page 3

Appendix I *(Continued)*

DOCUMENTS THAT ESTABLISH EMPLOYMENT ELIGIBILITY

Social Security card
An original or certified copy of a birth certificate issued by a state, county, or
   municipal authority
Unexpired INS employment authorization
Unexpired reentry permit (INS Form I-327)
Unexpired Refugee Travel Document (INS Form I-571)
Certificate of Birth issued by the Department of State (Form FS-545)
Certificate of Birth Abroad issued by the Department of State (Form DS-1350)
United States Citizen identification (INS Form I-197)
Native American tribal document
Identification used by Resident Citizen in the United States

DOCUMENTS THAT ESTABLISH IDENTITY ONLY

State driver's license or identification card containing a photograph
School or university identification card with photograph
Voter's registration card
United States military identification card or draft record
Identification card issued by federal, state, or local governmental agencies
Military dependent's identification card
Native American tribal documents
United States Coast Guard Merchant Mariner card
Driver's license issued by a Canadian government authority

DOCUMENTS THAT ESTABLISH IDENTITY
AND EMPLOYMENT ELIGIBILITY

Current United States passport
Alien Registration Receipt Card (INS Form I-151)
Resident Alien Card (INS Form I-551), which must contain a photograph of the
   bearer
Temporary Resident Card (INS Form I-688)
Employment Authorization Card (INS Form I-688A)

Appendix J   Form I-9 Qualifying Documents

January 15, 20XX
Via Certified Mail: Z 123 456 789

Nina Phillips, General Manager
XYZ Restaurant
Re: My client: Ginny Mayes
Date of Accident: January 1, 20XX

Dear Ms. Phillips:

Please be advised that I represent Ginny Mayes. Ms. Mayes has retained my firm to represent her in her claim for damages against the XYZ Restaurant and others that might be responsible for causing the incident that led to her injuries.

As you are aware, my client attended the New Year's Eve Gala that was hosted by the XYZ Restaurant on December 31, 1999. At midnight, and until a few minutes thereafter, employees of the XYZ Restaurant began opening champagne bottles by "popping the corks" (releasing the corks and allowing them to fly into the air).

My client was dancing on the dance floor when she was suddenly struck in her left eye by one of the corks. The cork was traveling at a high rate of speed, and when it struck her eye, she lost her balance and fell, striking her head on the wooden dance floor.

As a result of the negligent acts of the employees/agents of the XYZ Restaurant, my client suffered severe injuries including a subdural hematoma, a concussion, facial lacerations, and a permanent partial loss of sight in her left eye.

You are further advised that my client's occupation for the past fifteen (15) years has been as a pilot for a major airline. Airlines require high vision standards to be met by their pilots. Ms. Mayes's physicians have advised her that she will no longer meet the minimum vision standards required to be a pilot (report enclosed), as a direct result of the injuries she sustained while attending the New Year's Eve Gala.

Accordingly, demand is hereby made for the sum of $25,000,000 (twenty-five million dollars) to compensate my client for the injuries she suffered due to the negligence and gross negligence of the employees of XYZ Restaurant Company; including past, present, and future pain and suffering; past, present, and future medical expenses for both treatment and rehabilitation; and past, present, and future lost wages.

If you have liability insurance, you are strongly urged to advise the carrier of this claim, as most policies require prompt notification when a claim is made.

Please be advised that in the event this matter is not resolved to my client's satisfaction within ten (10) days of your receipt of this correspondence, she has authorized me to pursue any and all legal remedies available to her in this regard, including filing suit seeking the recovery of compensatory damages, punitive damages, costs of court, and reasonable attorney fees.

Finally, you are advised that time is of the essence in this regard and that your silence will be deemed an admission. Please contact me or have your attorney contact me as soon as possible if you have any questions.

Thank you for your courtesy and cooperation.

Very truly yours,

Ms. Alixandre Caroline, Attorney at Law

Appendix K Sample Demand Letter

INCIDENT REPORT

Business _____   Date _____

Address _____   City _____ State_____

Complainant

_____

Last Name   First Name   Initial

_____

Address   City   State   Zip

_____

Home Telephone   Business Telephone

Type of Incident

_____

Theft   Accident   Property Damage   Other

Injury

First aid given?   Yes_____   No_____

First aid refused?   Yes_____   No_____

EMS called?   Yes_____   No_____

Taken to emergency?   Yes_____   No_____

Nature of injury_____

_____

_____

Detail of Incident

_____

_____

_____

_____

_____

_____

_____

_____

Appendix L   Sample Incident Report Form

Property and Value

Damaged/Missing Property Description   Estimated Value

_____   _____

_____   _____

_____   _____

_____   _____

_____   _____

Police Report

Police Officer Name _____

Shield # _____   Report # _____

Arrest made? _____   Citation issued? _____

Witnesses:

Name _____   Tel: _____

Address _____ City _____ State _____

Name _____   Tel: _____

Address _____ City _____ State _____

Name _____   Tel: _____

Address _____ City _____ State _____

Comments: _____

_____

_____

_____

_____

_____

_____   _____
Prepared by   Reviewed by

_____   _____
Date   Date

Appendix L *(Continued)*

Lost and Found Ticket

Facility Name _____ Today's Date _____

Item Description _____

_____

_____

_____

_____

_____

Location found _____ Room Number _____

Name of finder _____

Supervisor who received item(s) _____

_____

DISPOSITION OF PROPERTY

Date item returned to owner _____

Owner Name _____ Owner Address _____

Owner Telephone _____ _____

Returned to owner by _____

Date item:

Returned to finder _____ Disposed of _____

Appendix M   Sample Lost and Found Tracking Form

Policy Regarding Employee Privacy

The Company respects the individual privacy of its employees. However, an employee may not expect privacy rights to be extended to work-related conduct or the use of company-owned equipment, supplies, systems, or property. The purpose of this policy is to notify you that no reasonable expectation of privacy exists in connection with your use of such equipment, supplies, systems, or property, including computer files, computer databases, office cabinets, or lockers. It is for that reason the following policy should be read; if you do not understand it, ask for clarification before you sign it.

I, _____, understand that all electronic communications systems and all information transmitted by, received from, or stored in these systems are the property of the Company. I also understand that these systems are to be used solely for job-related purposes and not for personal purposes, and that I do not have any personal privacy right in connection with the use of this equipment or with the transmission, receipt, or storage of information in this equipment.

I consent to the Company monitoring my use of company equipment at any time at its discretion. Such monitoring may include printing and reading all electronic mail entering, leaving, or stored in these systems.

I agree to abide by this Company policy and I understand that the policy prohibits me from using electronic communication systems to transmit lewd, offensive, or racially related messages.

_____   _____

Signature of employee   Date

Appendix N   Sample Employee Privacy Policy

Property Safety and Security Checklist

Property Name _____

Manager's Name _____

Month/Year Inspected _____ Inspected By _____

Check "OK" for items in compliance. For those items not in compliance, assign someone to correct the problem and provide a target completion date. For any item appearing two months in succession, attach a sheet explaining progress toward problem resolution.

OK	Not OK	Property Area	Correction Assigned To	Target Correction Date
		Outside/Parking Areas		
_____	_____	Paved areas free of cracks and uneven surfaces	_____	_____
_____	_____	Walkways uncluttered and unobstructed	_____	_____
_____	_____	Lighting adequate; in working condition	_____	_____
_____	_____	Required warning; caution signage in place	_____	_____
_____	_____	Landscape void of hiding areas	_____	_____
_____	_____	Fences in good repair	_____	_____
		Transportation/Valet		
_____	_____	Driving records of drivers on file	_____	_____
_____	_____	Daily vehicle inspection on file	_____	_____
_____	_____	Vehicle maintenance records on file	_____	_____
		Elevators		
_____	_____	Lights operational	_____	_____
_____	_____	Telephones operational	_____	_____
_____	_____	Elevator inspection current; posted	_____	_____
_____	_____	Signage includes Braille	_____	_____

Appendix O Property Safety and Security Checklist

OK	Not OK	Property Area	Correction Assigned To	Target Correction Date
		Dining Areas		
_____	_____	Floor covering in good repair	_____	_____
_____	_____	Adequate lighting	_____	_____
_____	_____	Seating inspected	_____	_____
_____	_____	Tables inspected	_____	_____
_____	_____	Signage appropriate	_____	_____
_____	_____	Evacuation plan posted (if required)	_____	_____
_____	_____	Room capacity posted (if required)	_____	_____
_____	_____	Wiring on public space equipment inspected	_____	_____
		Kitchen Areas		
_____	_____	Floor tile in good repair	_____	_____
_____	_____	Chemicals stored away from food	_____	_____
_____	_____	Safe food storage practices	_____	_____
_____	_____	Outlets properly grounded	_____	_____
_____	_____	Hood ducts and filters cleaned; documented	_____	_____
_____	_____	Fire extinguishing system inspection posted	_____	_____
_____	_____	Kitchen inspection scores reviewed with manager	_____	_____
_____	_____	Fire extinguisher training held; documented	_____	_____
_____	_____	Material Safety Data Sheets available	_____	_____
		Laundry Areas		
_____	_____	Dryer vents cleaned; documented	_____	_____
_____	_____	Chemicals stored properly	_____	_____
_____	_____	Material Safety Data Sheets available	_____	_____

Appendix O *(Continued)*

OK	Not OK	Property Area	Correction Assigned To	Target Correction Date
		Private Meeting/Banquet Room Areas		
_____	_____	Floor covering in good condition	_____	_____
_____	_____	Entrance doors open/close properly	_____	_____
_____	_____	Kitchen doors open/close properly	_____	_____
_____	_____	Evacuation procedures posted	_____	_____
_____	_____	Appropriate signage	_____	_____
_____	_____	Lights installed and operable	_____	_____
		Back of House Areas		
_____	_____	Floor covering in good condition	_____	_____
_____	_____	Proper storage techniques used	_____	_____
_____	_____	Hot water temperature tested	_____	_____
_____	_____	Power shutoff identified/labeled	_____	_____
_____	_____	Gas shutoff identified/labeled	_____	_____
_____	_____	Appropriate signage	_____	_____
_____	_____	Lights installed and operable	_____	_____
		Other Concerns		
		Lobby/Entrance Areas		
_____	_____	Steps/stairways marked; in good repair	_____	_____
_____	_____	Handrails installed	_____	_____
_____	_____	Floors, carpets in good condition	_____	_____
_____	_____	Lighting levels adequate	_____	_____

Appendix O *(Continued)*

OK	Not OK	Property Area	Correction Assigned To	Target Correction Date
		Fire and Safety		
_____	_____	Fire alarm system tested; documented	_____	_____
_____	_____	Sprinkler system tested; documented	_____	_____
_____	_____	Fire extinguisher tests current	_____	_____
_____	_____	Kitchen hood fire extinguishing system tested; documented	_____	_____
_____	_____	All exit signs illuminated	_____	_____
_____	_____	Smoke alarms tested; documented	_____	_____
_____	_____	Meeting with local fire officials held; documented	_____	_____

General/Additional Comments: _____

_____

_____

_____

_____

Inspection Form filed on: _____

Reviewed By: _____ Title: _____

Appendix O *(Continued)*

EMERGENCY TELEPHONE NUMBERS

Property Manager _____

Emergency Services

Fire Department _____

Fire Alarm Service Provider _____

Police Department _____

Ambulance _____

Paramedics _____

Elevator Service Company _____

Insurance Company Representative _____

Telephone Repair Service _____

Utility Services

Gas _____

Electric _____

Water _____

Property-Specific Numbers

District Manager _____

Owner (with approval) _____

Other _____   _____

Other _____   _____

Other _____   _____

Appendix P Sample Emergency Telephone List

FIRE ALARM PROCEDURES

1. When an alarm sounds: All nonemergency committee personnel will go out the first available exit that is safe and then to the parking lot.

FIRE RESPONSE INSTRUCTIONS

1. Without endangering yourself, notify any employees or guests in immediate danger of smoke, heat, or fire.
2. Close all doors to prevent the spread of the fire.
3. If possible, and if trained to do so, help extinguish the fire by using one of the public/department fire extinguishers.
4. Never permit the fire and or smoke to come between you and your route of escape.
5. Advise all guests/employees of the nearest safe fire exit.
6. Do not attempt to use the elevator under any circumstances.
7. If you encounter smoke in a hallway, stairwell, anywhere, *stop;* go back to a safe area and look for another means of escape.
8. Keep doors and windows in the area of the fire closed, to minimize further fire spreading.

EVACUATION

Evacuation of the building should be done quickly and calmly. Safety of guests should be the primary concern. Each department will appoint one of its staff to oversee fellow staff members' evacuation from the building. This employee will be responsible for needed supplies and the general safety of the department's staff members.

Time permitting, the manager in the following departments will be responsible to:

Food and Beverage

1. Secure food, storage, and liquor rooms.
2. Place cash in a sealed envelope and drop into safe.
3. Take kitchen keys.

Accounting

1. Back up computer programs onto disks.
2. Take current payroll register.
3. Take all master keys.

Appendix Q Sample Fire Emergency Plan

Sales

1. Take banquet event book and group/function book binder.

Engineering

1. Take master key log.
2. Deactivate all gas-operated equipment.
3. Shut down elevators.

General Manager (GM)/Manager on Duty (MOD)

1. Meet fire department outside and advise them of the current situation.
2. Assist police/fire personnel to secure exit and entrance to the restaurant.

Appendix Q   *(Continued)*

MANAGER'S RESPONSIBILITIES IN A CRISIS

1. Take the immediate action required to ensure the safety of guests and employees.
2. Contact the appropriate source of assistance; for example, the fire department, police, or a medical professional.
3. Implement the relevant portion of your emergency plan.
4. Contact those within the organization who need to be informed of the crisis, which may include your supervisor, owners, insurance companies, and company safety and security professionals.
5. Assume the leadership role expected of management during a crisis. Demonstrate your competence and professionalism by showing a genuine concern for the well-being of those affected by the crisis.
6. Communicate with your employees about the crisis.
7. Inform those guests who need to know what is being done and what will be done to deal with the crisis.
8. Secure organizational property, but only if it can be done without risking injury to guests or employees.
9. Prepare for and make yourself available to the media.
10. Using an incident report form or a narrative style, document in writing your efforts and activities during the crisis.

Appendix R   Manager's Responsibilities in a Crisis

INDEX